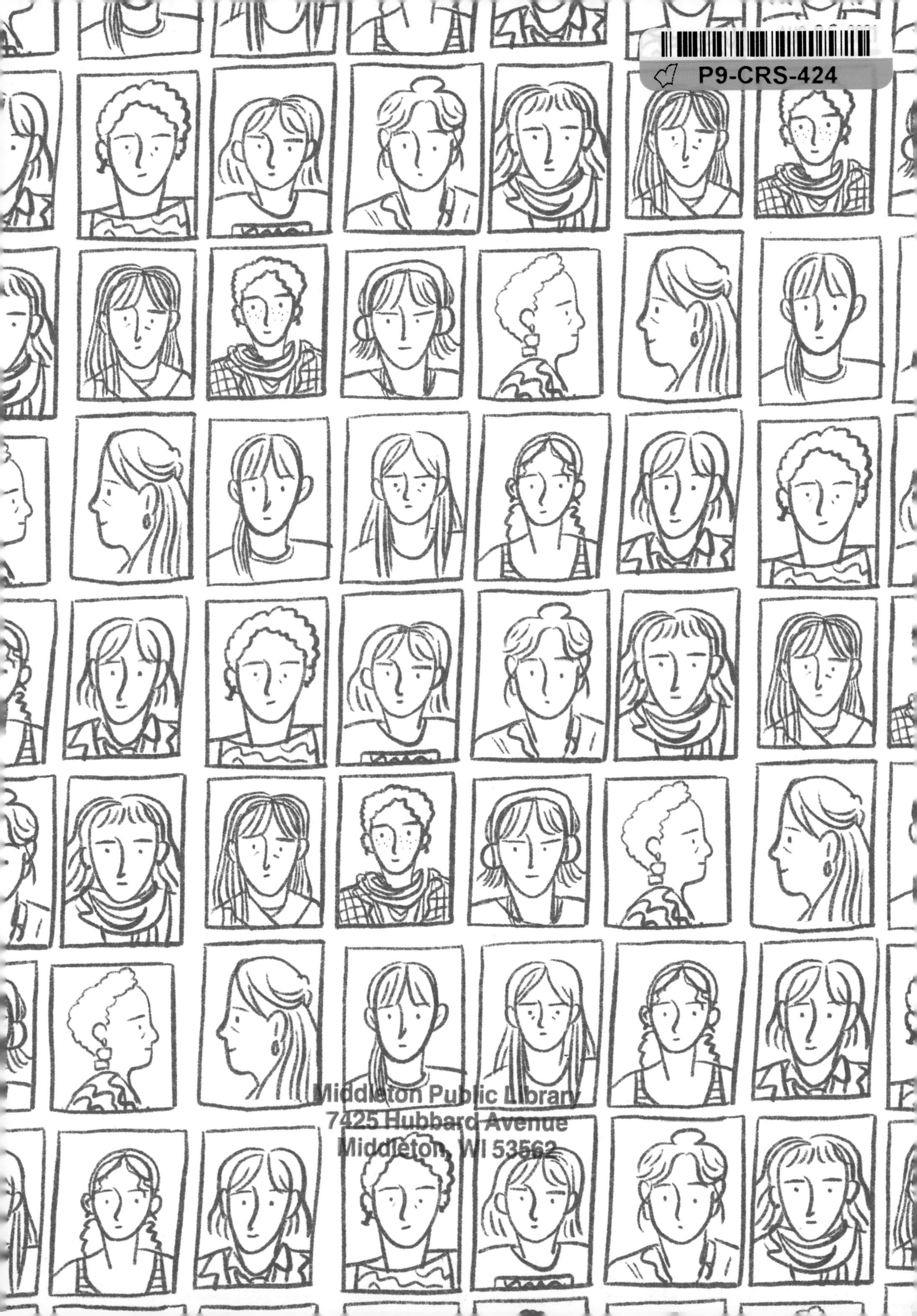

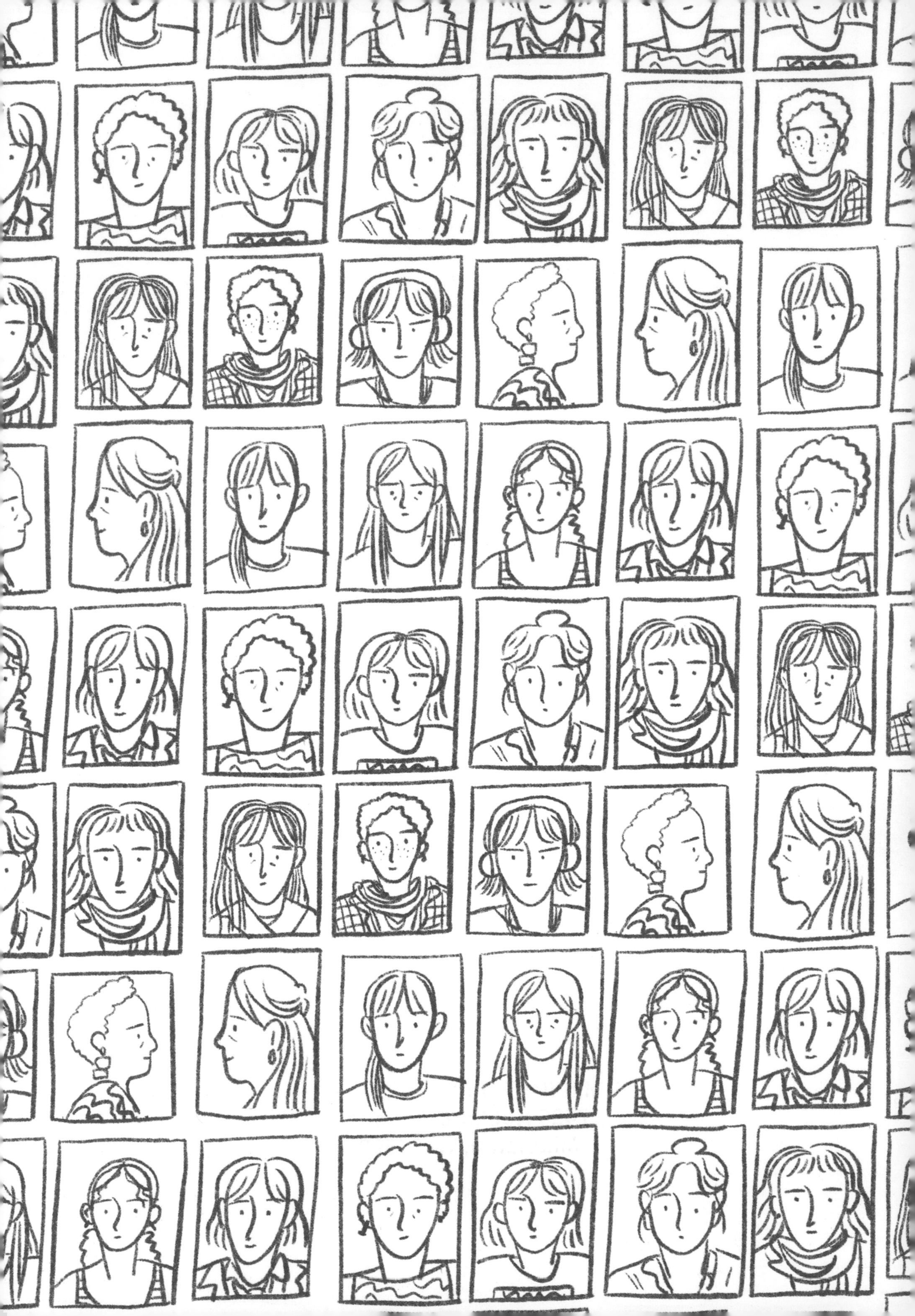

It's Not What You Thought It Would Be

Lizzy Stewart

It's not what you thought it would be

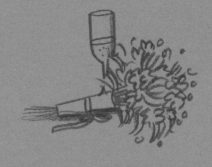

Thanks to: Jenny Whittam, Candy Brown,
Eleni Kalorkoti, Matthew Swan, Avery Hill,
Zainab Akhtar, Owen Pomery.

For my family, who think this is all a bit
weird but are very nice about it anyway.

FANTAGRAPHICS BOOKS, INC.
7563 Lake City Way NE • Seattle, WA 98115

www.fantagraphics.com
facebook.com/fantagraphics
@fantagraphics.com

Editor: Conrad Groth
Book Design: Lizzy Stewart
Production: Paul Baresh
Promotion: Jacq Cohen
Associate Publisher: Eric Reynolds
Publisher: Gary Groth

Heavy Air – 2016 (first appeared in Shortbox #2)
Blush – 2019
Dog Walk – 2016
Walking Home – 2019
A Quick Catch-Up – 2017
Lunch Break – 2019
It's Not What You Thought It Would Be – 2016
Quiet – 2018
The Wedding Guests – 2019

ISBN: 978-1-68396-435-3
Library of Congress Control Number: 2020948399
First Fantagraphics Books edition: July 2021
Printed in China

HEAVY AIR

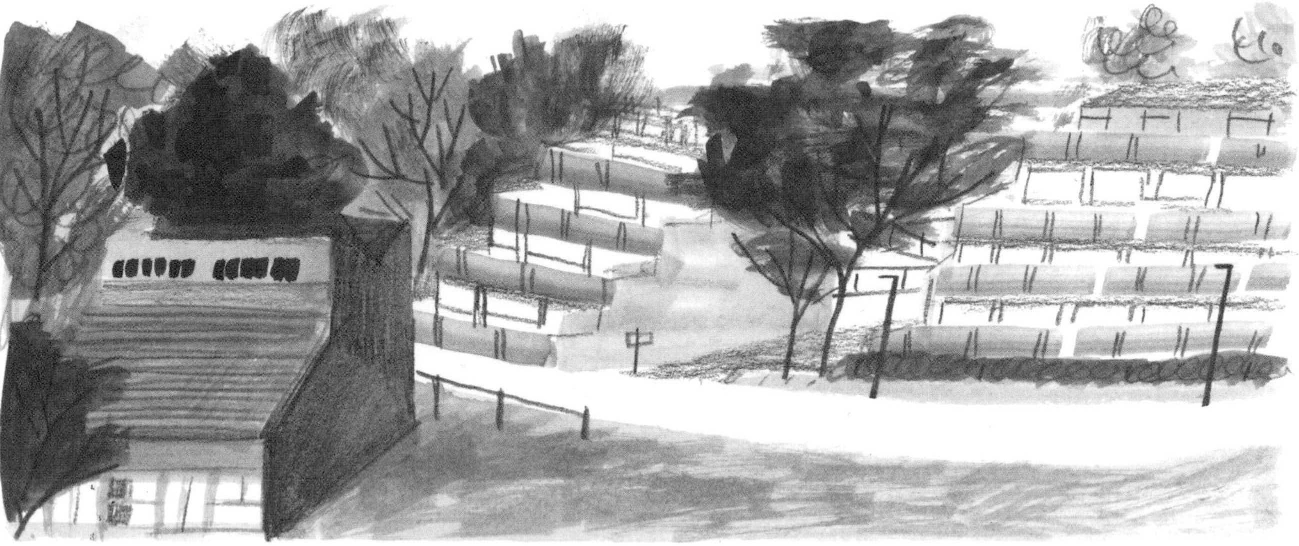

We lived on the estate.

At the top of the hill, a warren of small streets and walkways intersected with blocks built in the late '60s, stacked one on top of the other facing outwards towards the city.

I remember being told that the whole place had been built without knocking down a single tall tree. Instead, the streets were built around the towering elms.

We lived in the treetops.

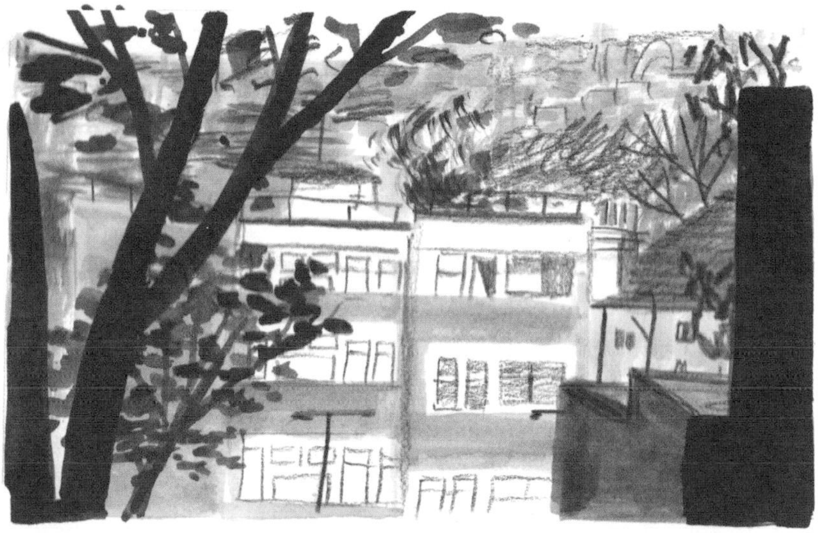

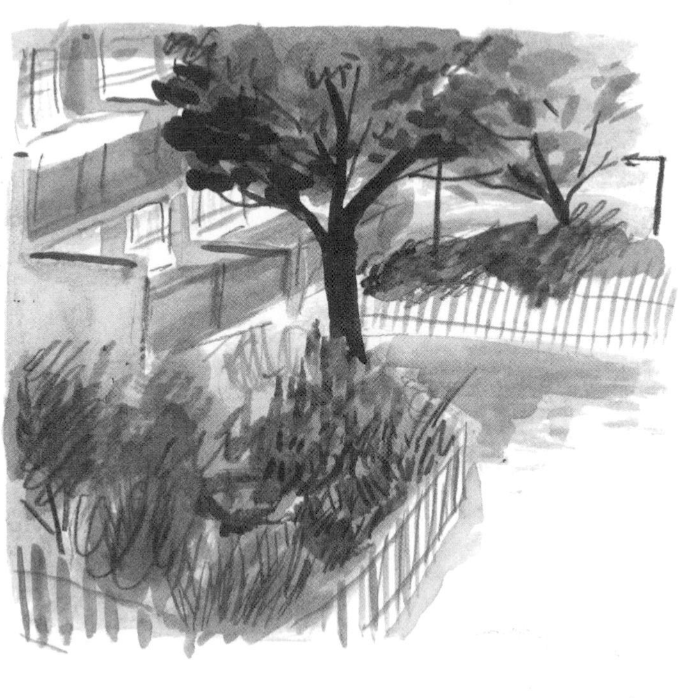

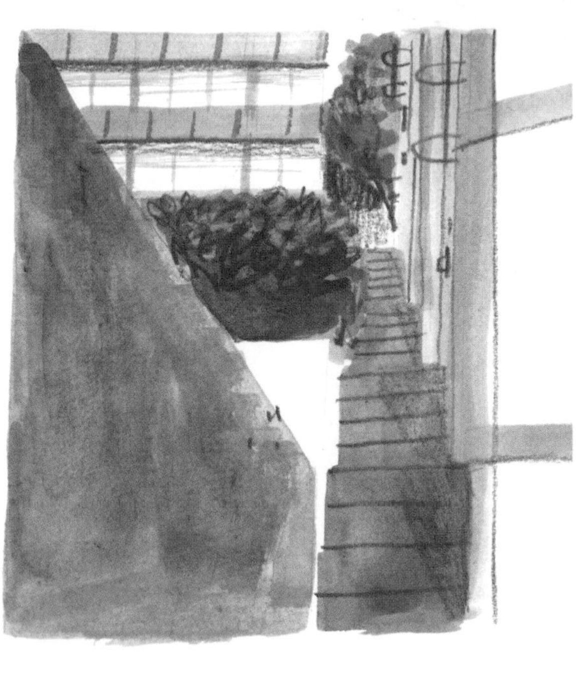

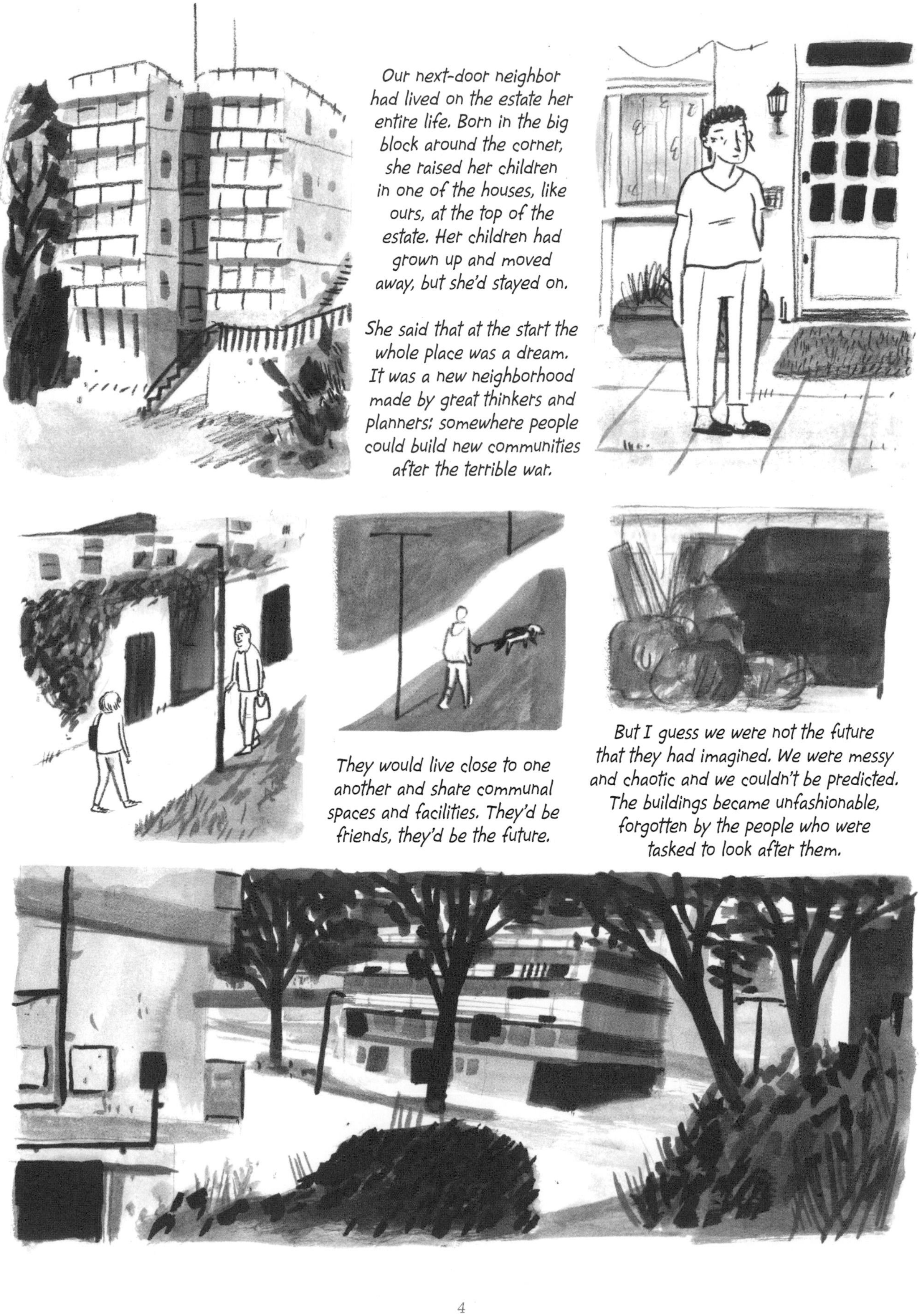
Our next-door neighbor had lived on the estate her entire life. Born in the big block around the corner, she raised her children in one of the houses, like ours, at the top of the estate. Her children had grown up and moved away, but she'd stayed on.
She said that at the start the whole place was a dream. It was a new neighborhood made by great thinkers and planners: somewhere people could build new communities after the terrible war.
They would live close to one another and share communal spaces and facilities. They'd be friends, they'd be the future.
But I guess we were not the future that they had imagined. We were messy and chaotic and we couldn't be predicted. The buildings became unfashionable, forgotten by the people who were tasked to look after them.

Some of my friends didn't like walking here at night. I liked it, though. It was beautiful – you could see the whole twinkling city. The view was so dazzling you wouldn't believe they let us have it. In the summer it smelled like BBQ, and you could always hear music from a house party somewhere.

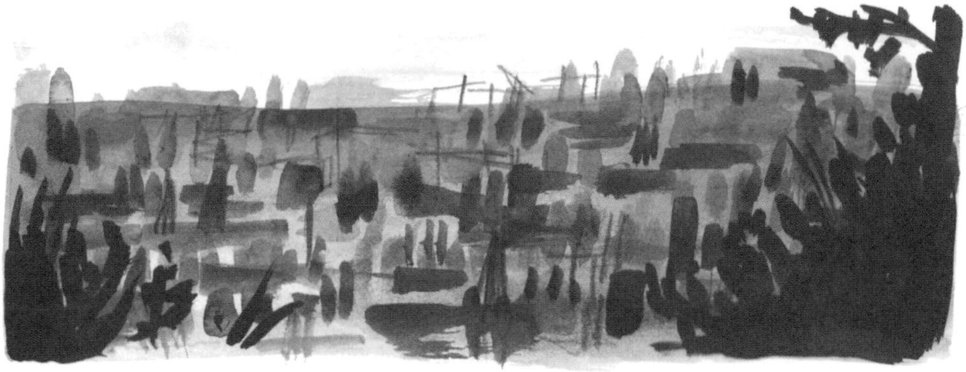

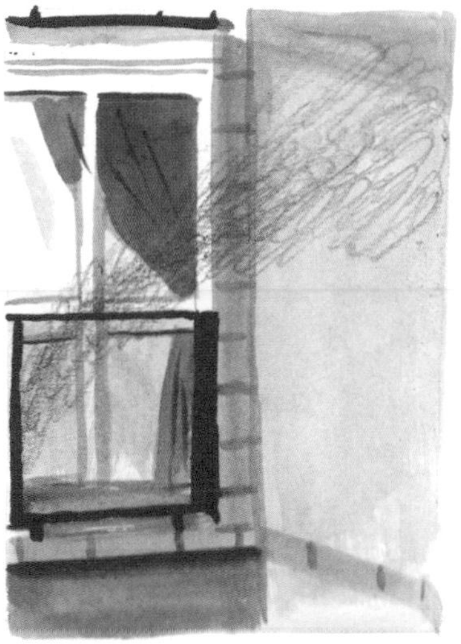

On my way home I'd take the long zig-zag ramp down to my house instead of the steps. I'd pass the yappy dog on number 12's balcony. I got a can of Coke at the shop and slipped a Snickers into my pocket. I wouldn't usually steal, but the shop guy called my little brother an idiot so it felt like revenge.

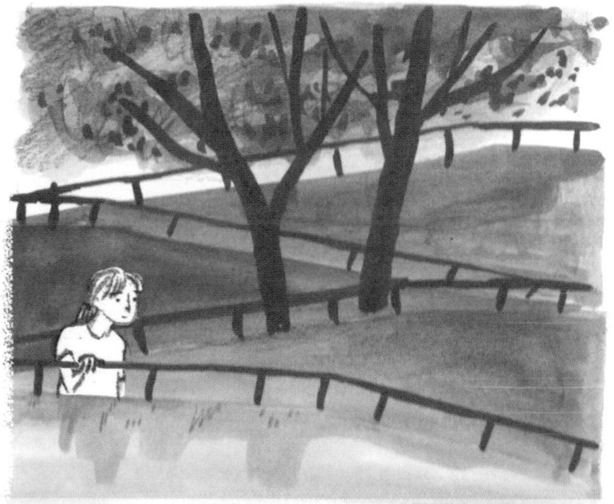

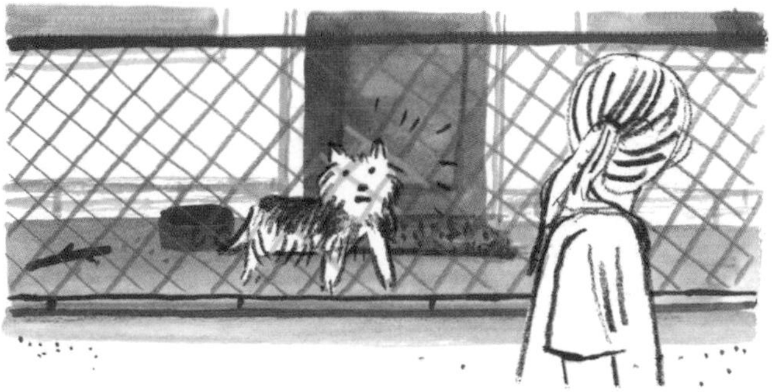

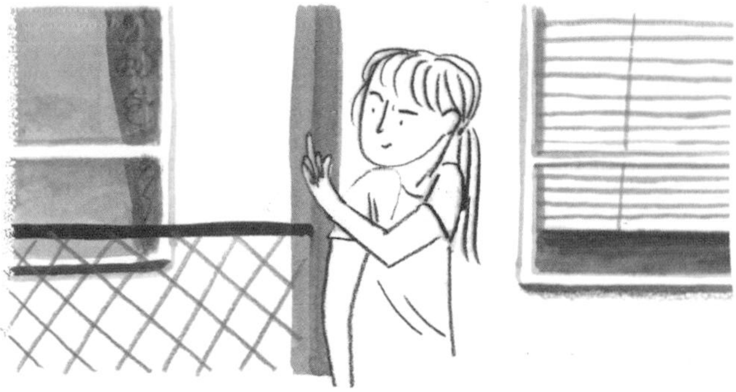

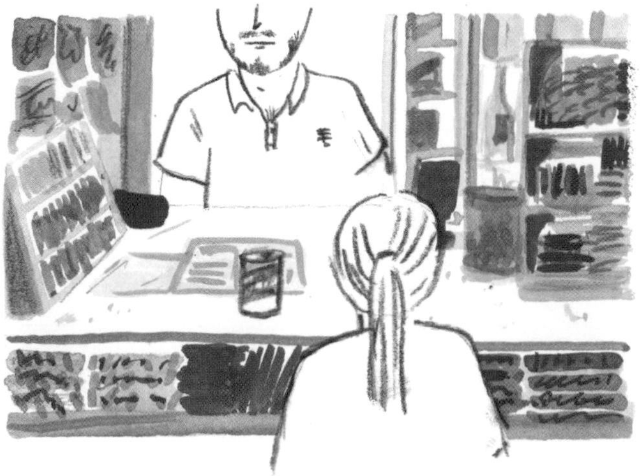

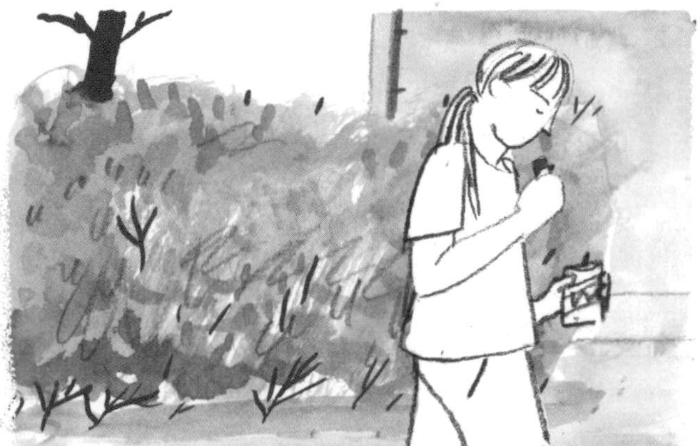

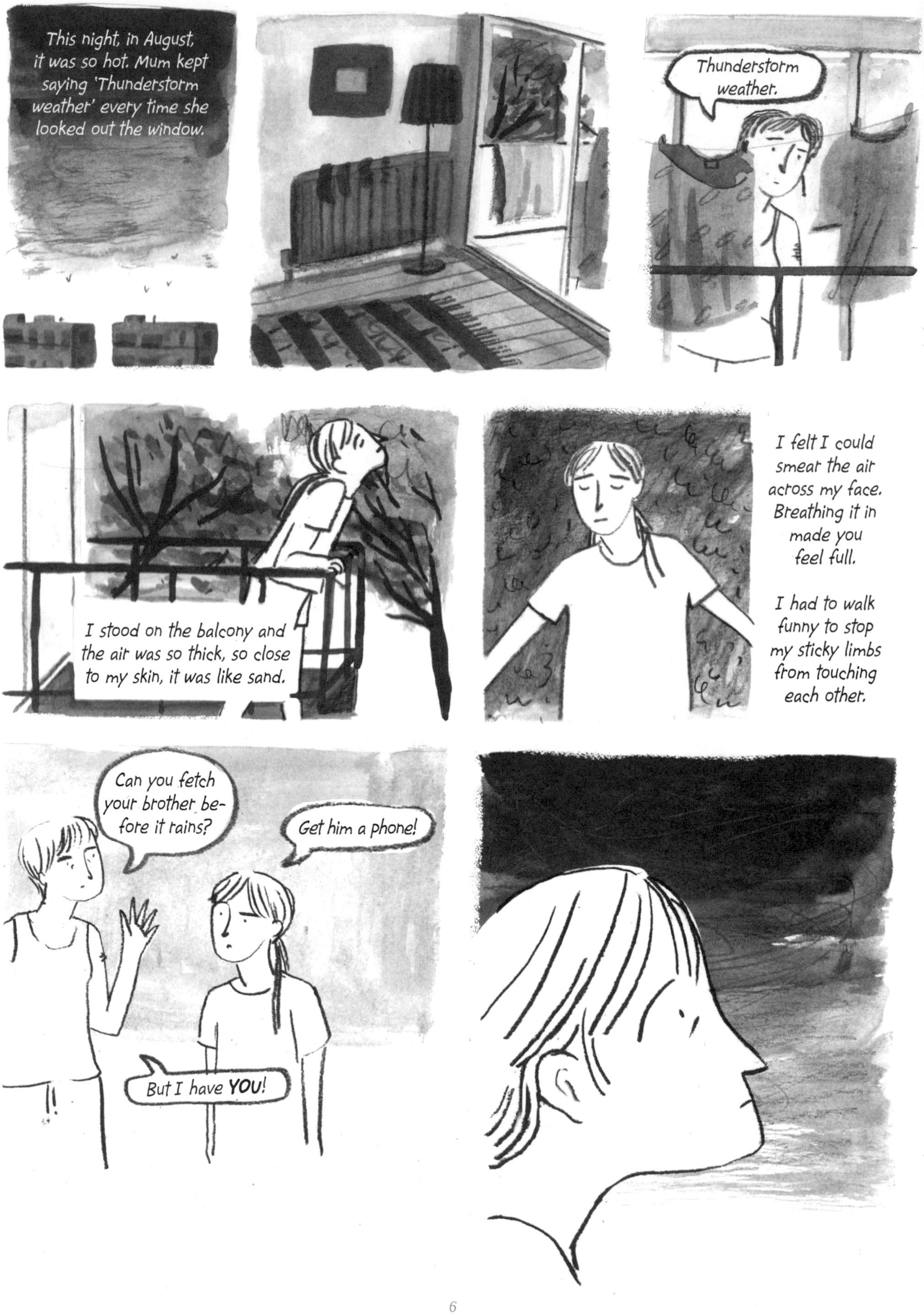
This night, in August, it was so hot. Mum kept saying 'Thunderstorm weather' every time she looked out the window.
Thunderstorm weather.
I stood on the balcony and the air was so thick, so close to my skin, it was like sand.
I felt I could smear the air across my face. Breathing it in made you feel full.
I had to walk funny to stop my sticky limbs from touching each other.
Can you fetch your brother before it rains?
Get him a phone!
But I have YOU!

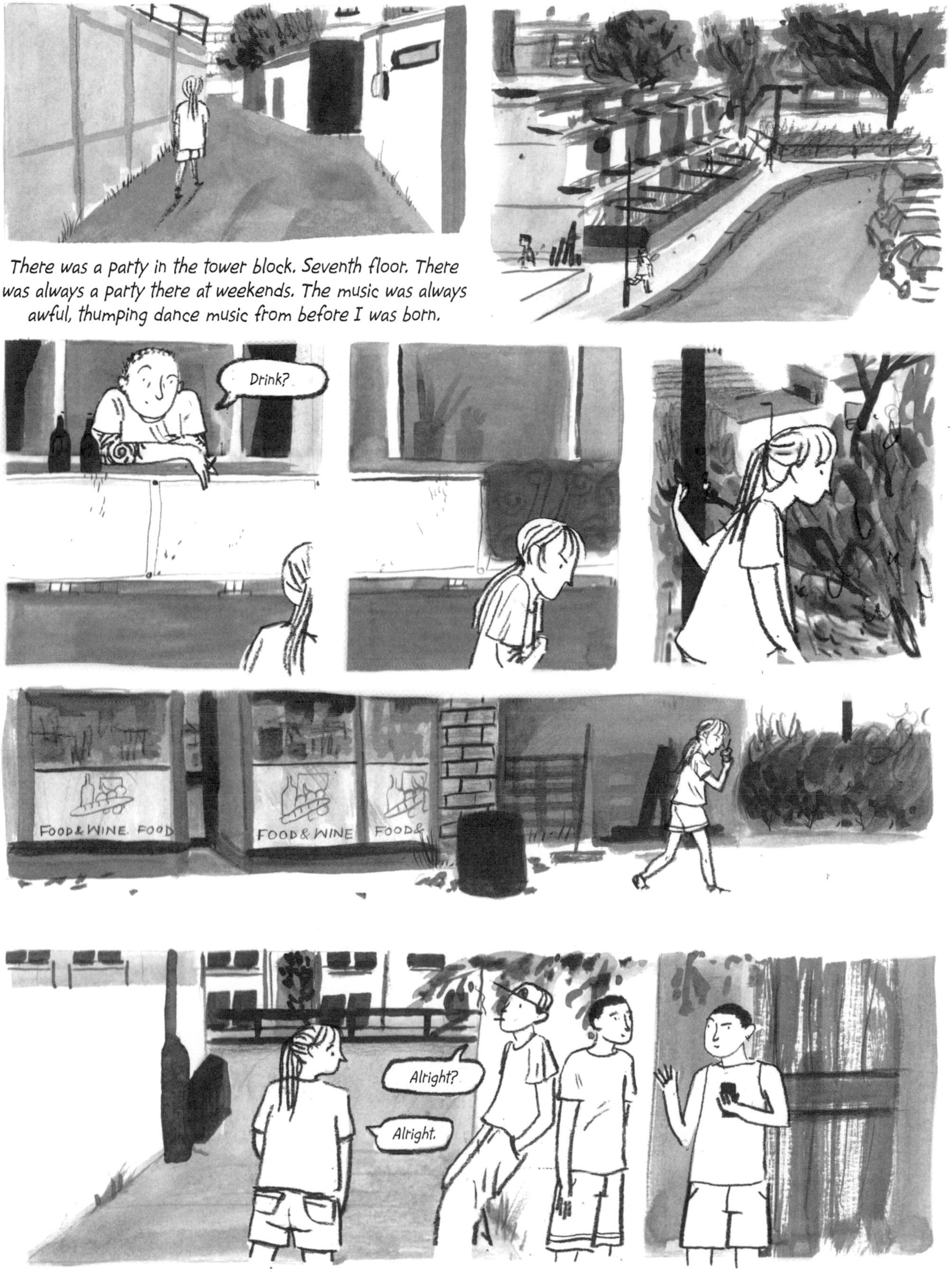
There was a party in the tower block. Seventh floor. There was always a party there at weekends. The music was always awful, thumping dance music from before I was born.
Drink?
FOOD&WINE. FOOD
FOOD& WINE
FOOD&
Alright?
Alright.

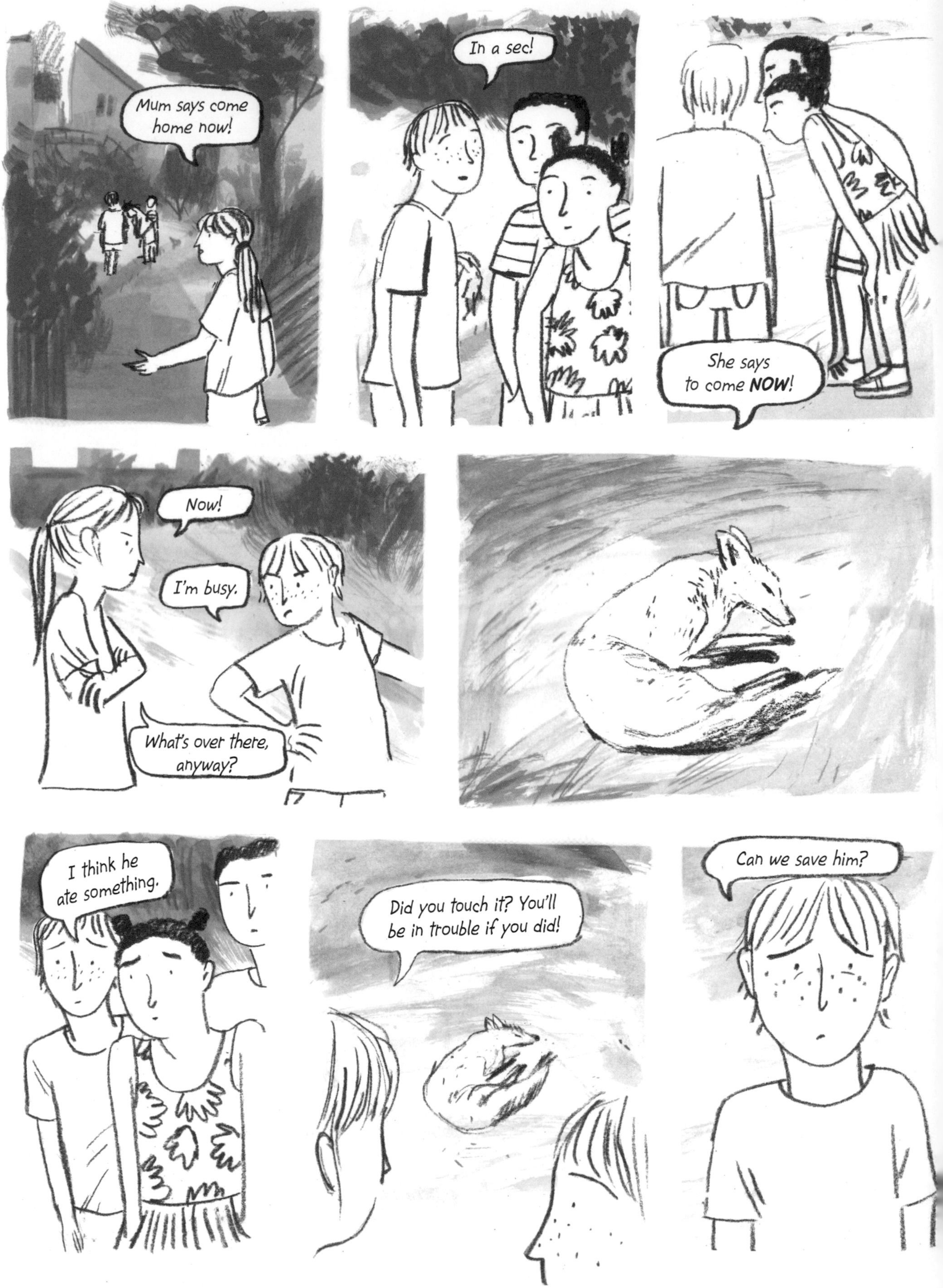
Mum says come home now!
In a sec!
She says to come NOW!
Now!
I'm busy.
What's over there, anyway?
I think he ate something.
Did you touch it? You'll be in trouble if you did!
Can we save him?

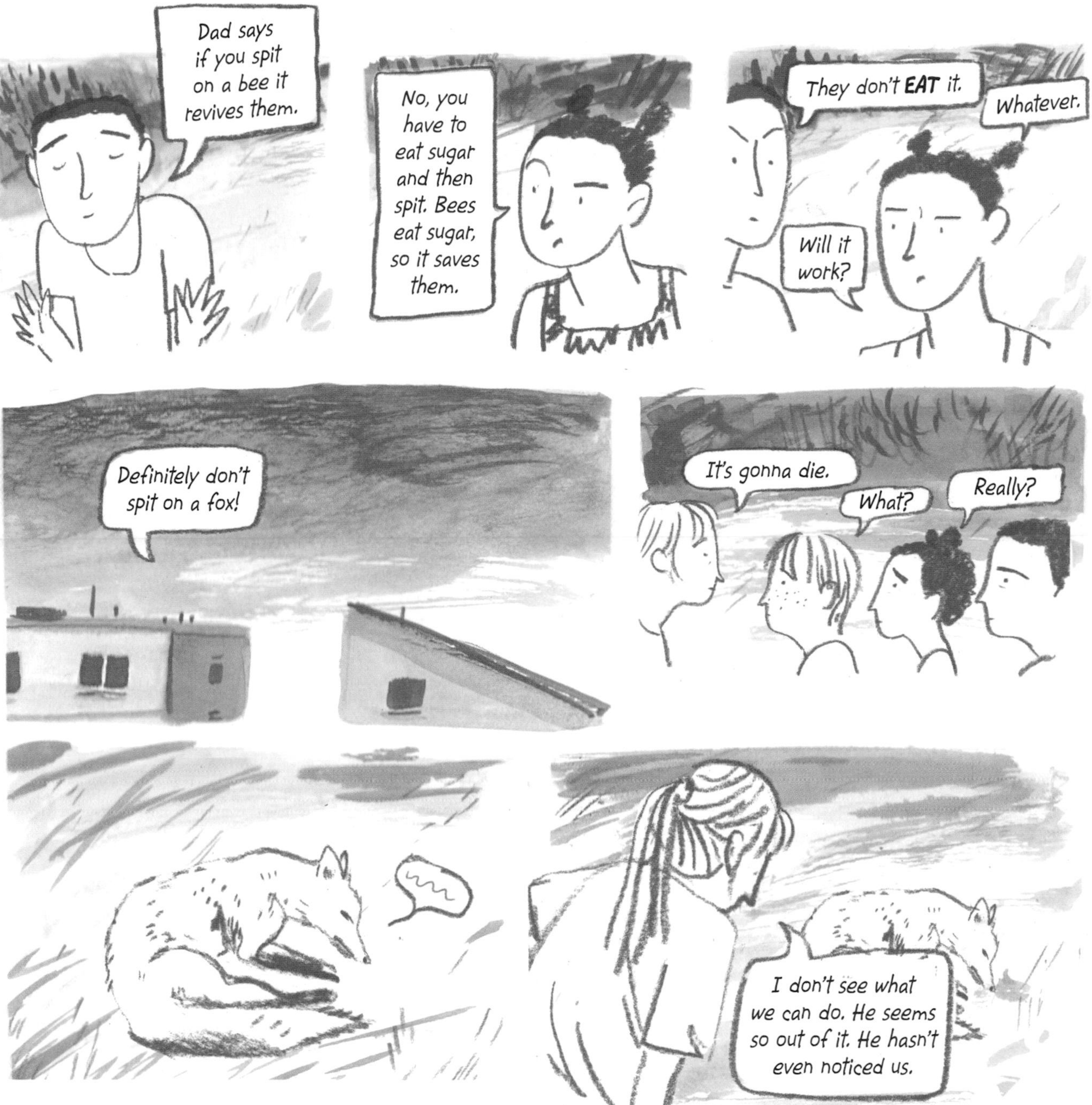
Dad says if you spit on a bee it revives them.
No, you have to eat sugar and then spit. Bees eat sugar, so it saves them.
They don't **EAT** it.
Whatever.
Will it work?
Definitely don't spit on a fox!
It's gonna die.
What?
Really?
I don't see what we can do. He seems so out of it. He hasn't even noticed us.

The fox wheezed and rattled but it didn't move.

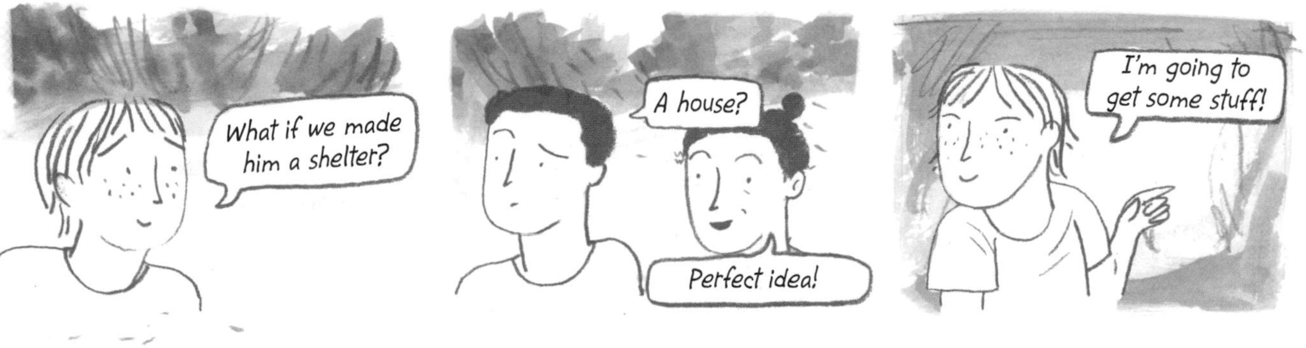
What if we made him a shelter?
A house?
Perfect idea!
I'm going to get some stuff!

I waited...

In a few years I'll be at university. I will iron out the kinks in my accent without even noticing that I'm doing it. I'll get a good job and nice friends who also have good jobs.

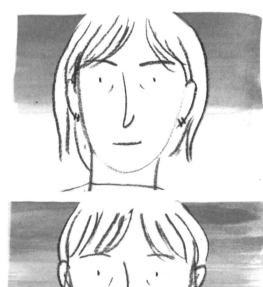

One day someone will ask me where I grew up and I will say 'an *estate*' and they will be surprised and say, salaciously, 'Was it rough?' and I'll shrug and wonder if I even remember it clearly anymore.

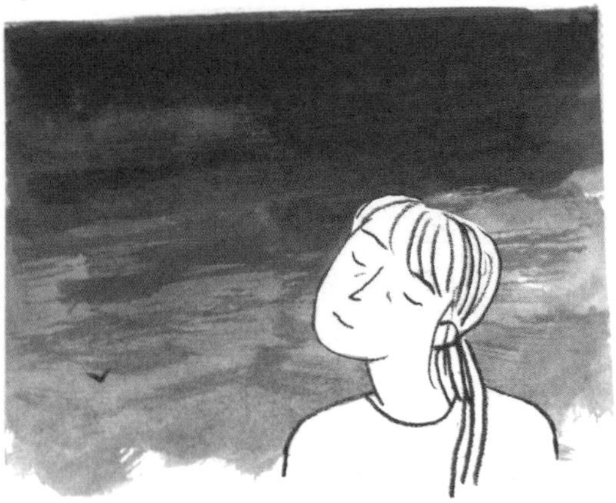

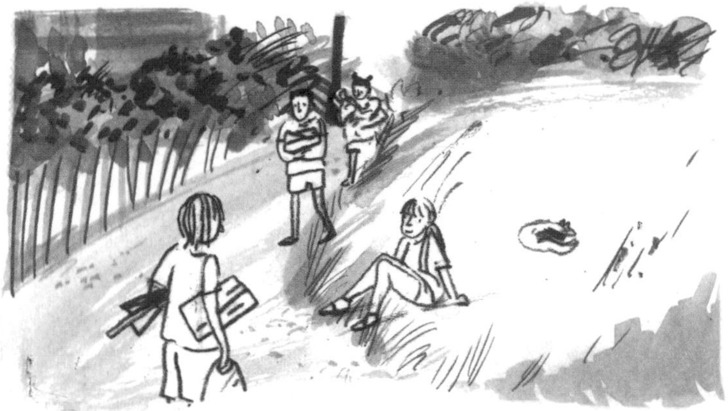

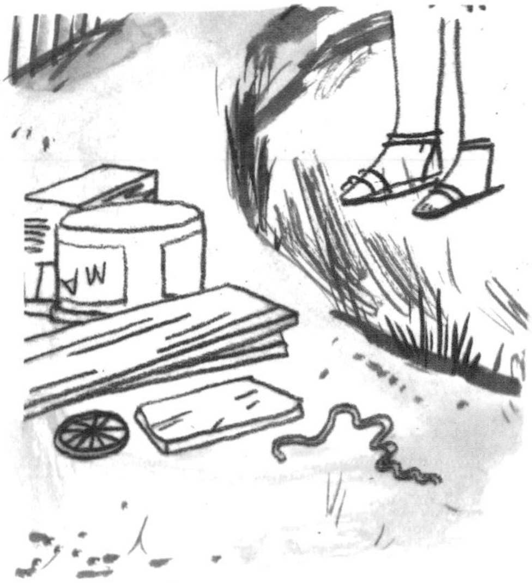

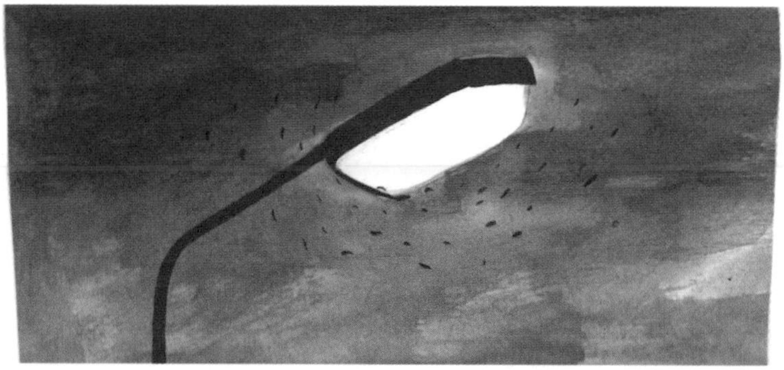

The sky turned purple and the orange street lights pinged on. The oscillatory buzz of the lights sounded as though something inside the light was contracting. Everything sounded like it was building. The whole estate was coiling up and the sky was getting lower.

We didn't notice the slowly swelling group of people watching us. We let them help out, but there was no question that the four of us were in charge. I didn't even know the other boy and girl before that day. I'm not sure I saw them after either. The estate was funny like that.

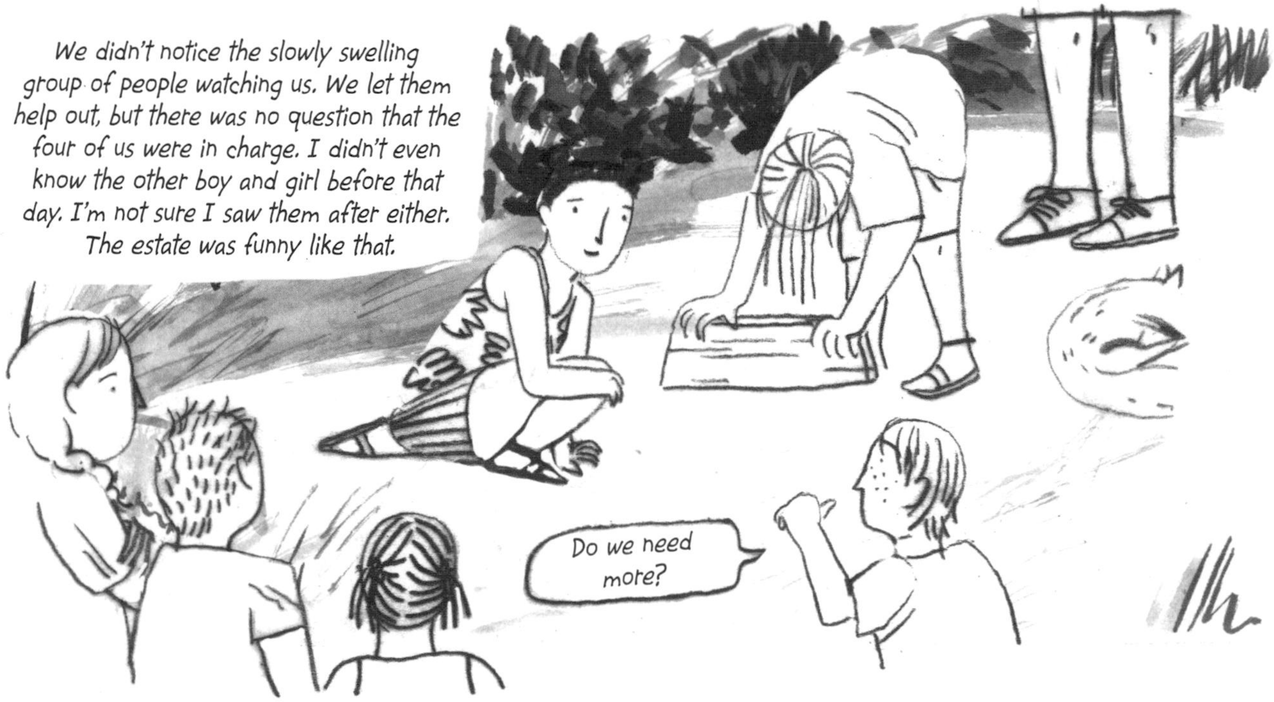
Do we need more?

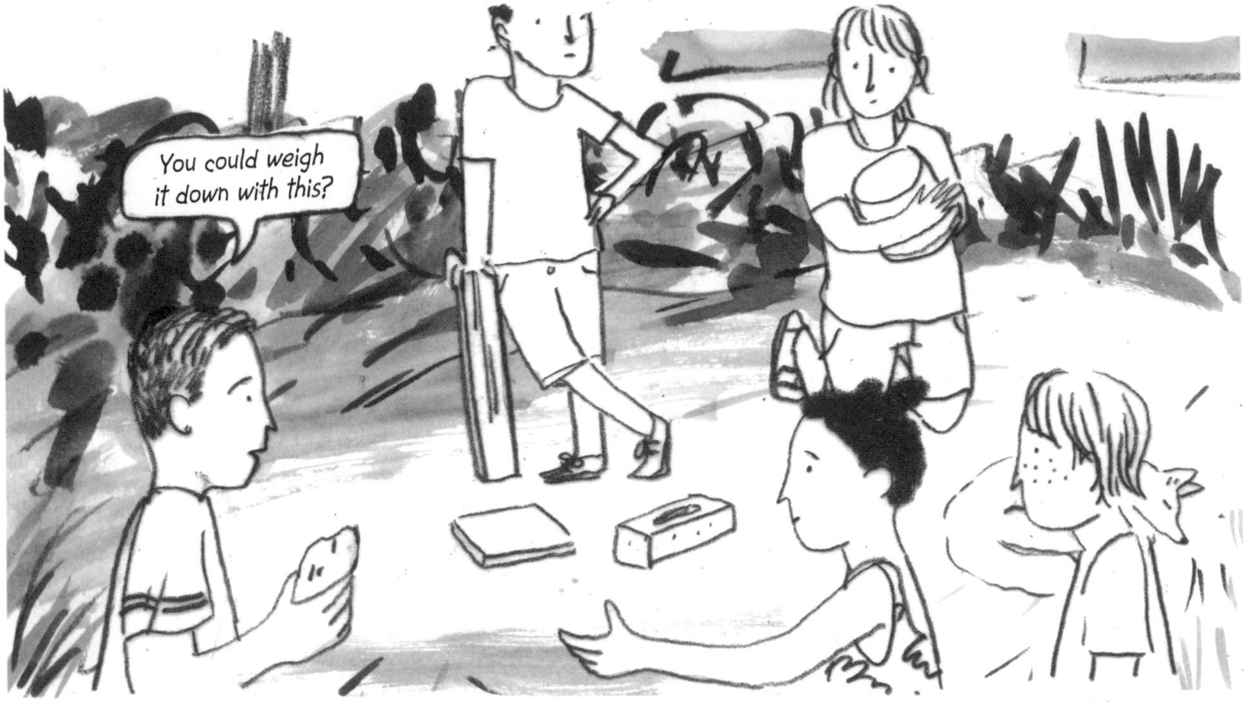
You could weigh it down with this?

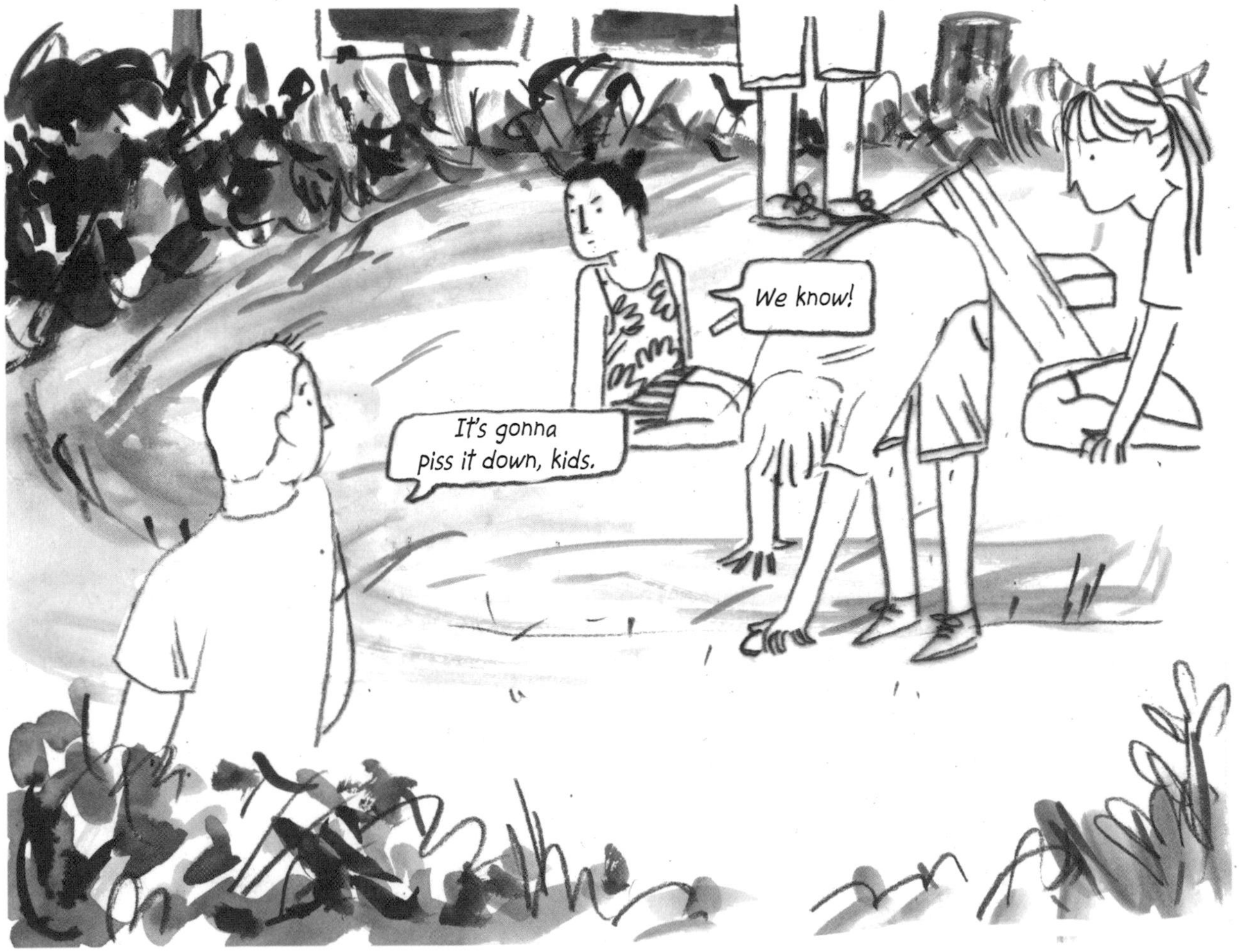
We know!
It's gonna piss it down, kids.

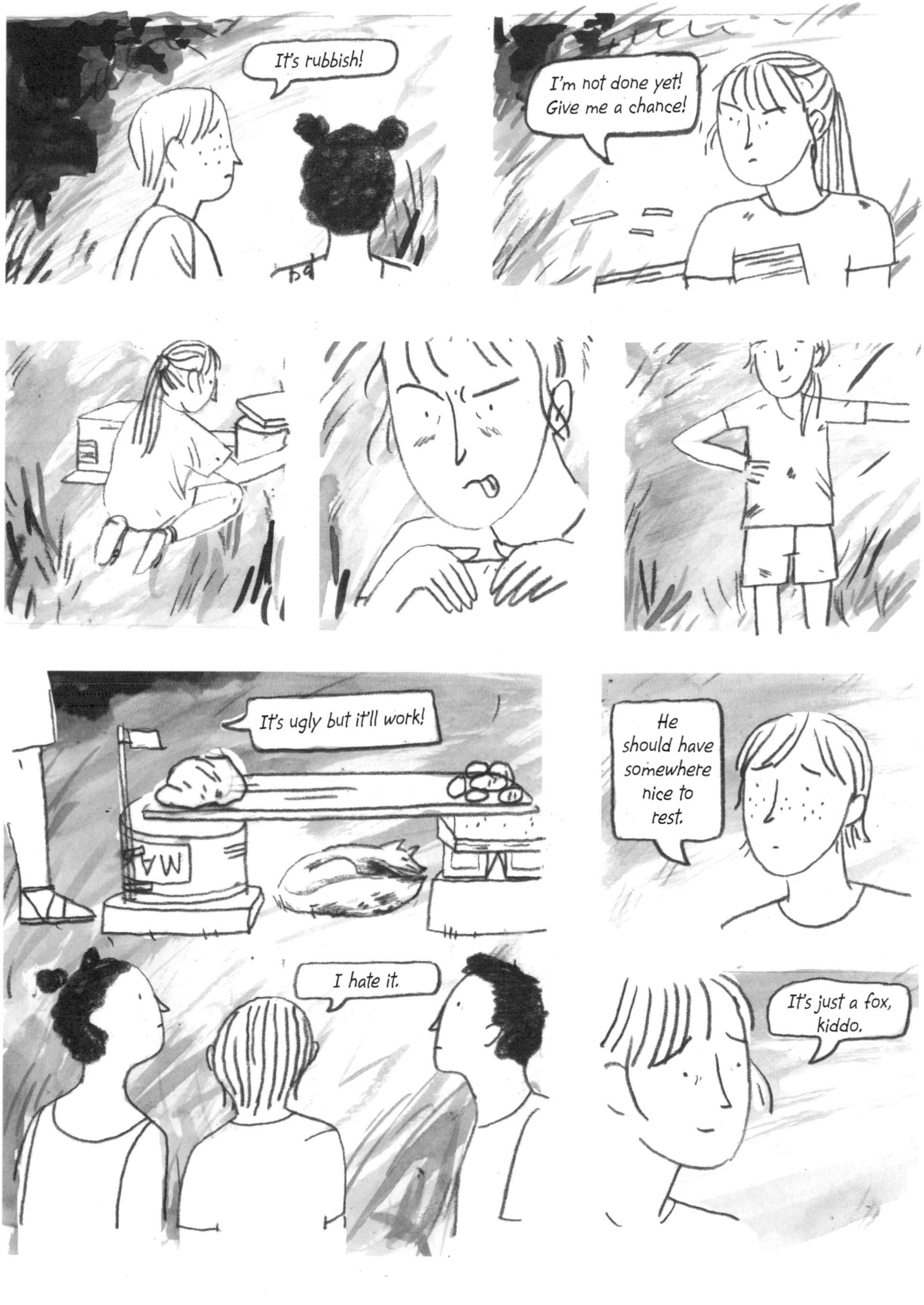
It's rubbish!
I'm not done yet! Give me a chance!
It's ugly but it'll work!
MAX
He should have somewhere nice to rest.
I hate it.
It's just a fox, kiddo.

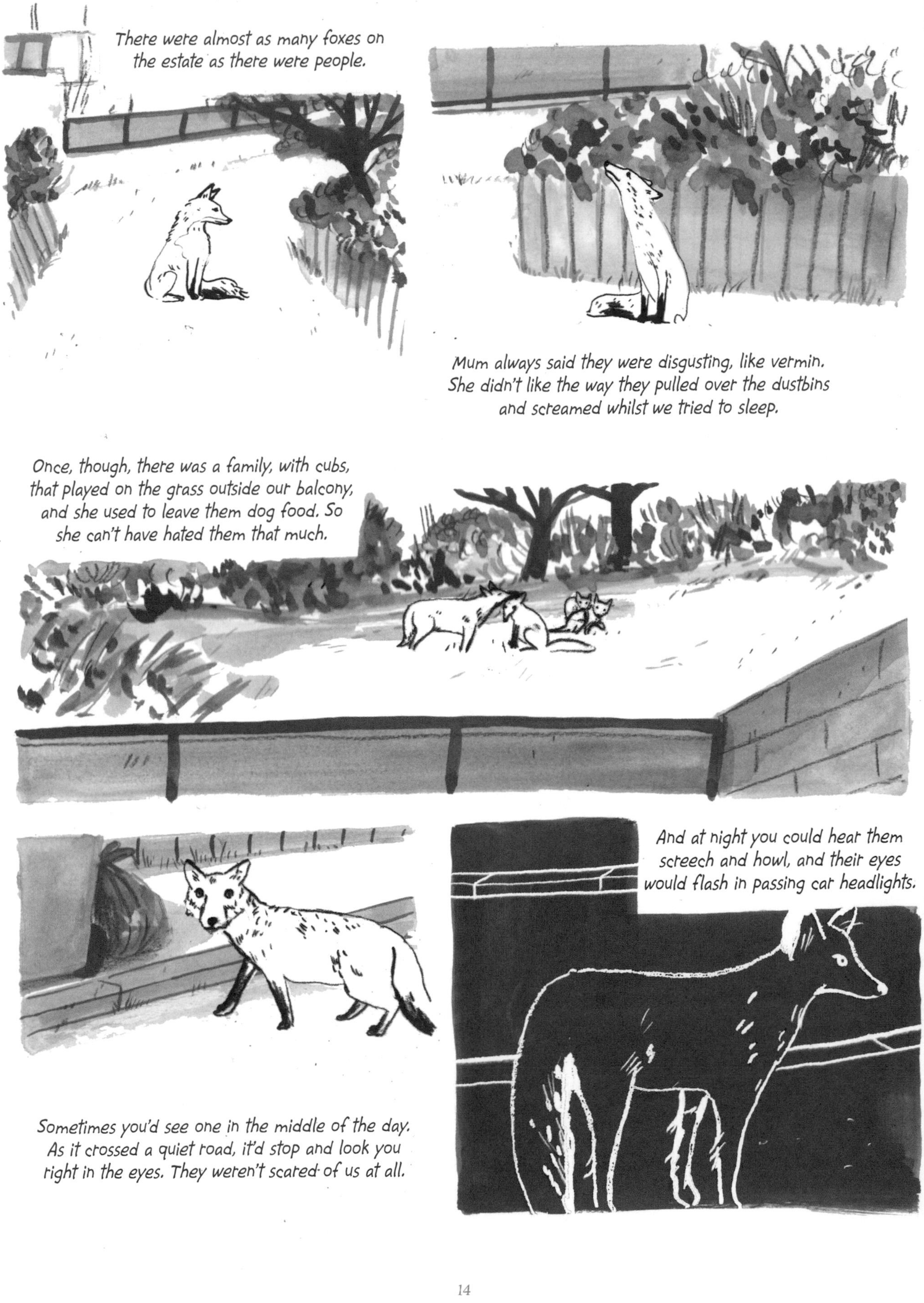
There were almost as many foxes on the estate as there were people.
Mum always said they were disgusting, like vermin. She didn't like the way they pulled over the dustbins and screamed whilst we tried to sleep.
Once, though, there was a family, with cubs, that played on the grass outside our balcony, and she used to leave them dog food. So she can't have hated them that much.
Sometimes you'd see one in the middle of the day. As it crossed a quiet road, it'd stop and look you right in the eyes. They weren't scared of us at all.
And at night you could hear them screech and howl, and their eyes would flash in passing car headlights.

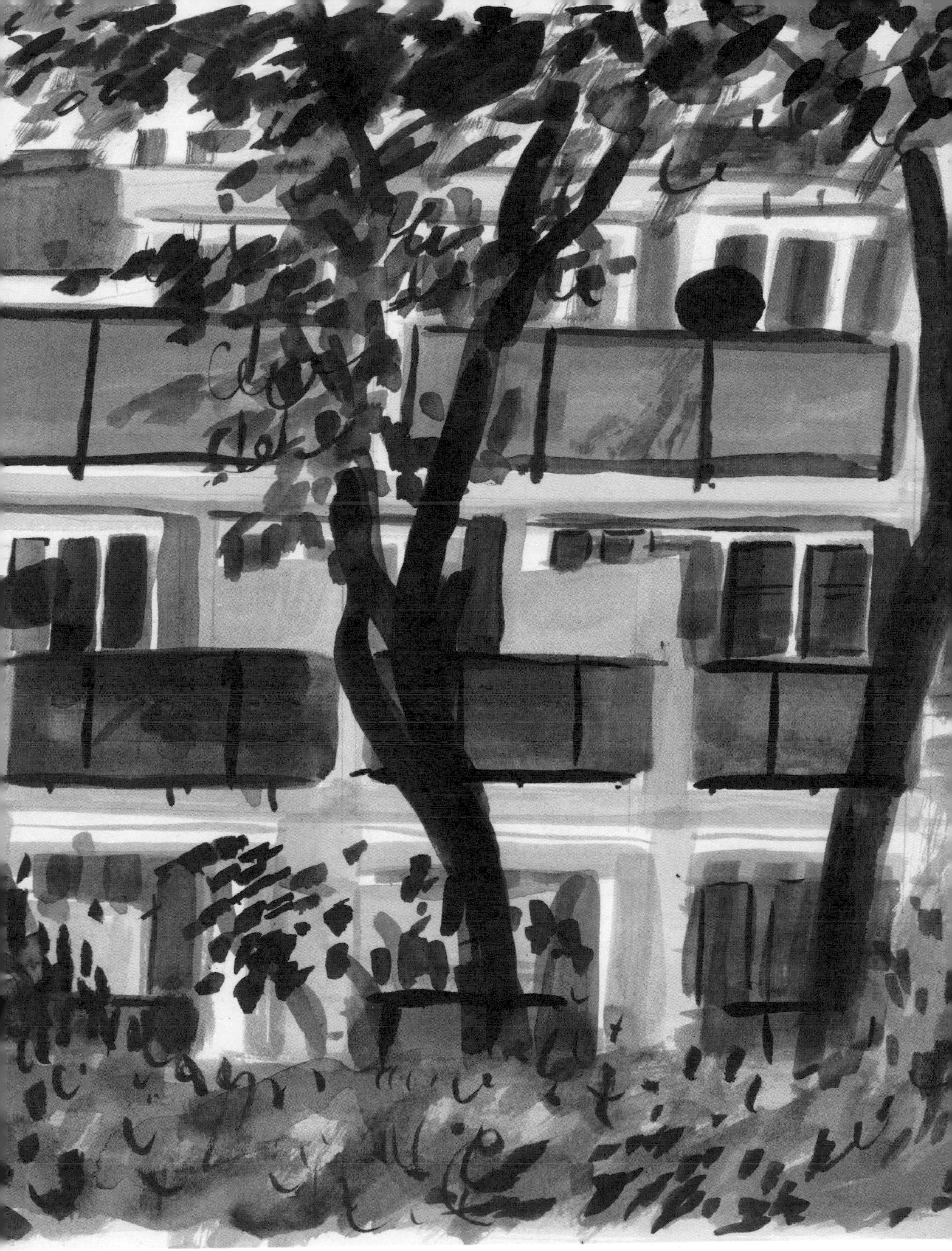

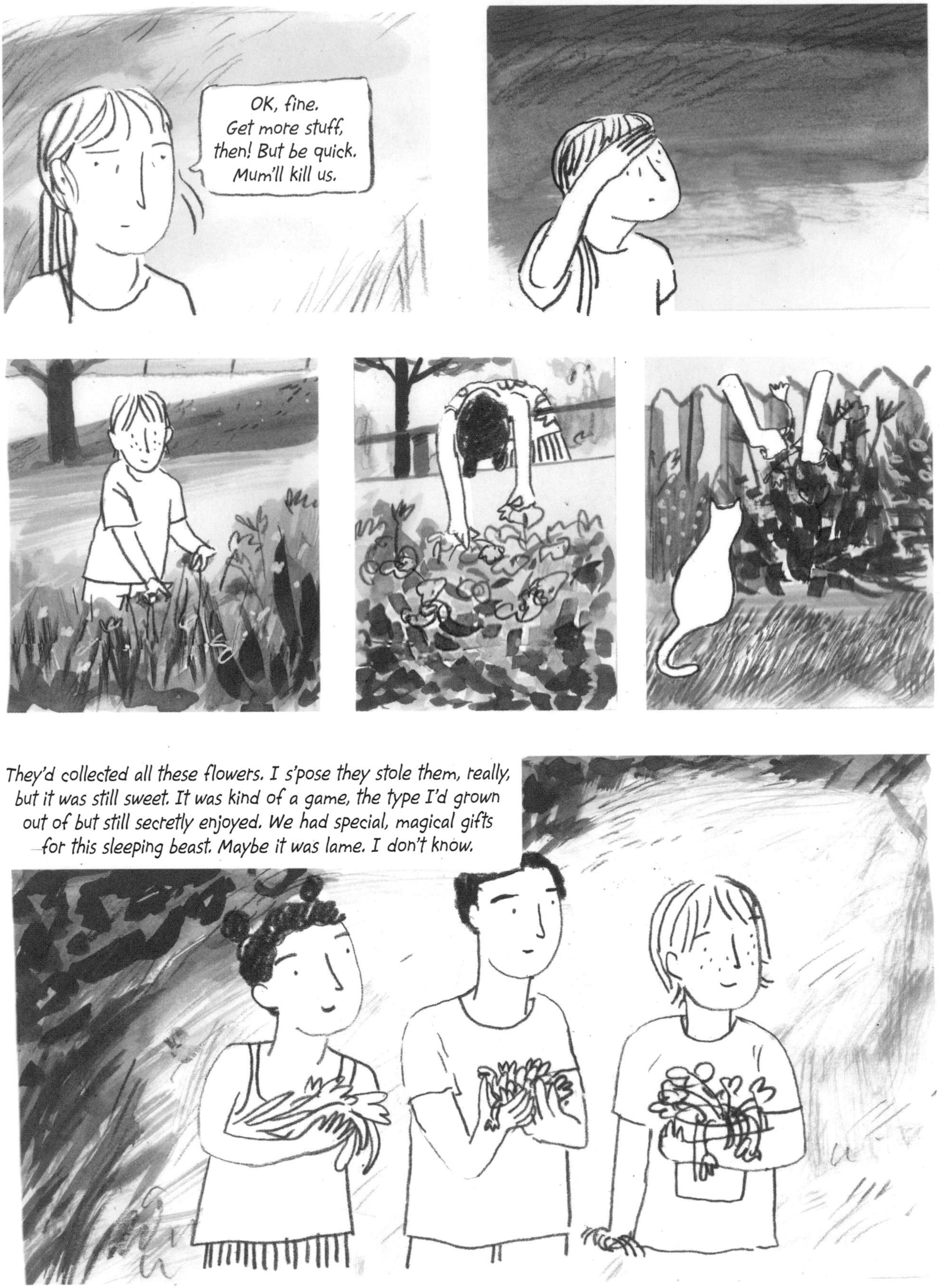
OK, fine. Get more stuff, then! But be quick. Mum'll kill us.
They'd collected all these flowers. I s'pose they stole them, really, but it was still sweet. It was kind of a game, the type I'd grown out of but still secretly enjoyed. We had special, magical gifts for this sleeping beast. Maybe it was lame. I don't know.

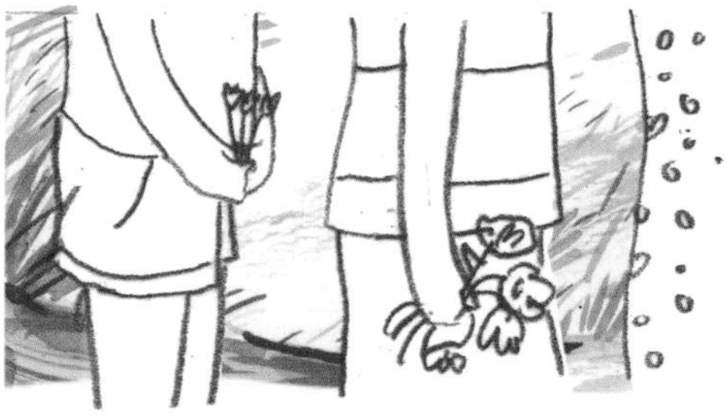

People lined up and offered flowers and Coke cans with dandelions stuffed inside and lollipop wrappers tied like flags. It was sweet but weird.

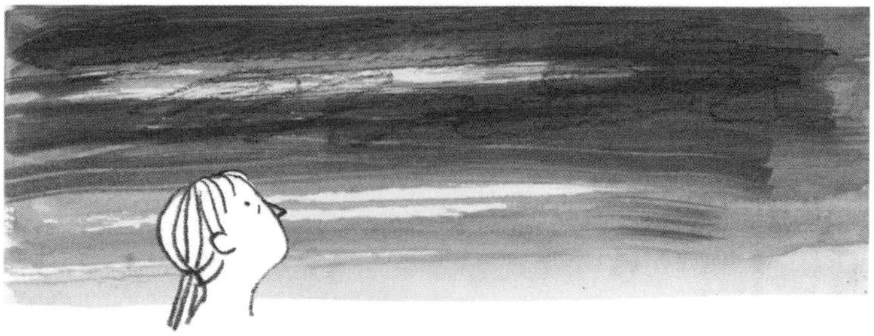

Maybe the sky was making us crazy. It felt a bit like going crazy, but it also felt completely the right thing to do. So we all waited to give our gifts to the sickly fox, and we all waited for the rain.

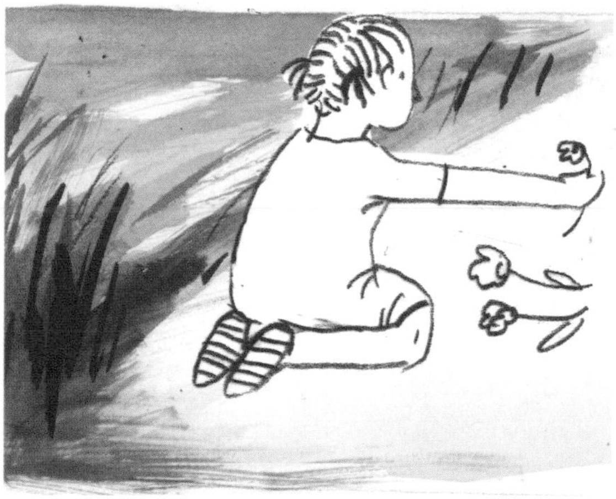

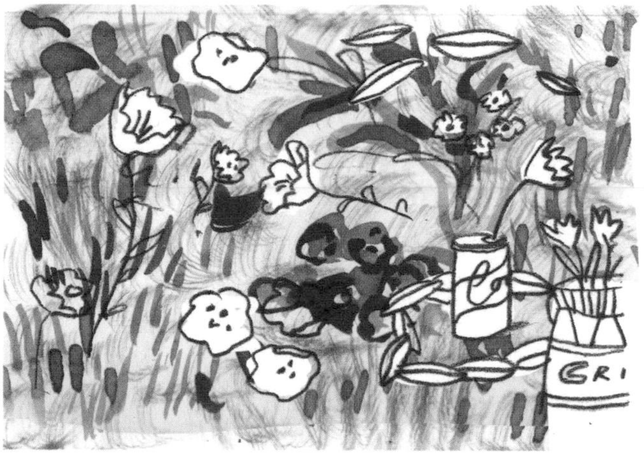

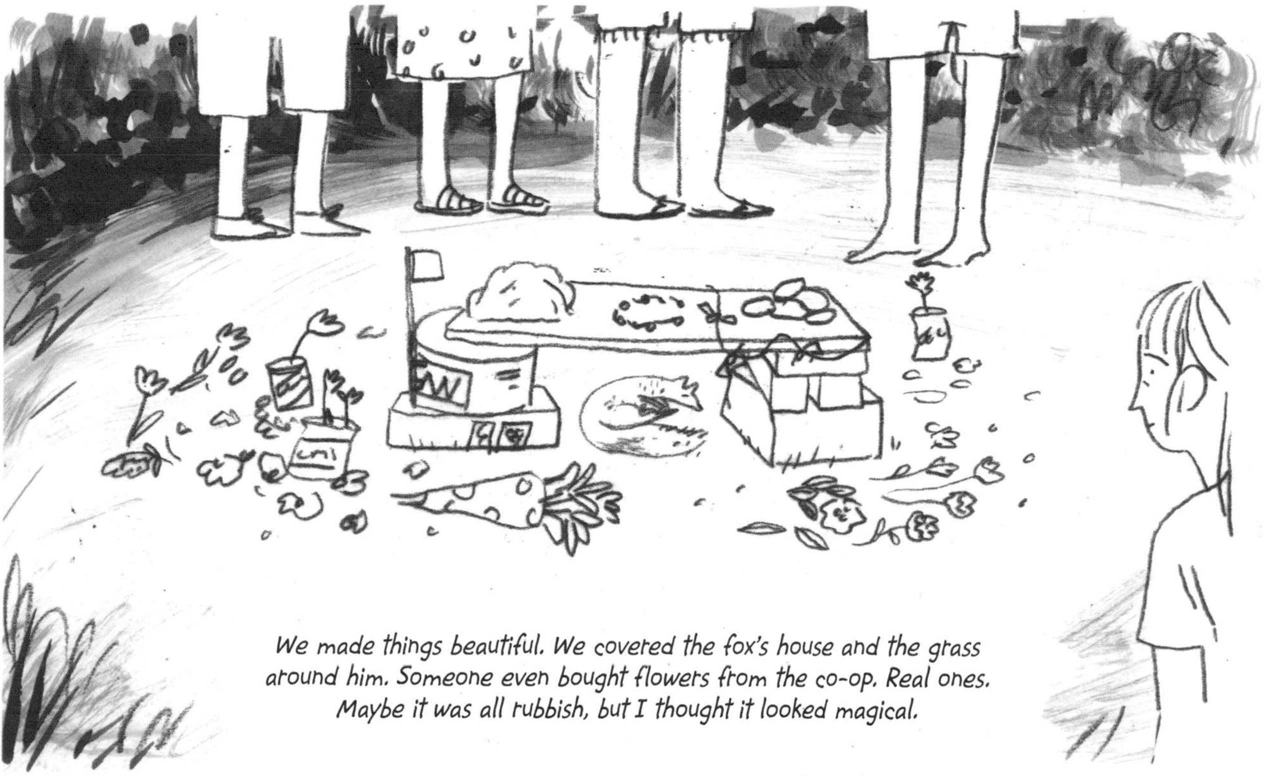
We made things beautiful. We covered the fox's house and the grass around him. Someone even bought flowers from the co-op. Real ones. Maybe it was all rubbish, but I thought it looked magical.

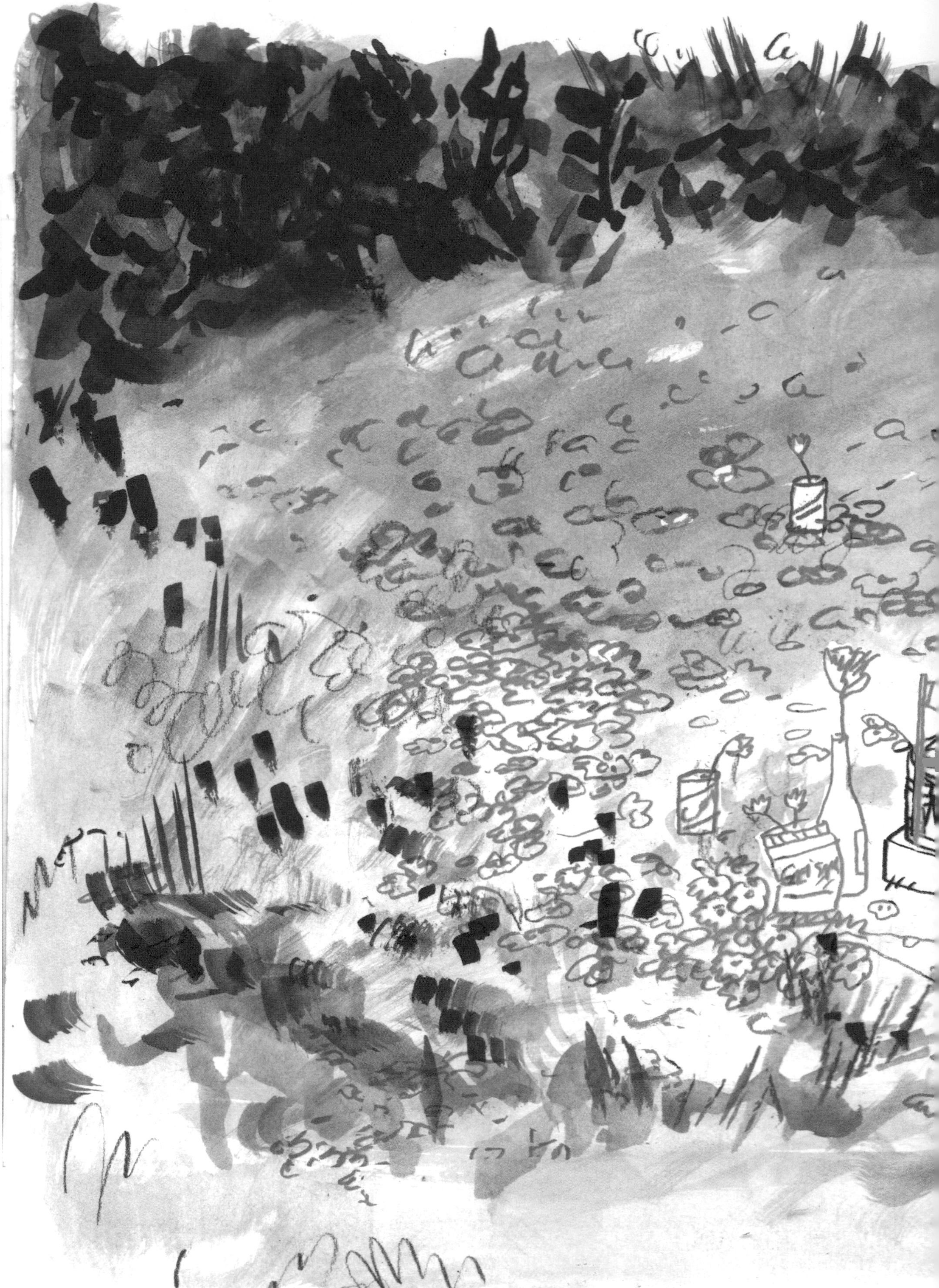

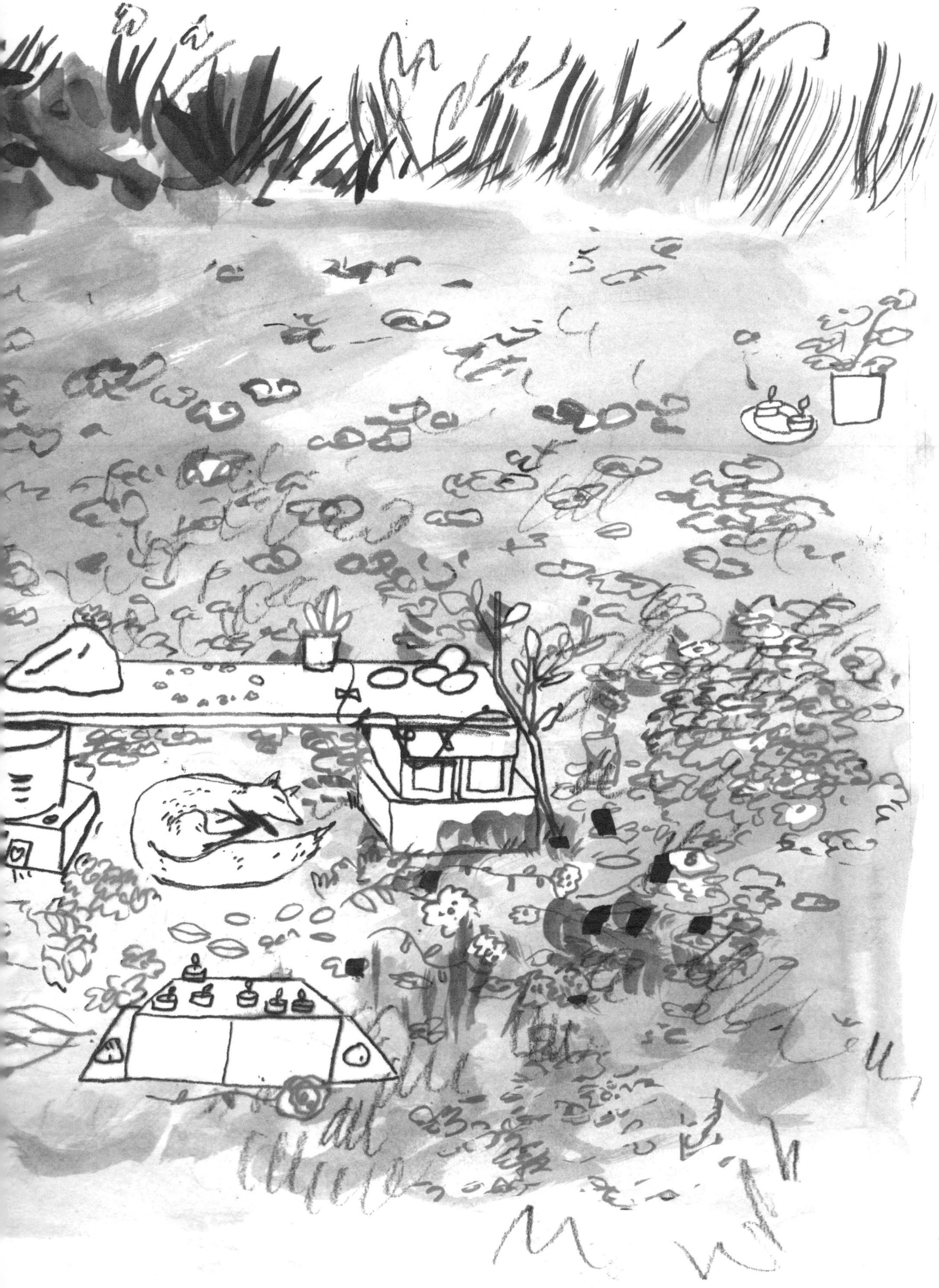

The storm was so close now.

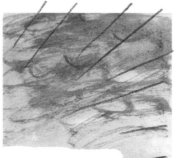

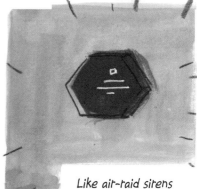

All the car alarms started going off at once. Like they'd all been nudged.

High-pitched electronic squeals shook the sludgy-thick air.

Like air-raid sirens in a war.

Whose car is that?

Neighbors came outside to yell at nobody in particular.

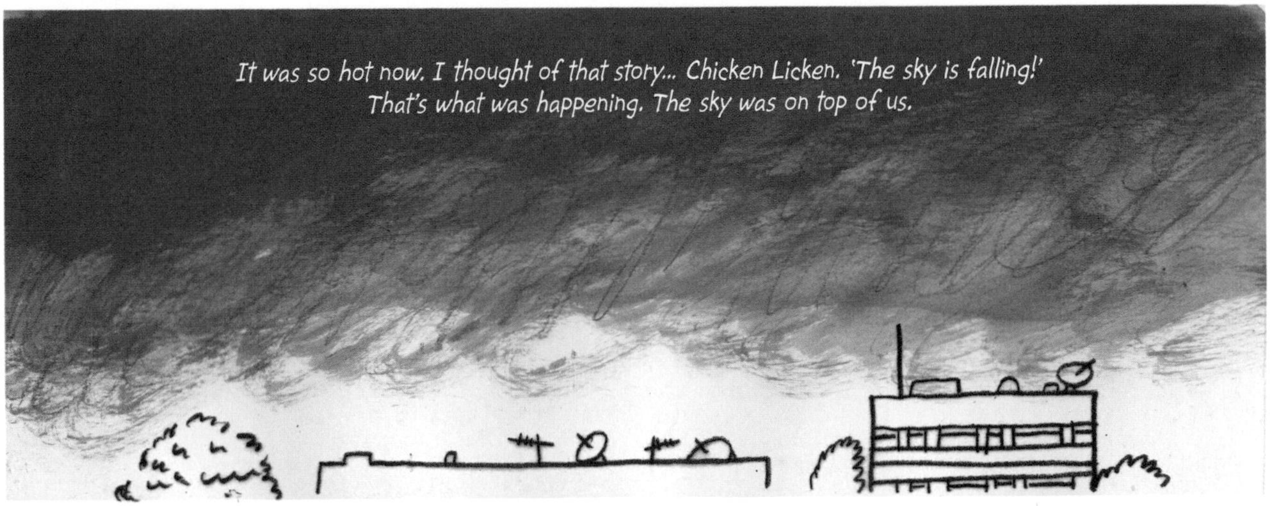
It was so hot now. I thought of that story... Chicken Licken. 'The sky is falling!' That's what was happening. The sky was on top of us.

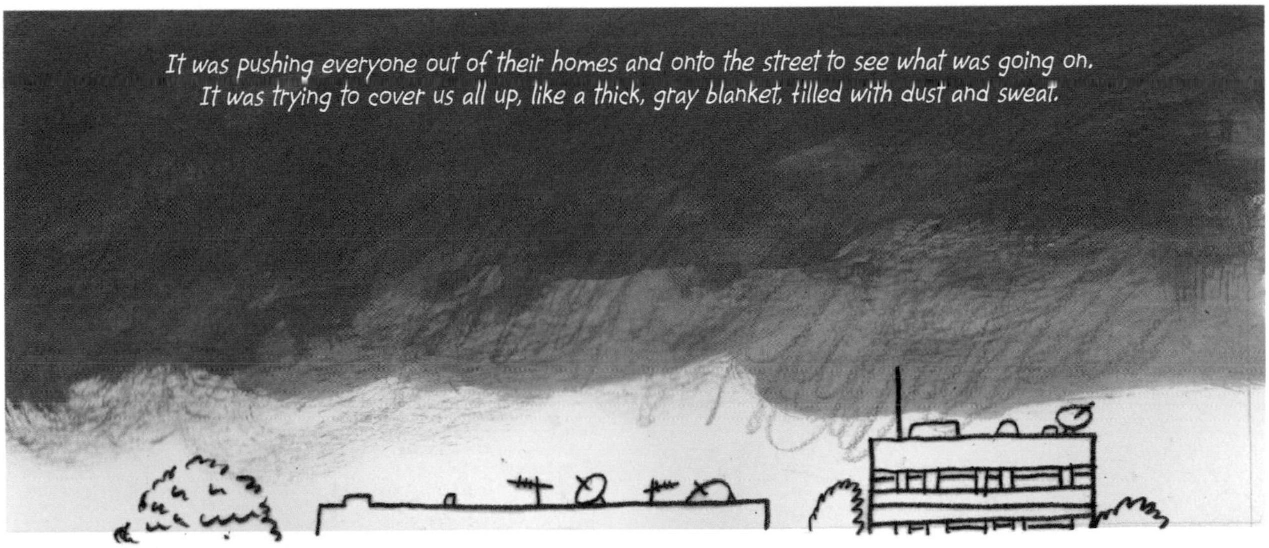
It was pushing everyone out of their homes and onto the street to see what was going on. It was trying to cover us all up, like a thick, gray blanket, filled with dust and sweat.

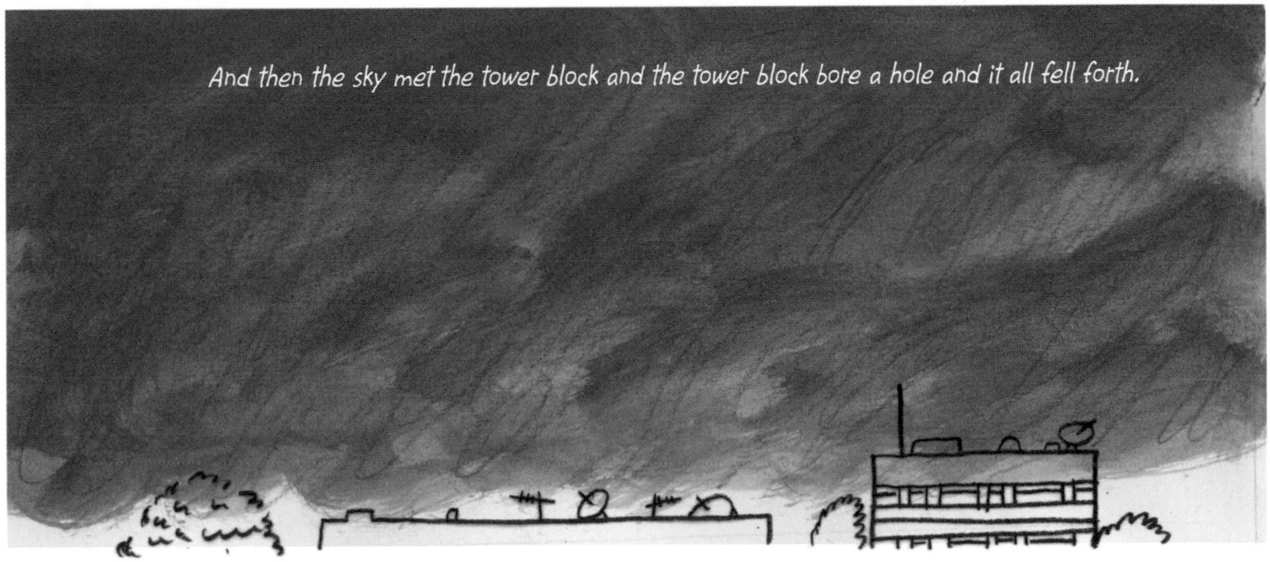
And then the sky met the tower block and the tower block bore a hole and it all fell forth.

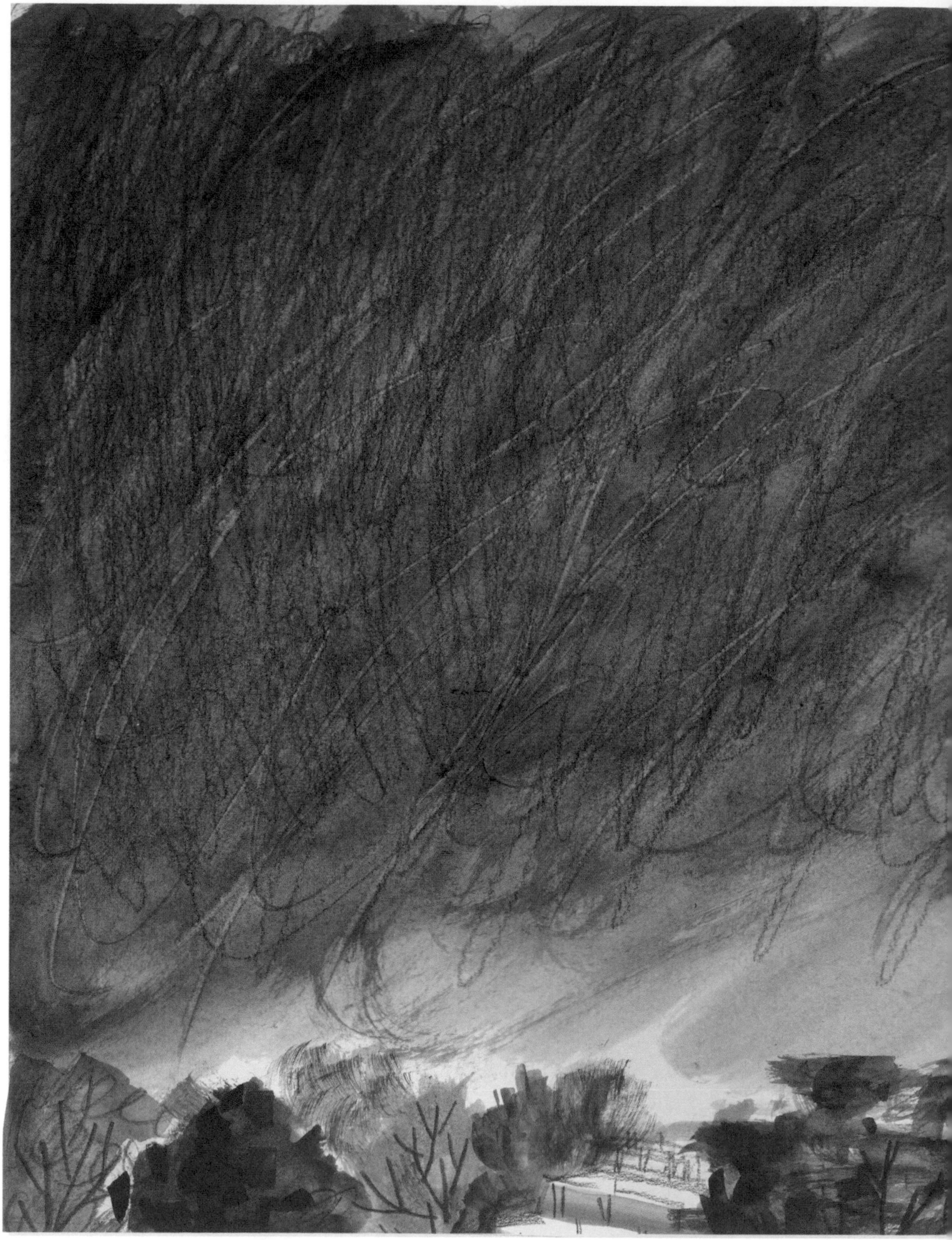

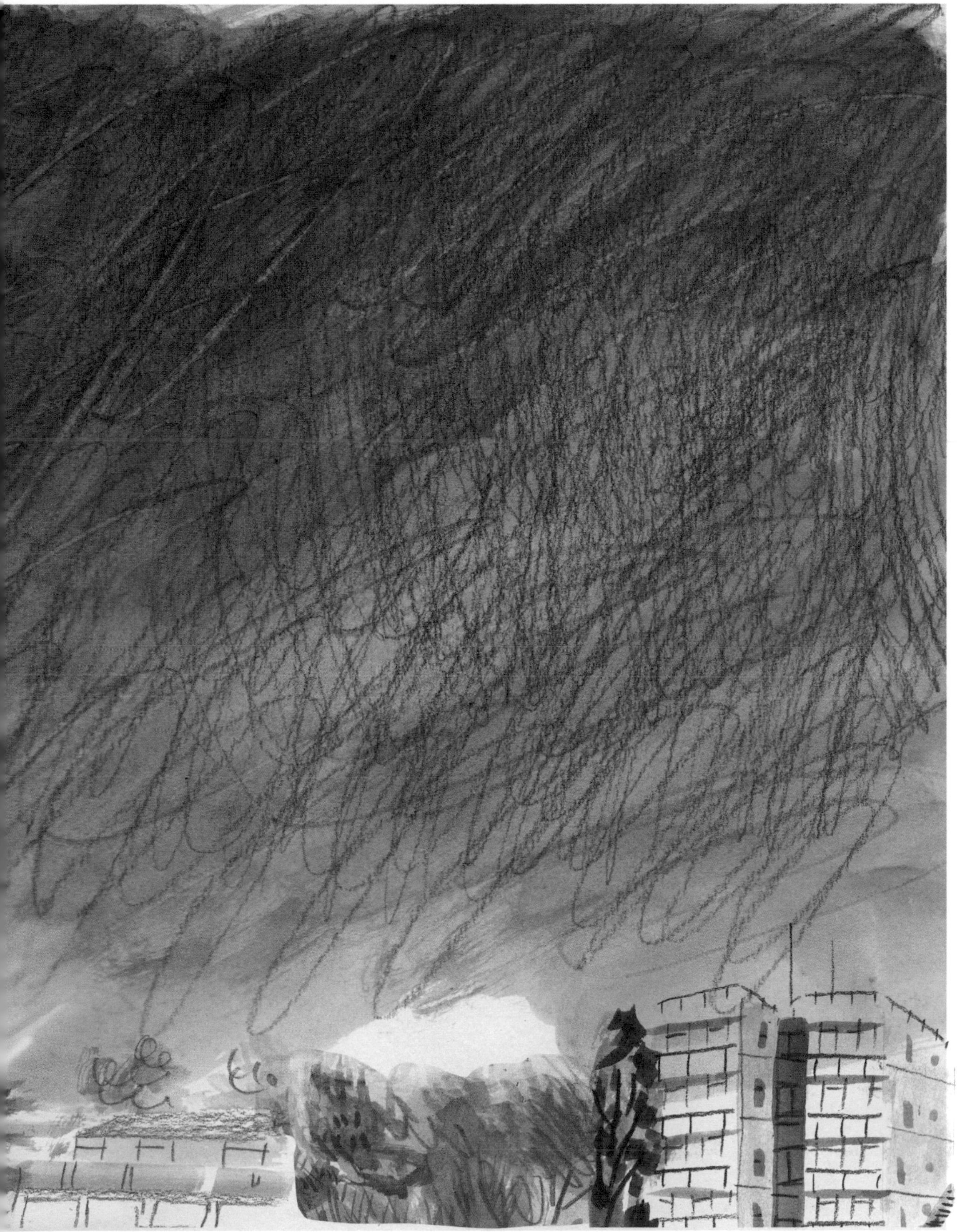

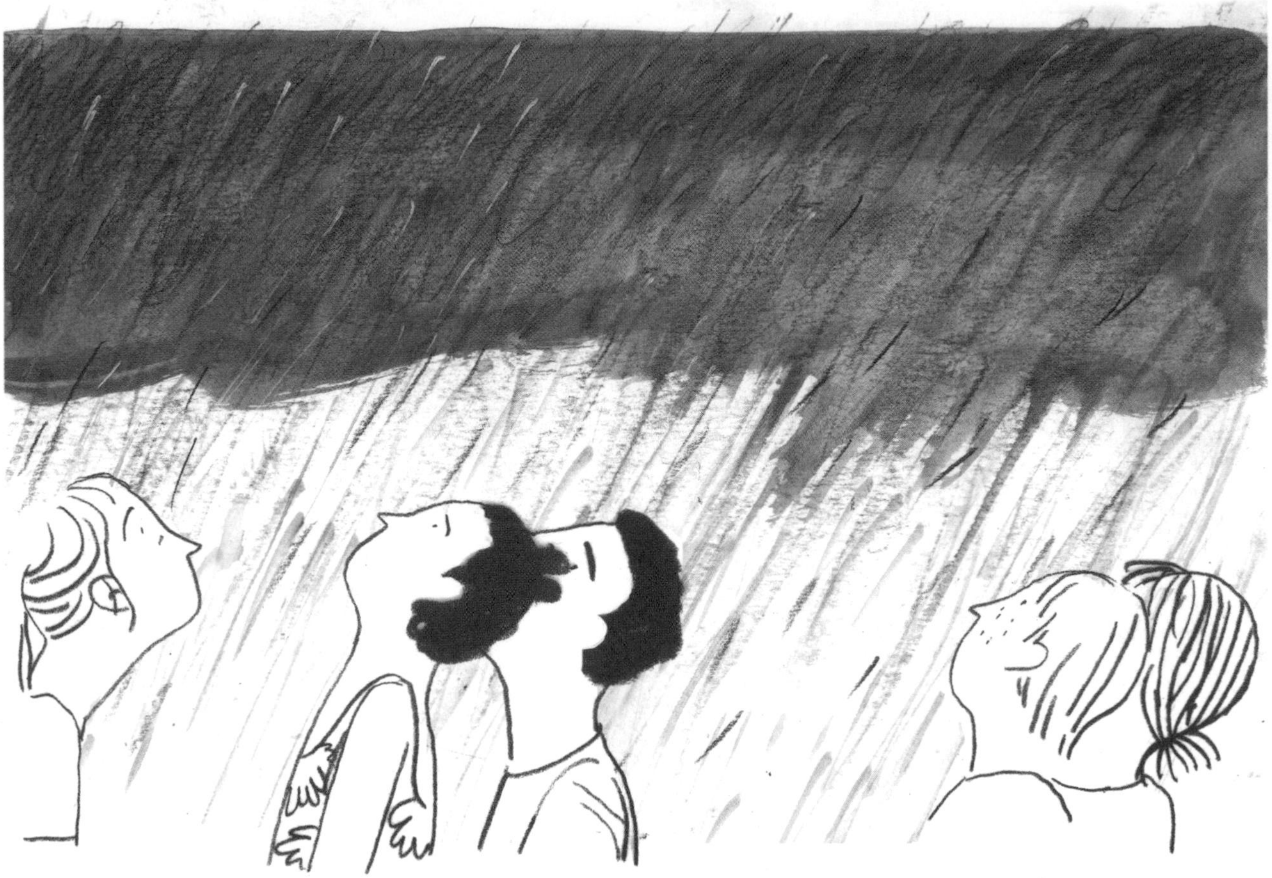

For a moment we didn't move. We'd never seen so much rain—fat, heavy drops
that seemed far more full of water than the average raindrop. They fell and fell and fell.

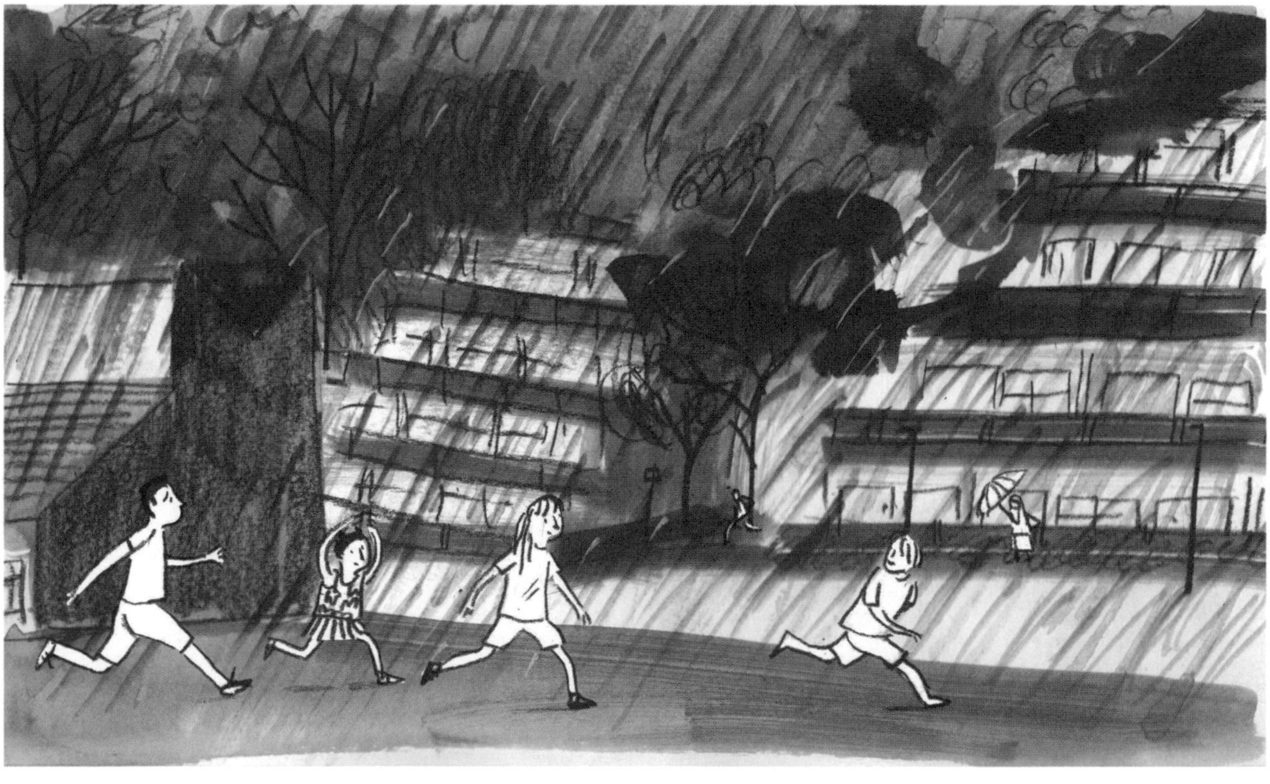

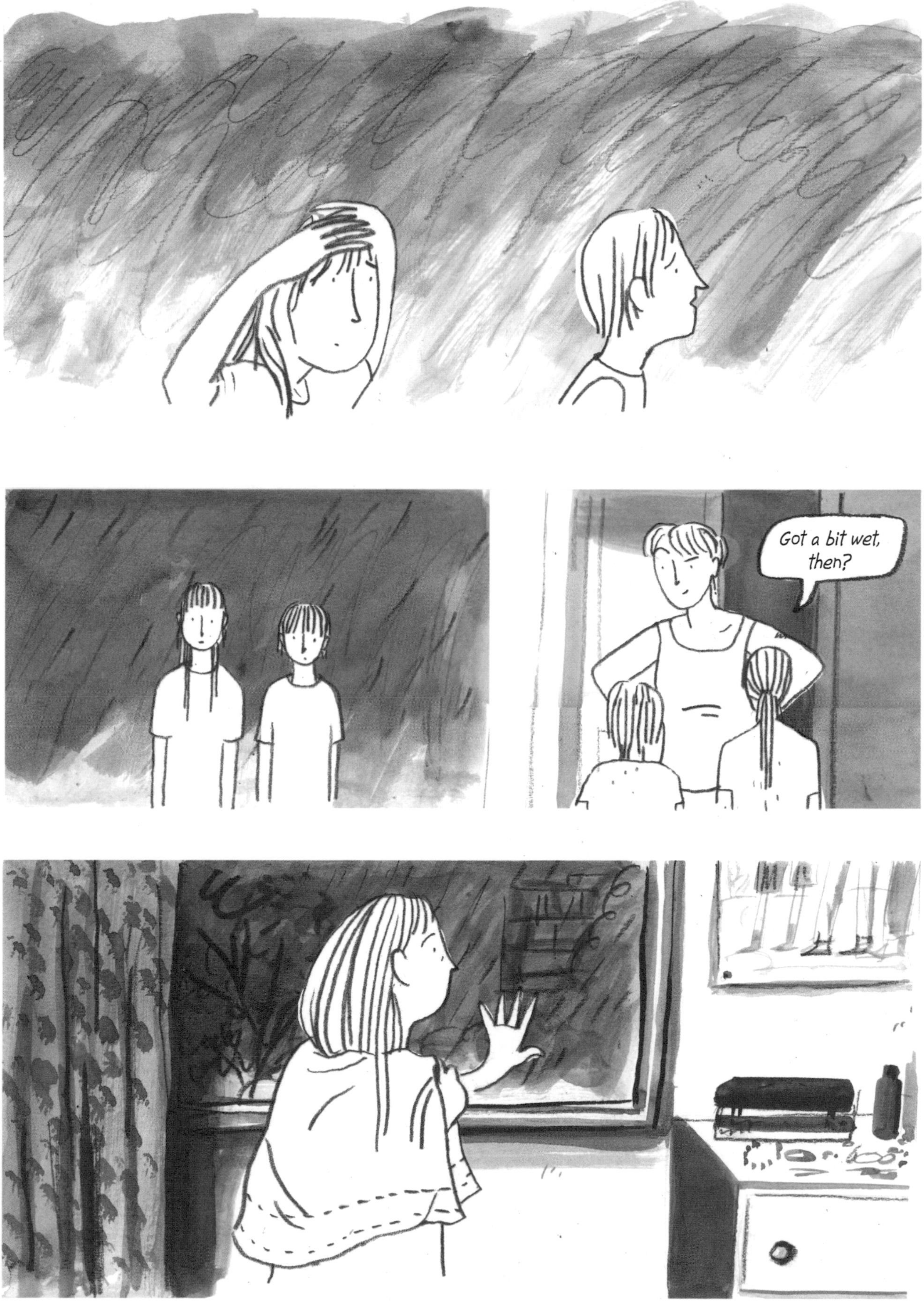
Got a bit wet, then?

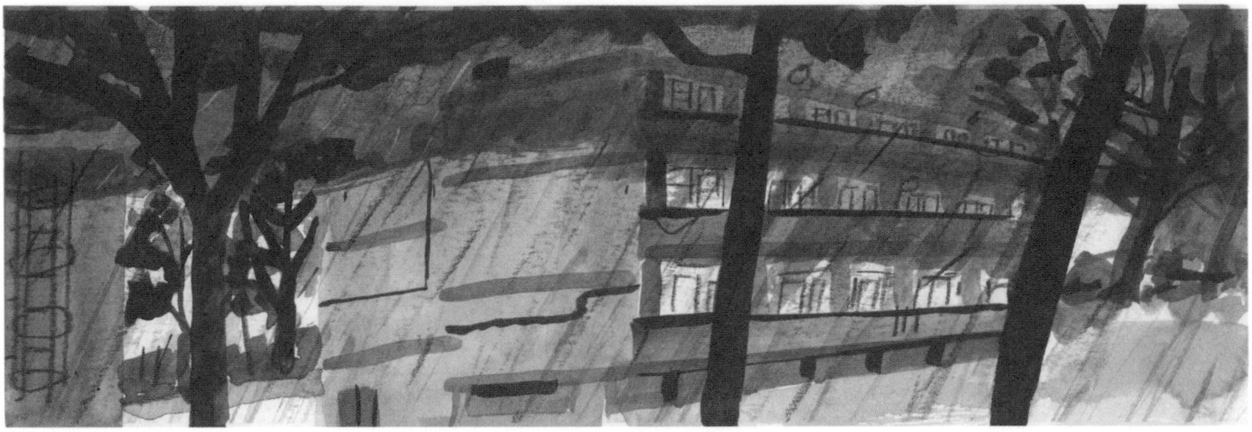

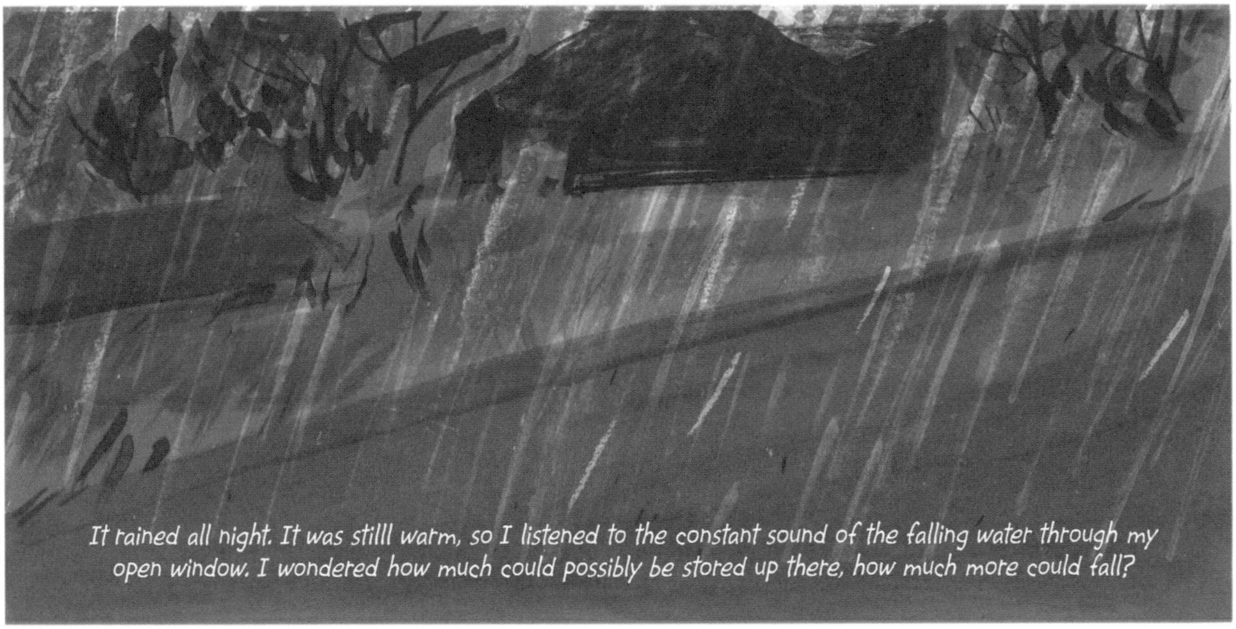
It rained all night. It was stilll warm, so I listened to the constant sound of the falling water through my open window. I wondered how much could possibly be stored up there, how much more could fall?

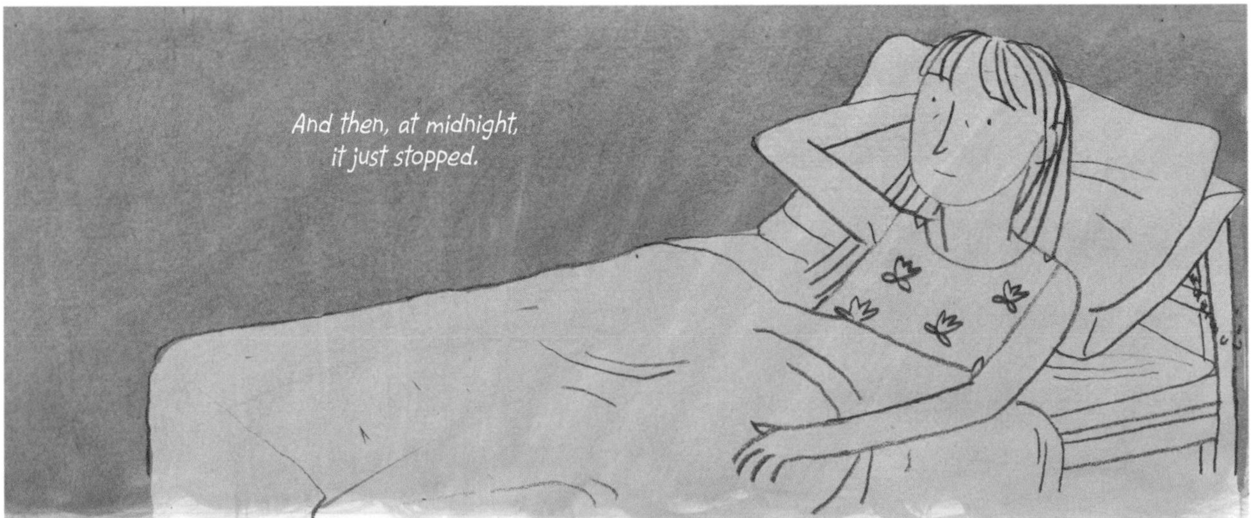
And then, at midnight, it just stopped.

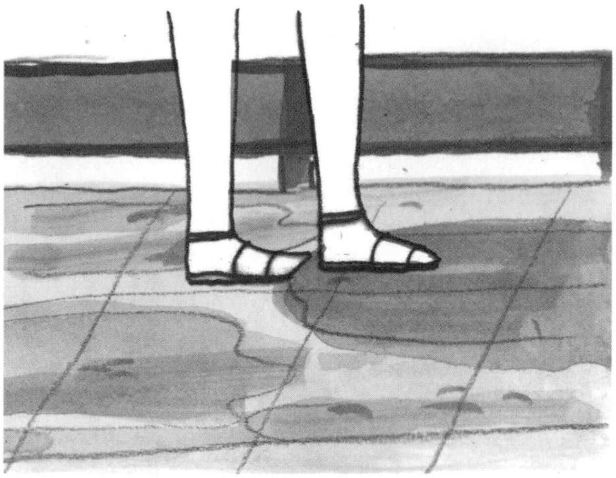

The patio was covered in puddles.

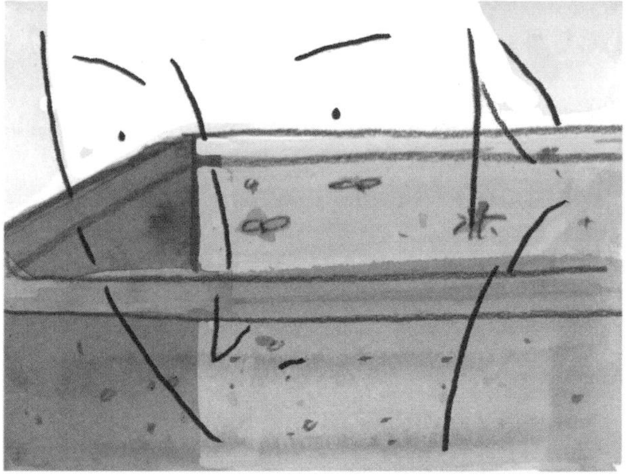

And a Tupperware box, left out all night, was
filled with murky brown water and dead bugs.

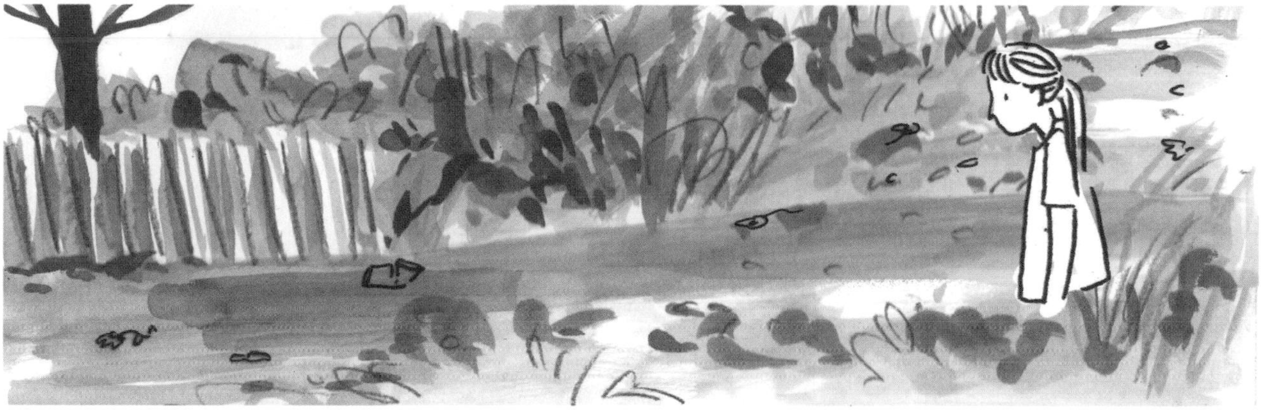

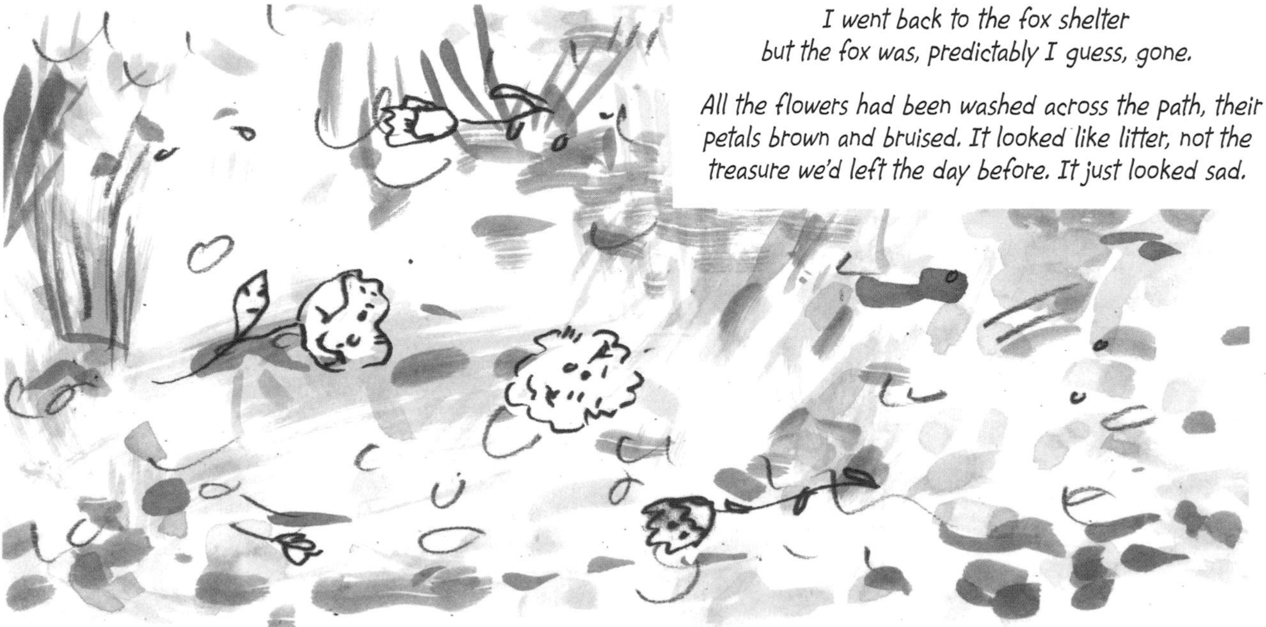
I went back to the fox shelter
but the fox was, predictably I guess, gone.
All the flowers had been washed across the path, their petals brown and bruised. It looked like litter, not the treasure we'd left the day before. It just looked sad.

We were all moved out
six months after the storm.
The estate was being refurbished
and we couldn't stay whilst the
contractors were there. Nor could
we afford the fancy new flats
they would leave behind.

What they don't tell you
about the end of the world,
the lunatics and the scientists,
is that it happens every day.

The world from before is gone
and there is a new world
and it is completely different.

B L U S H

WHEN I WAS YOUNG I WAS CONSTANTLY
EMBARRASSED. I SPENT EVERY DAY
TEETERING ON THE BRINK OF SOME
NON-SPECIFIC MORTIFICATION. ANY
LITTLE THING MIGHT SET IT OFF.

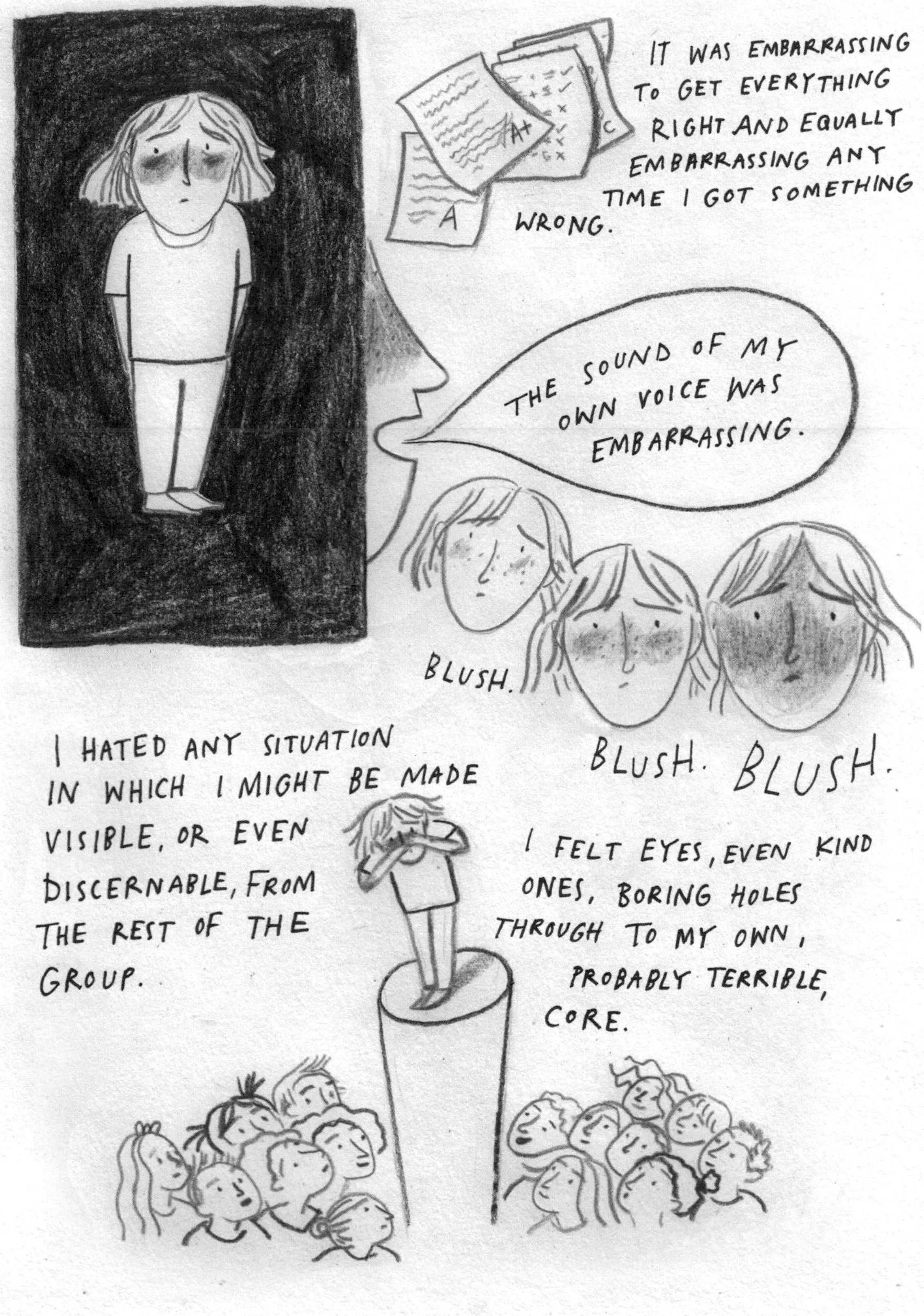
IT WAS EMBARRASSING TO GET EVERYTHING RIGHT AND EQUALLY EMBARRASSING ANY TIME I GOT SOMETHING WRONG.
A+
A
C
THE SOUND OF MY OWN VOICE WAS EMBARRASSING.
BLUSH.
BLUSH. BLUSH.
I HATED ANY SITUATION IN WHICH I MIGHT BE MADE VISIBLE, OR EVEN DISCERNABLE, FROM THE REST OF THE GROUP.
I FELT EYES, EVEN KIND ONES, BORING HOLES THROUGH TO MY OWN, PROBABLY TERRIBLE, CORE.

ONCE A TEACHER, WHO WAS RUNNING CHOIR, MADE ME SING A NOTE, ALONE.

AAAAAAA

I WASN'T MUSICAL. I'D JOINED COS MY FRIENDS WENT. I COULDN'T MATCH THE NOTE ON THE PIANO. SHE MADE ME DO IT OVER AND OVER TILL MY EYES WELLED WITH TEARS.

I REMEMBER HER AS A MONSTER FOR MAKING ME CRY SO PUBLICLY BUT PERHAPS SHE THOUGHT SHE WAS BEING ENCOURAGING, THAT I'D GET THERE EVENTUALLY. BUT I DIDN'T. INSTEAD, MY TONE-DEAF WAIL SNAKED AROUND THE ROOM AS MY CHEEKS BURNED RED.

I DON'T KNOW WHEN I STOPPED BEING EMBARRASSED. I SUPPOSE I DIDN'T STOP ALTOGETHER. BUT, AT SOME POINT, IT SORT OF PASSED.

I REMEMBER THE FEELING OF ALL THAT SHAME, HOW IT HELD ME STILL, CONTORTED INTO KNOTS. IT WAS A RELIEF TO DISCOVER I COULD LEAVE IT BEHIND AND FOCUS, SIMPLY, ON DOING THINGS. DOING THINGS WAS SO MUCH BETTER THAN WORRYING ABOUT WHO WAS WATCHING ME AND WHAT THEY THOUGHT. IT IS GOOD, SOMETIMES, TO STEP OUT OF YOUR OWN HEAD AND INTO THE WORLD.

DOG
WALK

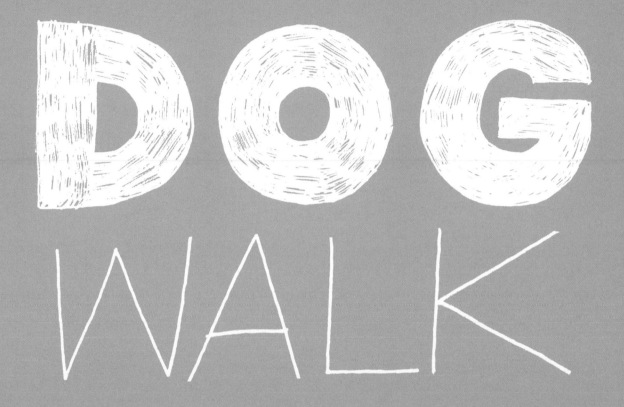

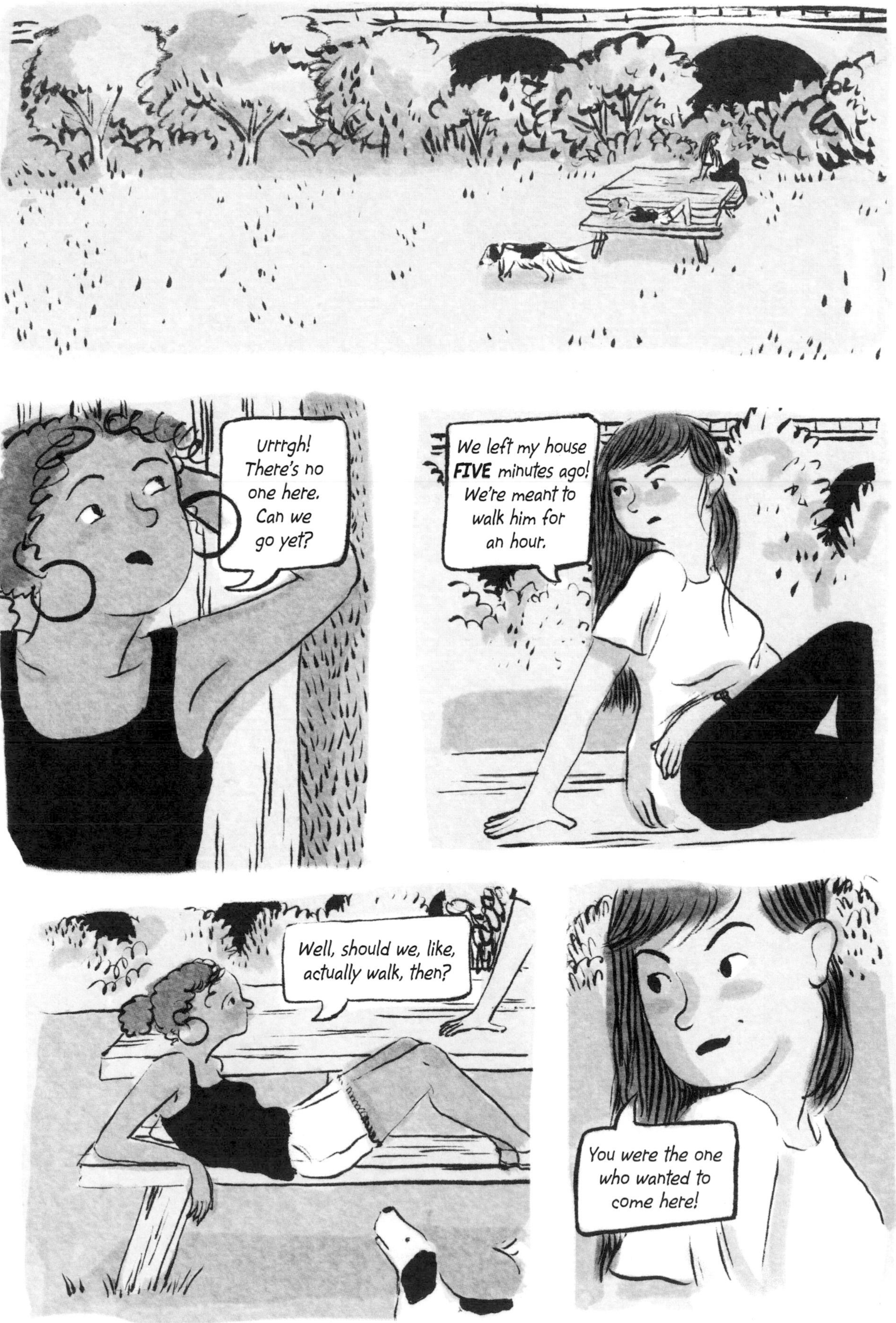
Urrrgh! There's no one here. Can we go yet?
We left my house FIVE minutes ago! We're meant to walk him for an hour.
Well, should we, like, actually walk, then?
You were the one who wanted to come here!

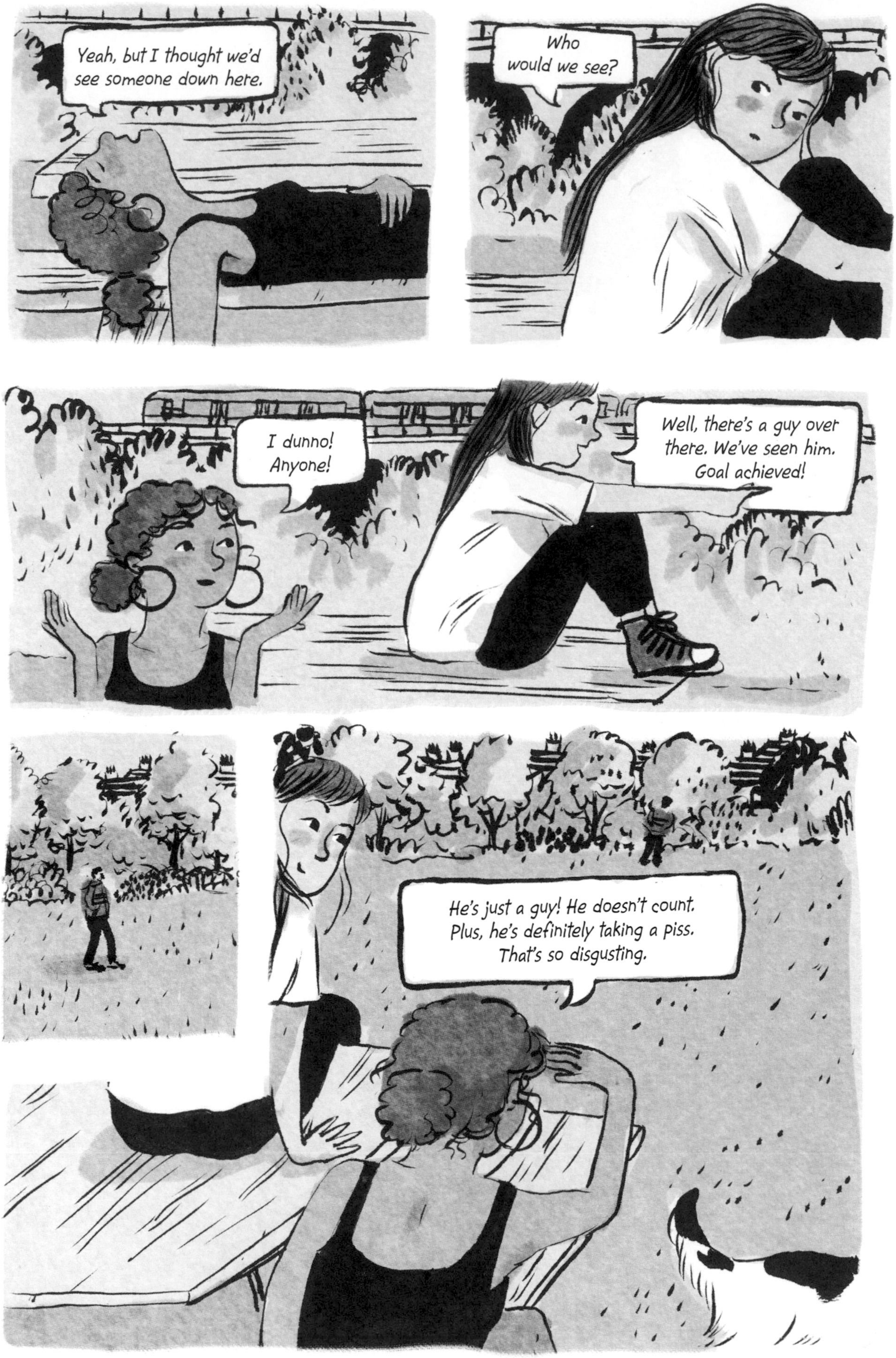
Yeah, but I thought we'd see someone down here.
Who would we see?
I dunno! Anyone!
Well, there's a guy over there. We've seen him. Goal achieved!
He's just a guy! He doesn't count. Plus, he's definitely taking a piss. That's so disgusting.

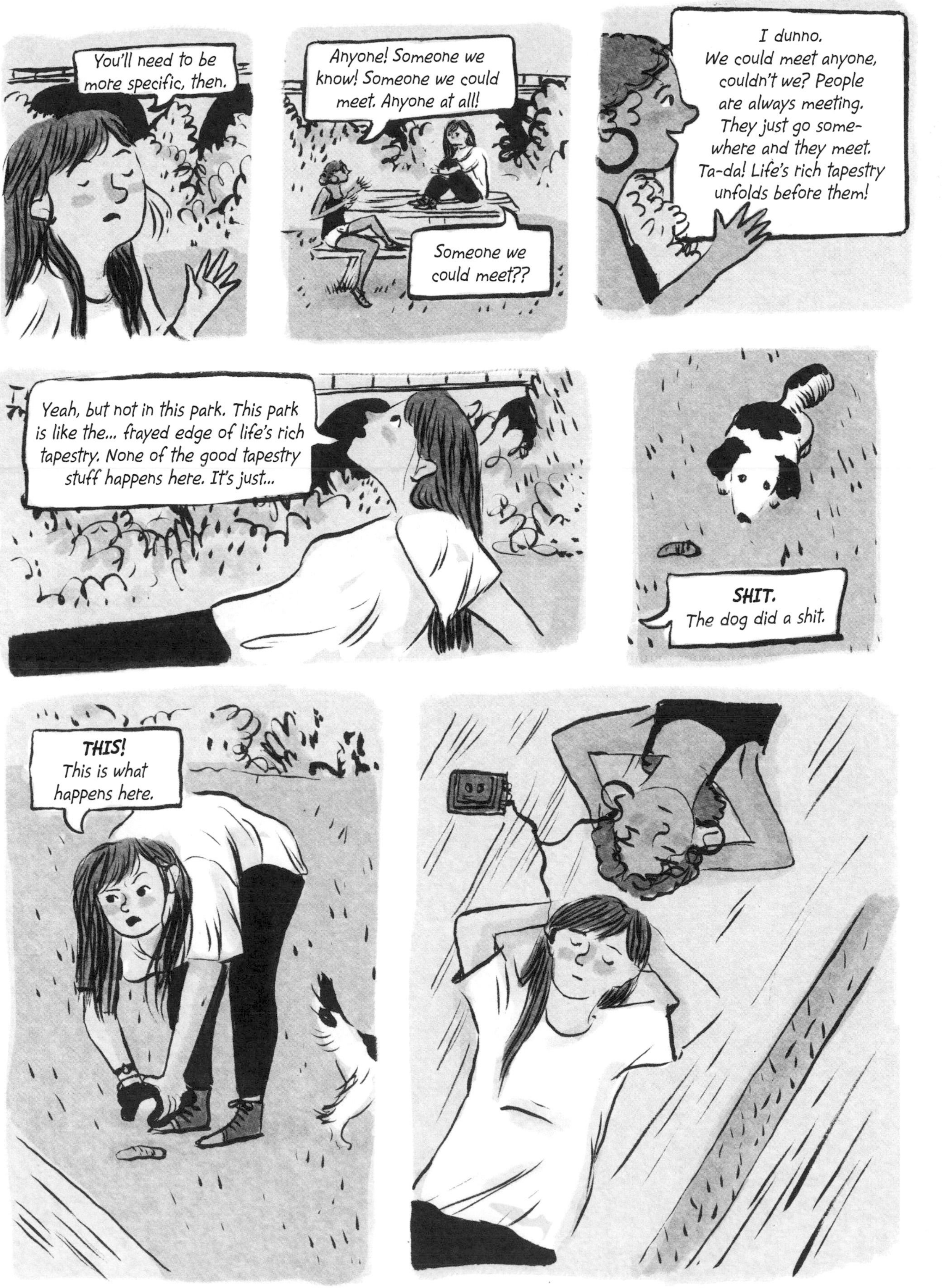
You'll need to be more specific, then.
Anyone! Someone we know! Someone we could meet. Anyone at all!
Someone we could meet??
I dunno. We could meet anyone, couldn't we? People are always meeting. They just go somewhere and they meet. Ta-da! Life's rich tapestry unfolds before them!
Yeah, but not in this park. This park is like the... frayed edge of life's rich tapestry. None of the good tapestry stuff happens here. It's just...
SHIT. The dog did a shit.
THIS! This is what happens here.

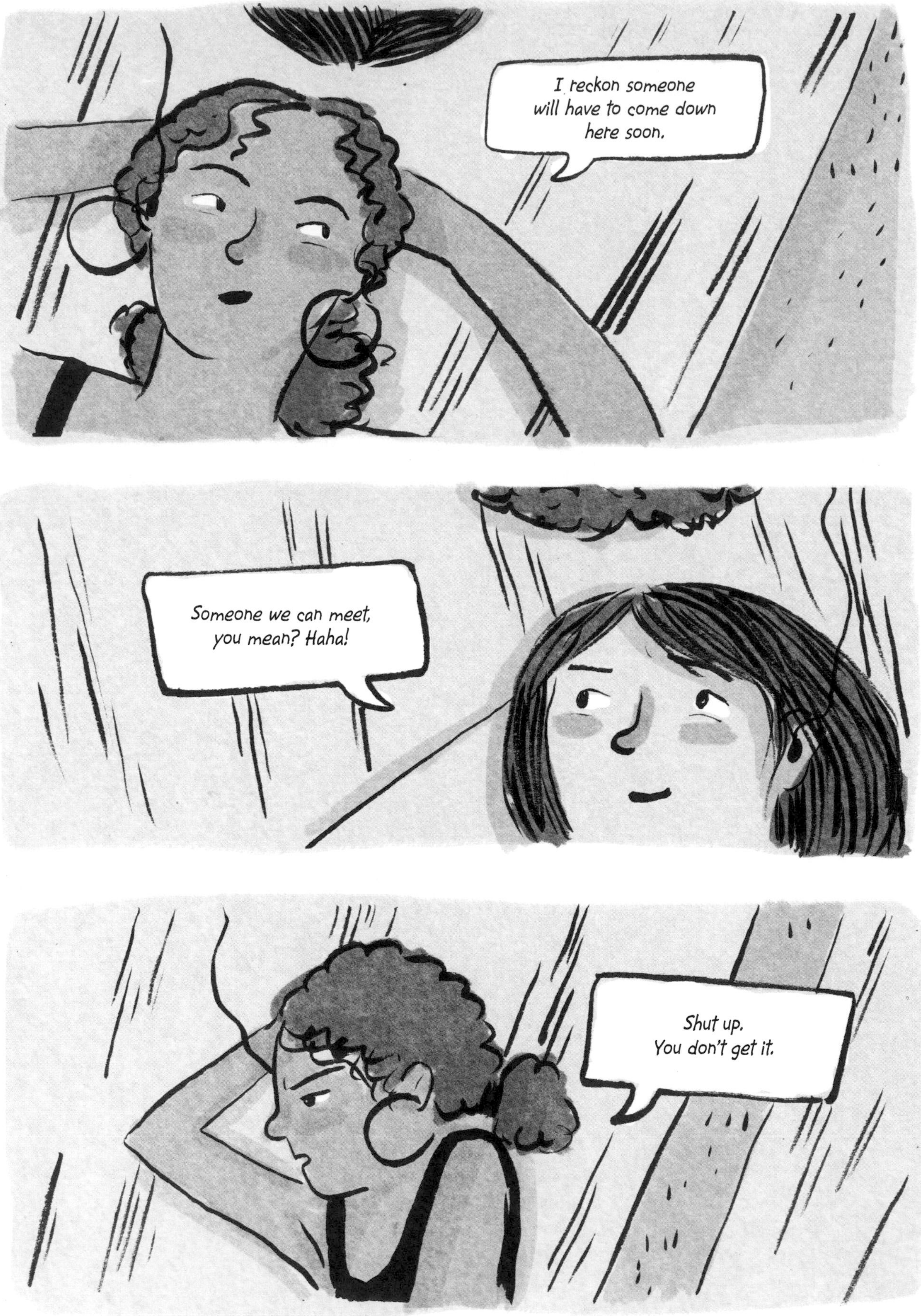
I reckon someone will have to come down here soon.
Someone we can meet, you mean? Haha!
Shut up. You don't get it.

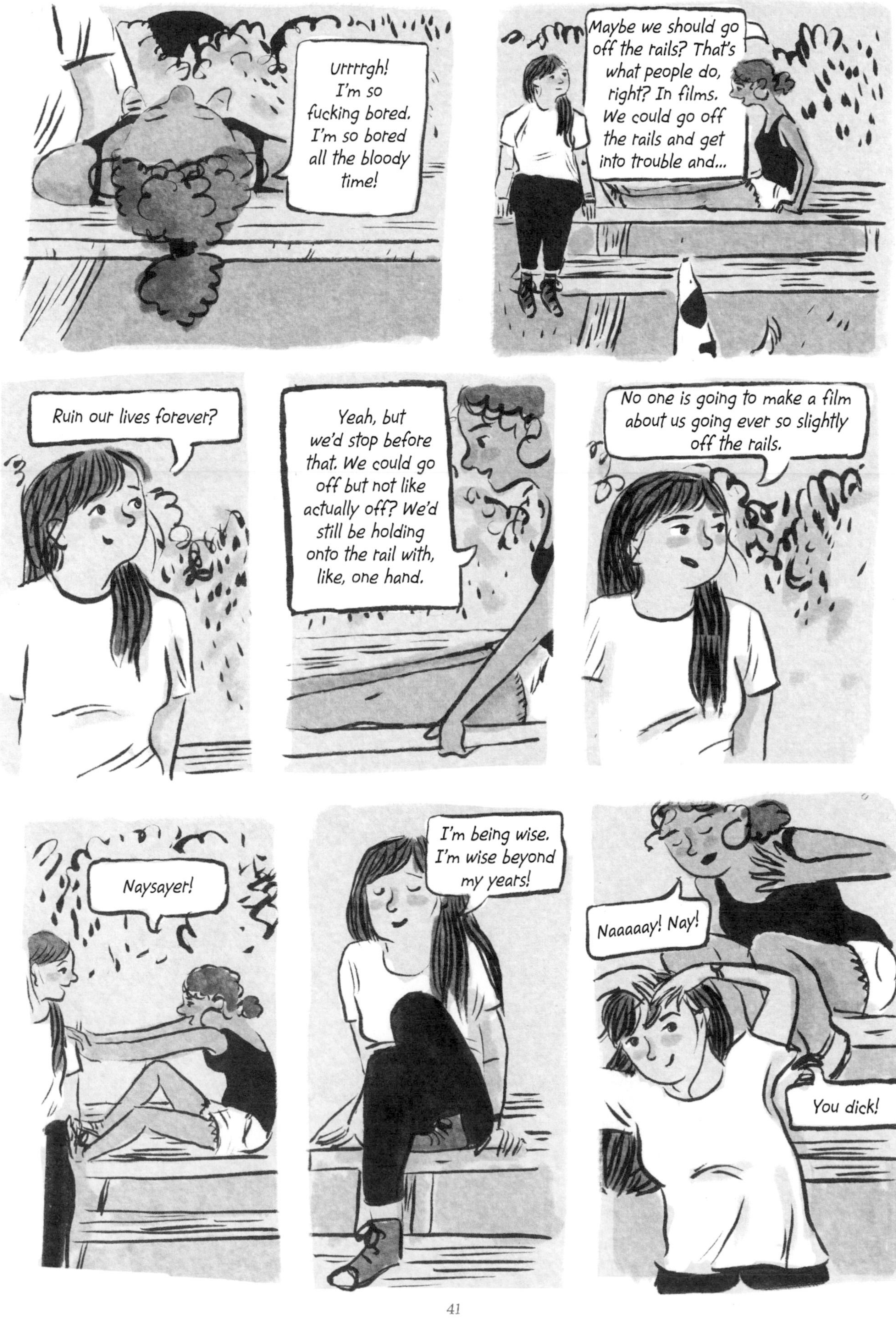
Urrrrgh! I'm so fucking bored. I'm so bored all the bloody time!
Maybe we should go off the rails? That's what people do, right? In films. We could go off the rails and get into trouble and...
Ruin our lives forever?
Yeah, but we'd stop before that. We could go off but not like actually off? We'd still be holding onto the rail with, like, one hand.
No one is going to make a film about us going ever so slightly off the rails.
Naysayer!
I'm being wise. I'm wise beyond my years!
Naaaaay! Nay!
You dick!

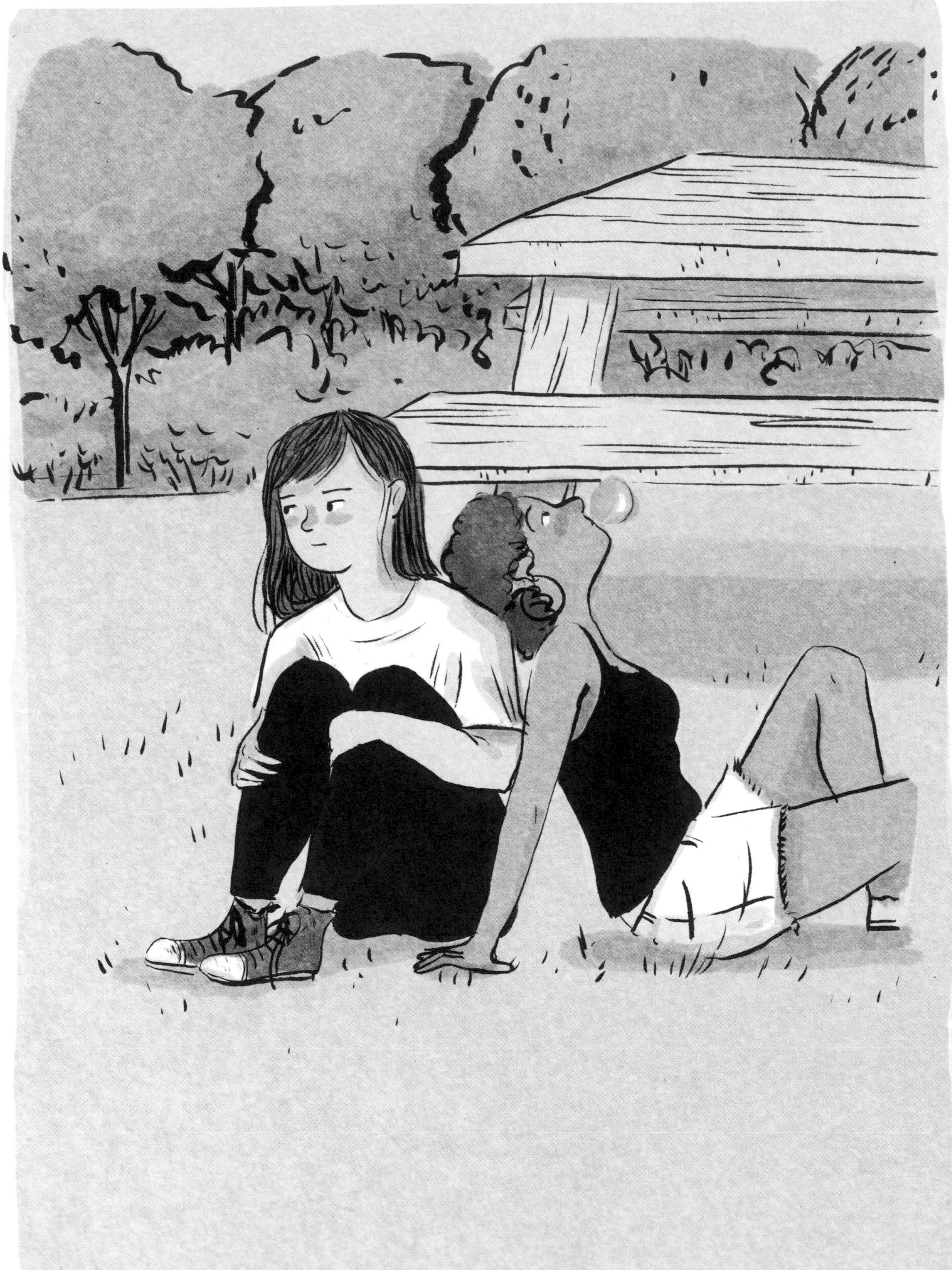

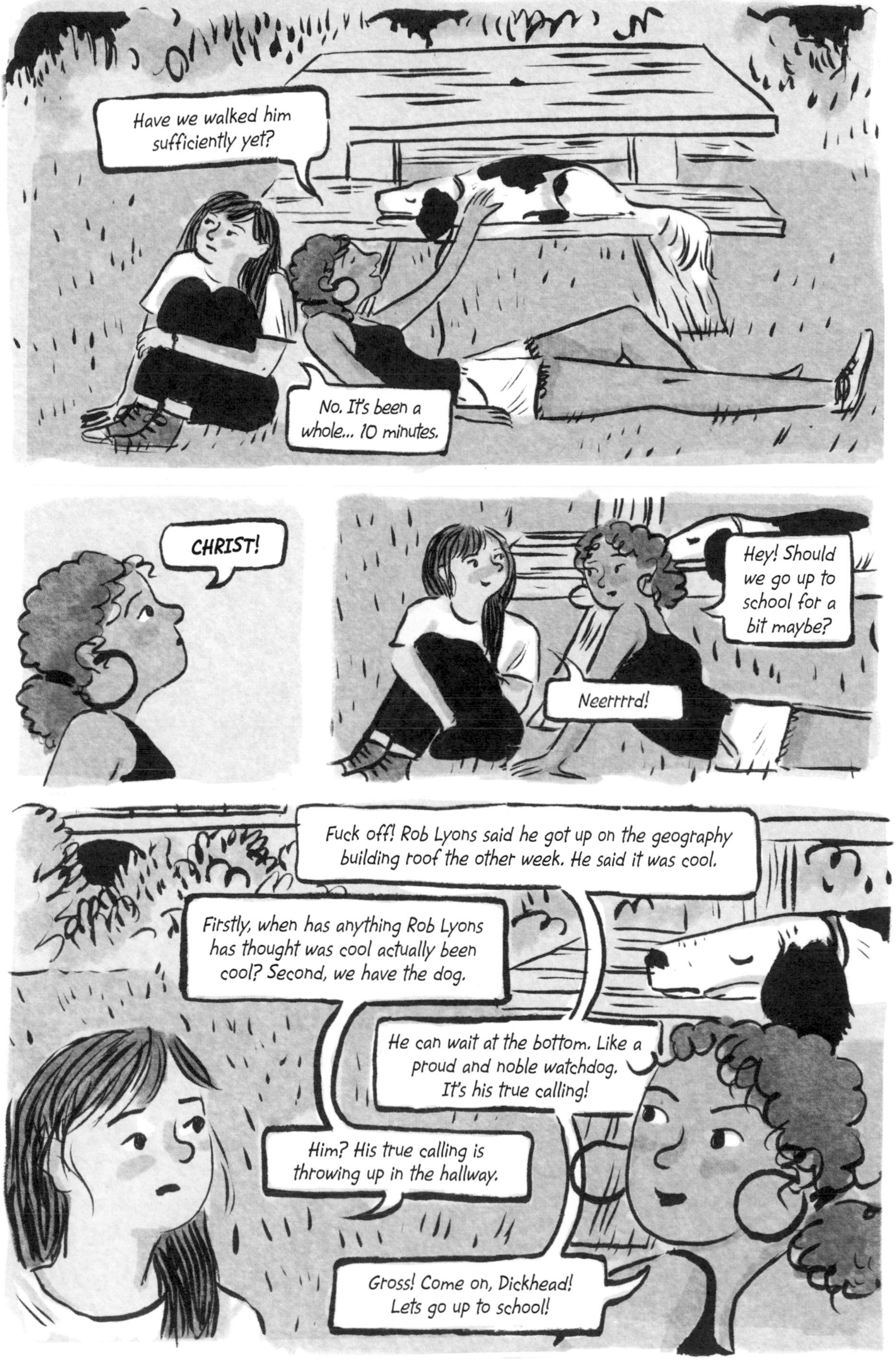
Have we walked him sufficiently yet?
No. It's been a whole... 10 minutes.
CHRIST!
Hey! Should we go up to school for a bit maybe?
Neerrrrd!
Fuck off! Rob Lyons said he got up on the geography building roof the other week. He said it was cool.
Firstly, when has anything Rob Lyons has thought was cool actually been cool? Second, we have the dog.
He can wait at the bottom. Like a proud and noble watchdog. It's his true calling!
Him? His true calling is throwing up in the hallway.
Gross! Come on, Dickhead! Lets go up to school!

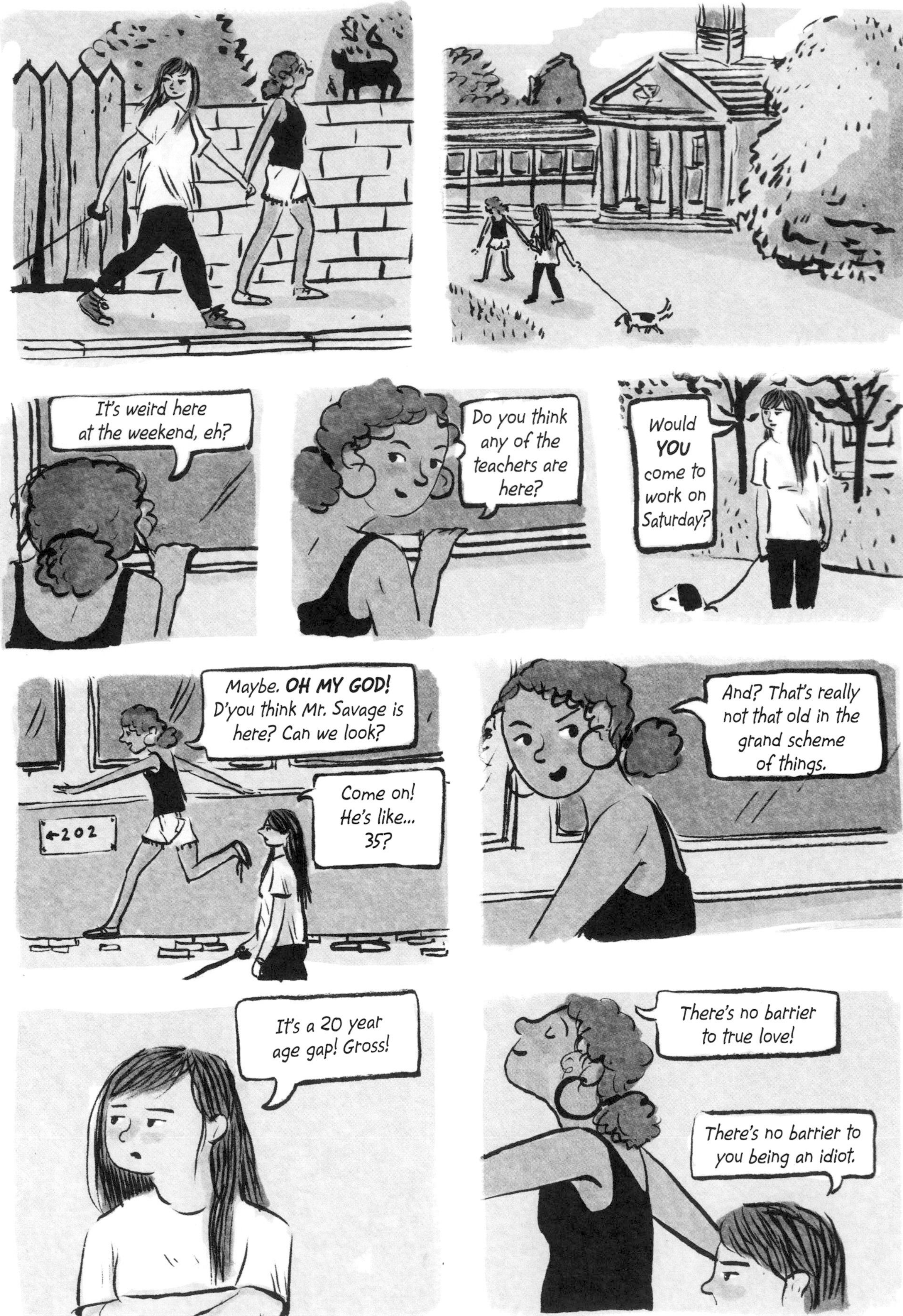

It's weird here at the weekend, eh?
Do you think any of the teachers are here?
Would YOU come to work on Saturday?
Maybe. OH MY GOD! D'you think Mr. Savage is here? Can we look?
Come on! He's like... 35?
←202
And? That's really not that old in the grand scheme of things.
It's a 20 year age gap! Gross!
There's no barrier to true love!
There's no barrier to you being an idiot.

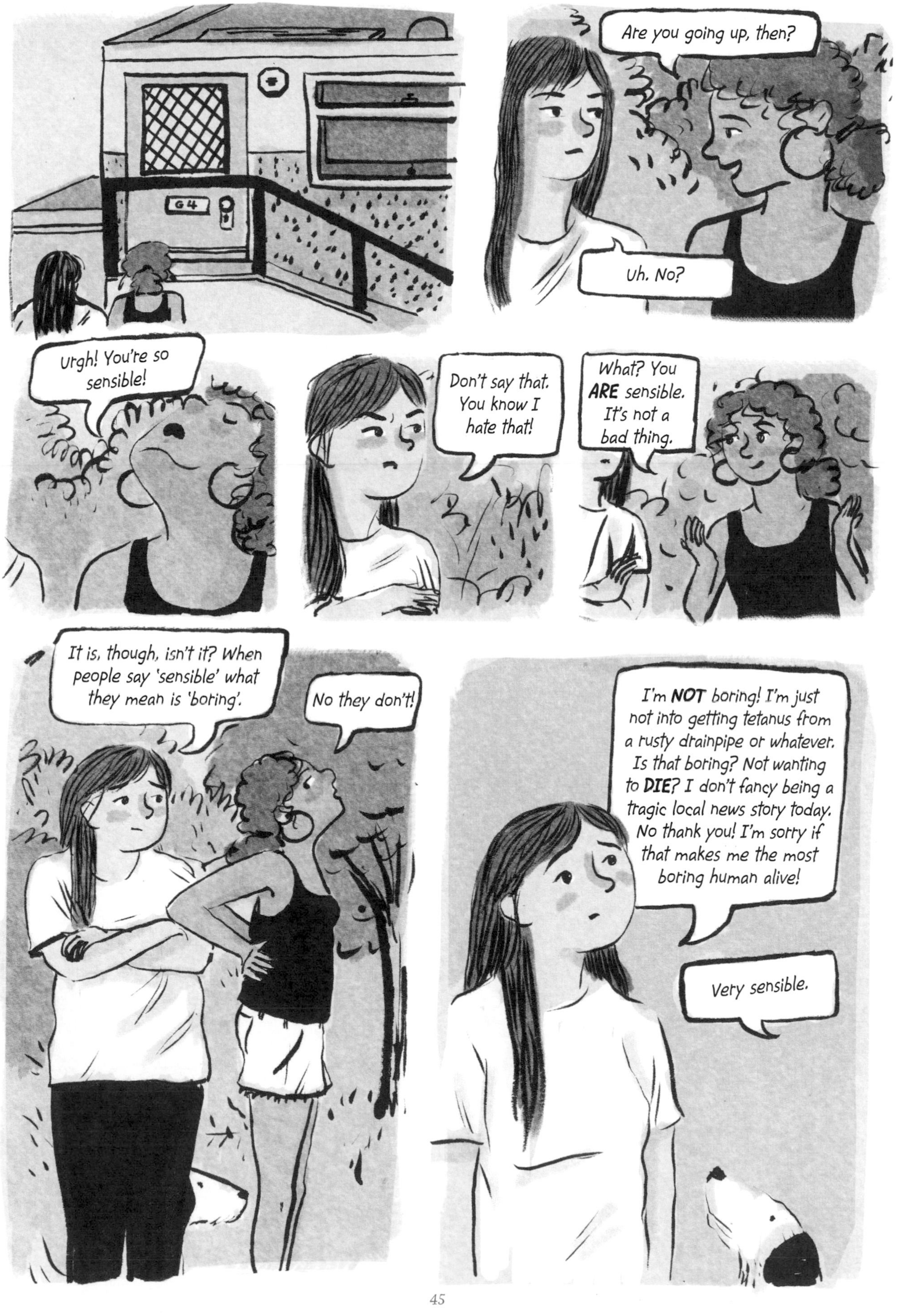
Are you going up, then?
Uh. No?
Urgh! You're so sensible!
Don't say that. You know I hate that!
What? You **ARE** sensible. It's not a bad thing.
It is, though, isn't it? When people say 'sensible' what they mean is 'boring'.
No they don't!
I'm **NOT** boring! I'm just not into getting tetanus from a rusty drainpipe or whatever. Is that boring? Not wanting to **DIE**? I don't fancy being a tragic local news story today. No thank you! I'm sorry if that makes me the most boring human alive!
Very sensible.

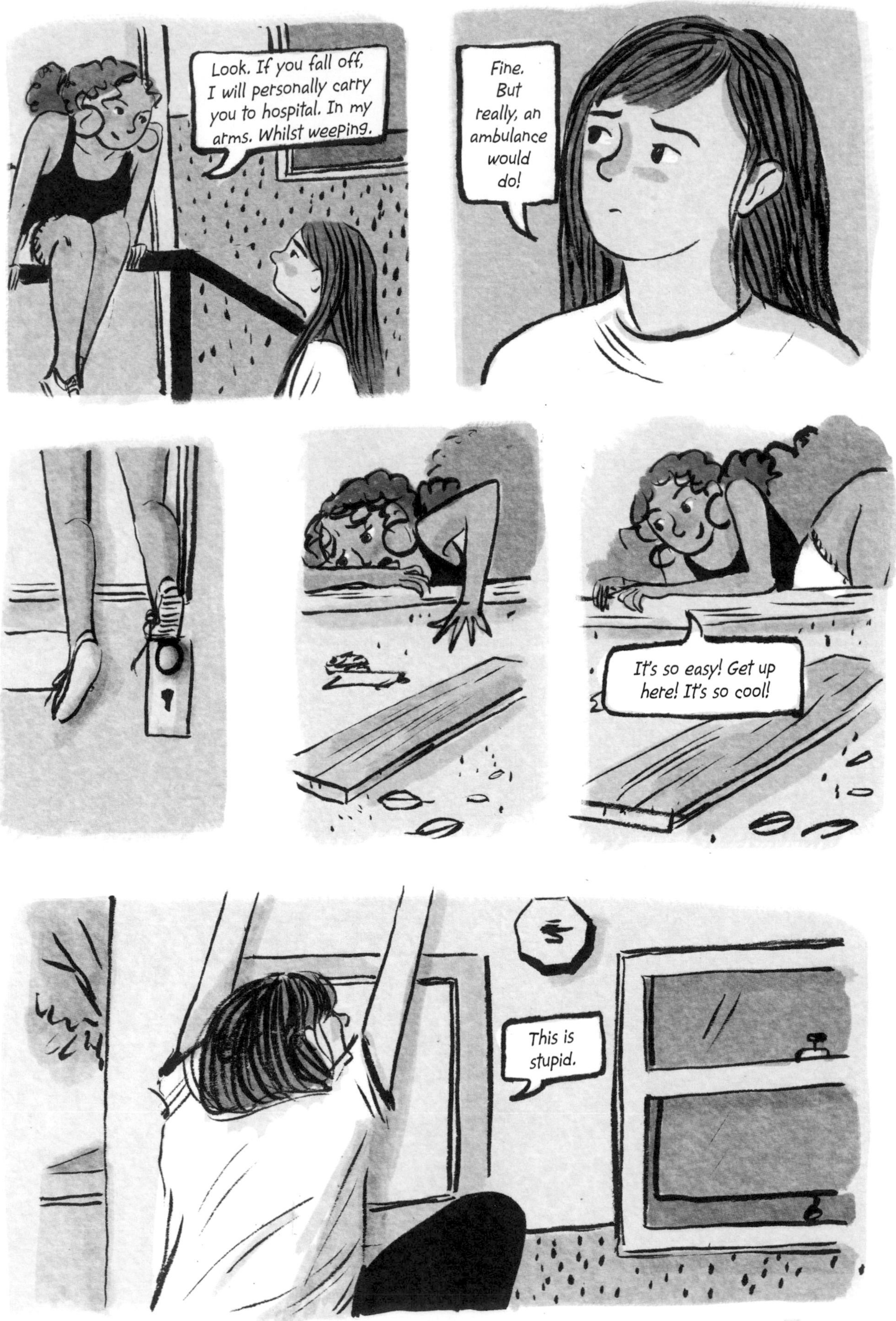
Look. If you fall off, I will personally carry you to hospital. In my arms. Whilst weeping.
Fine. But really, an ambulance would do!
It's so easy! Get up here! It's so cool!
This is stupid.

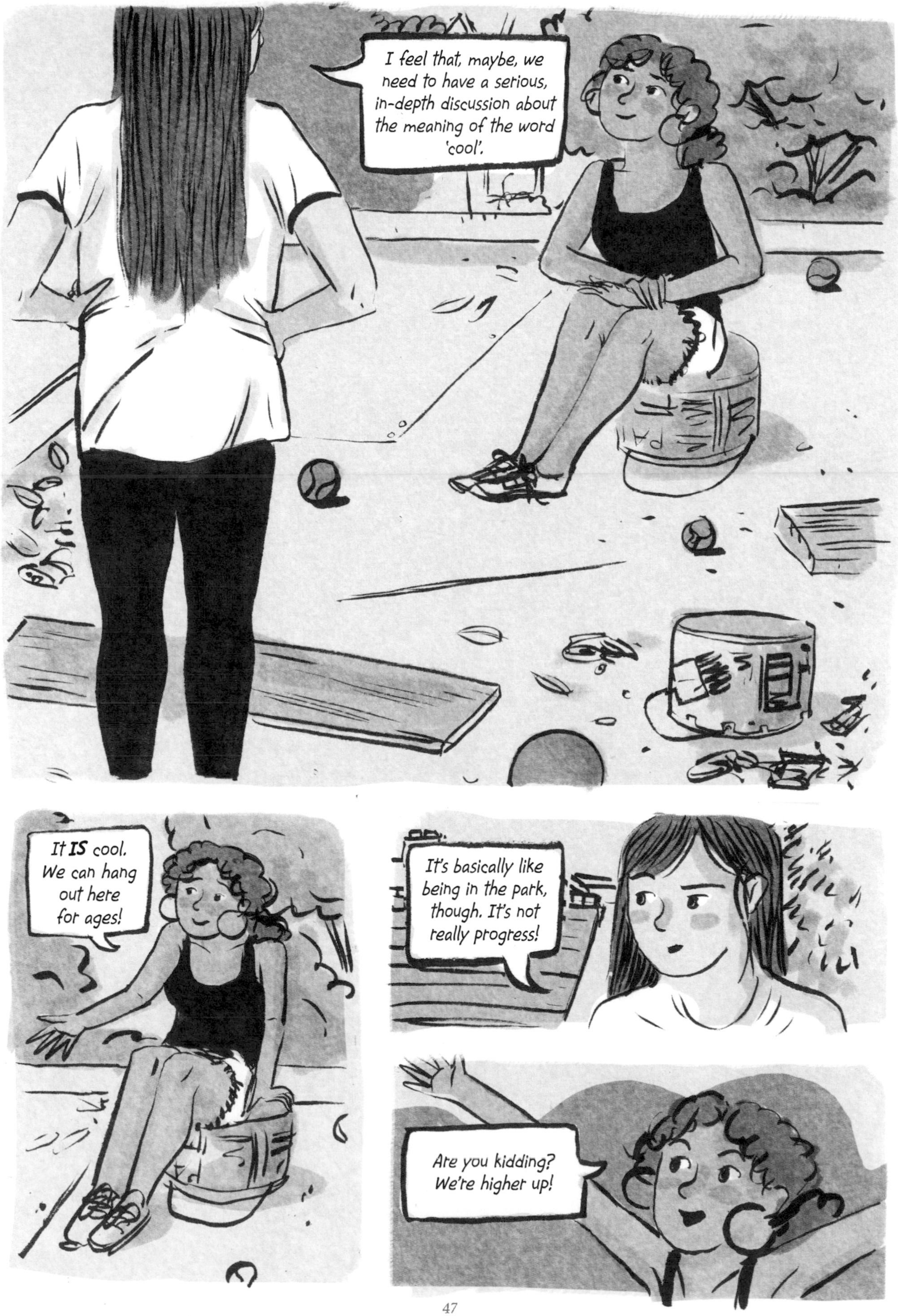

I feel that, maybe, we need to have a serious, in-depth discussion about the meaning of the word 'cool'.
It IS cool. We can hang out here for ages!
It's basically like being in the park, though. It's not really progress!
Are you kidding? We're higher up!

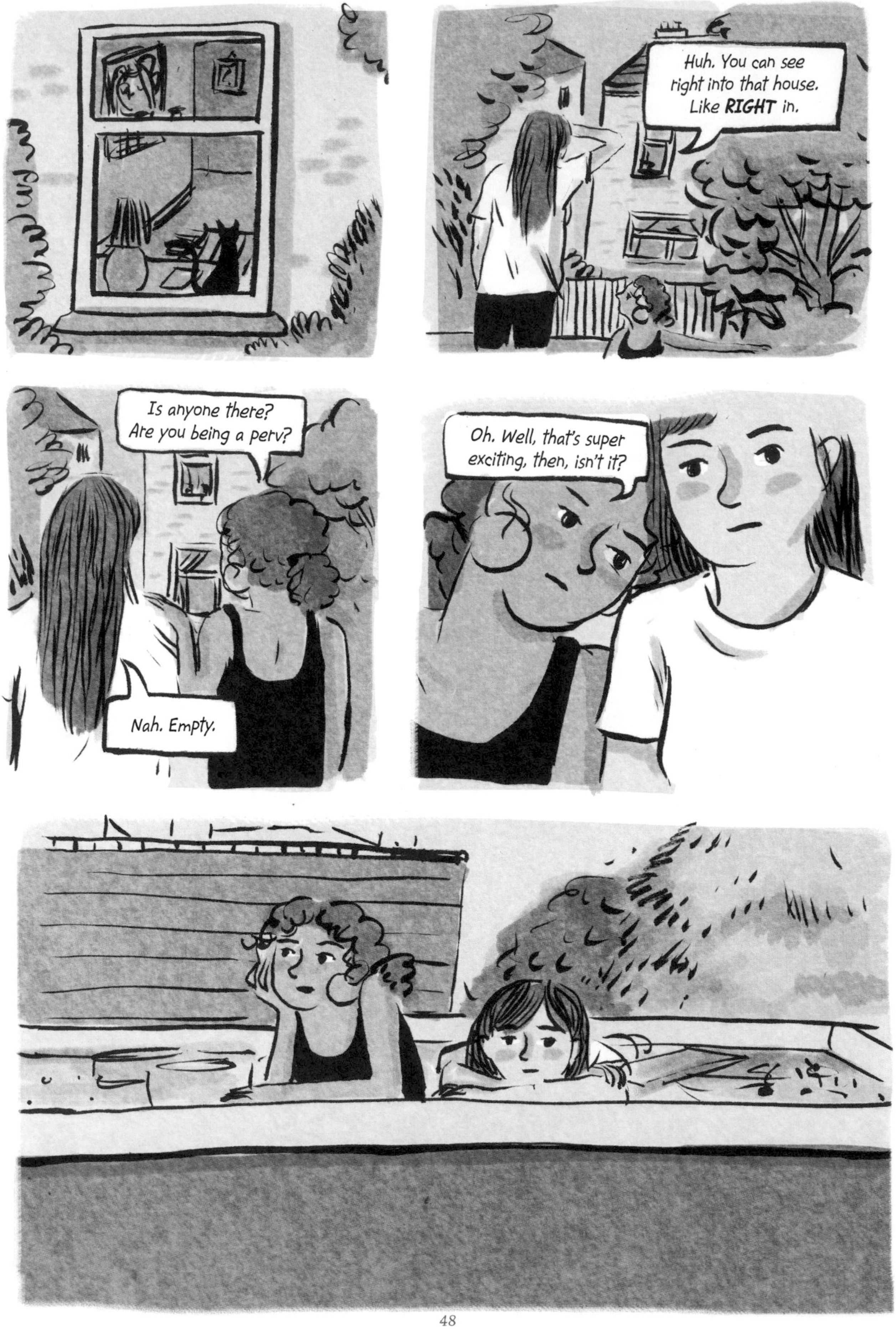
Huh. You can see right into that house. Like RIGHT in.
Is anyone there? Are you being a perv?
Nah. Empty.
Oh. Well, that's super exciting, then, isn't it?

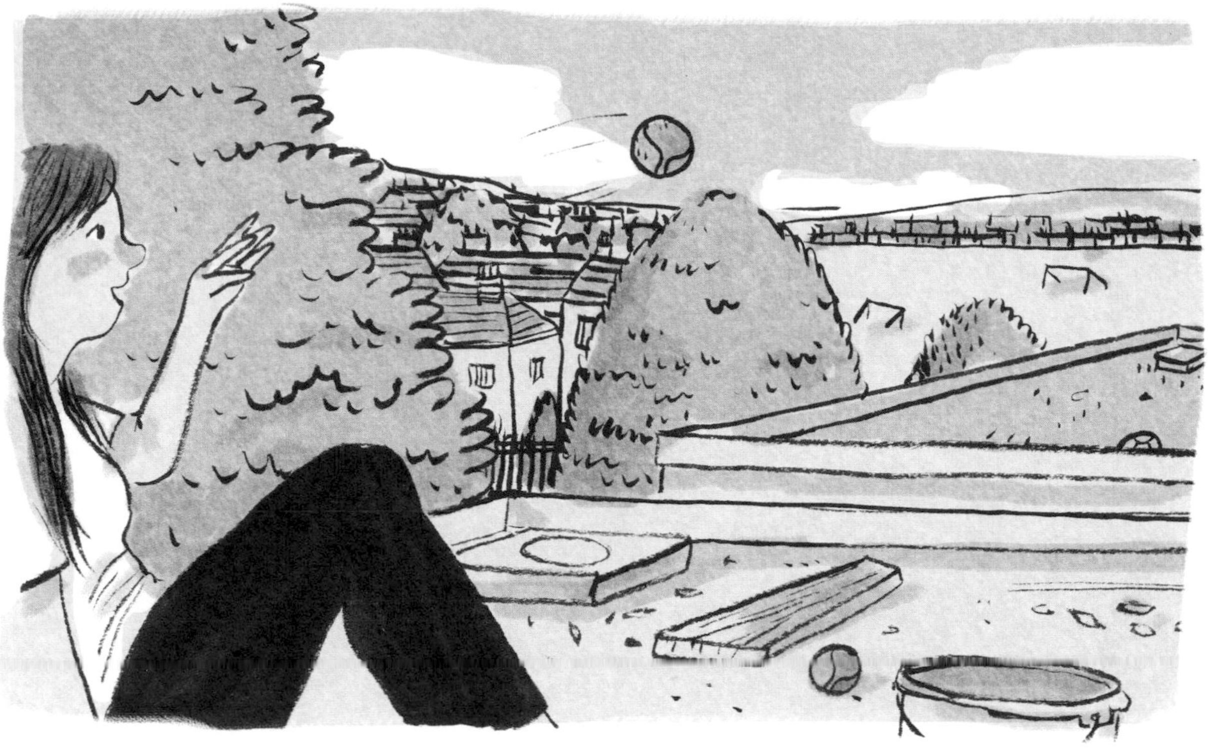

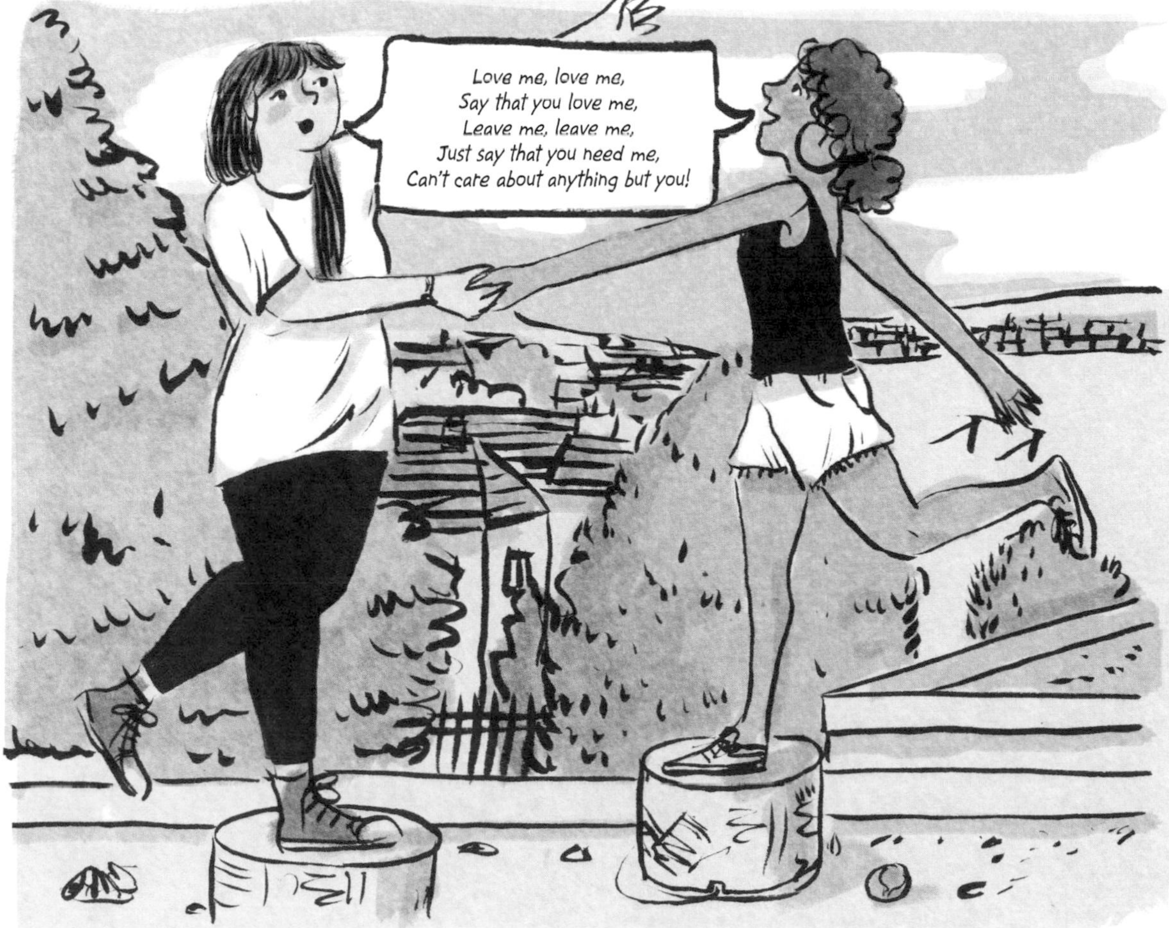
Love me, love me,
Say that you love me,
Leave me, leave me,
Just say that you need me,
Can't care about anything but you!

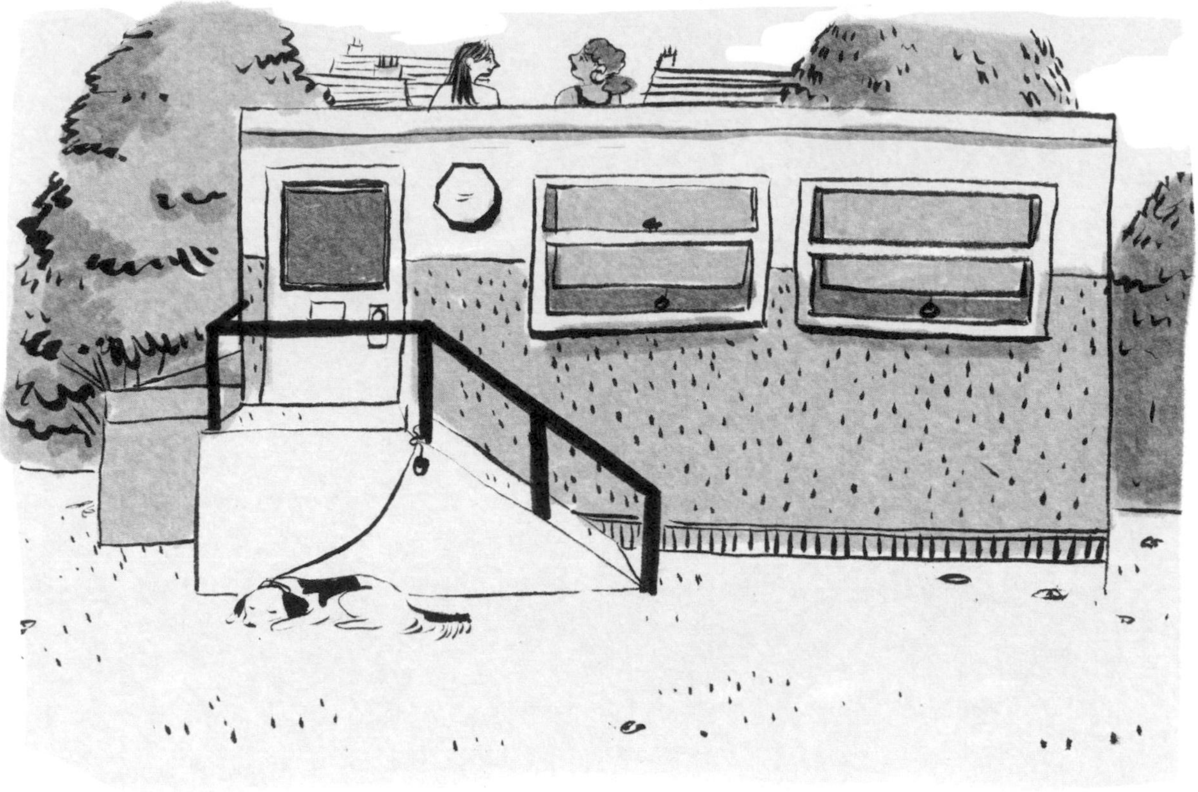

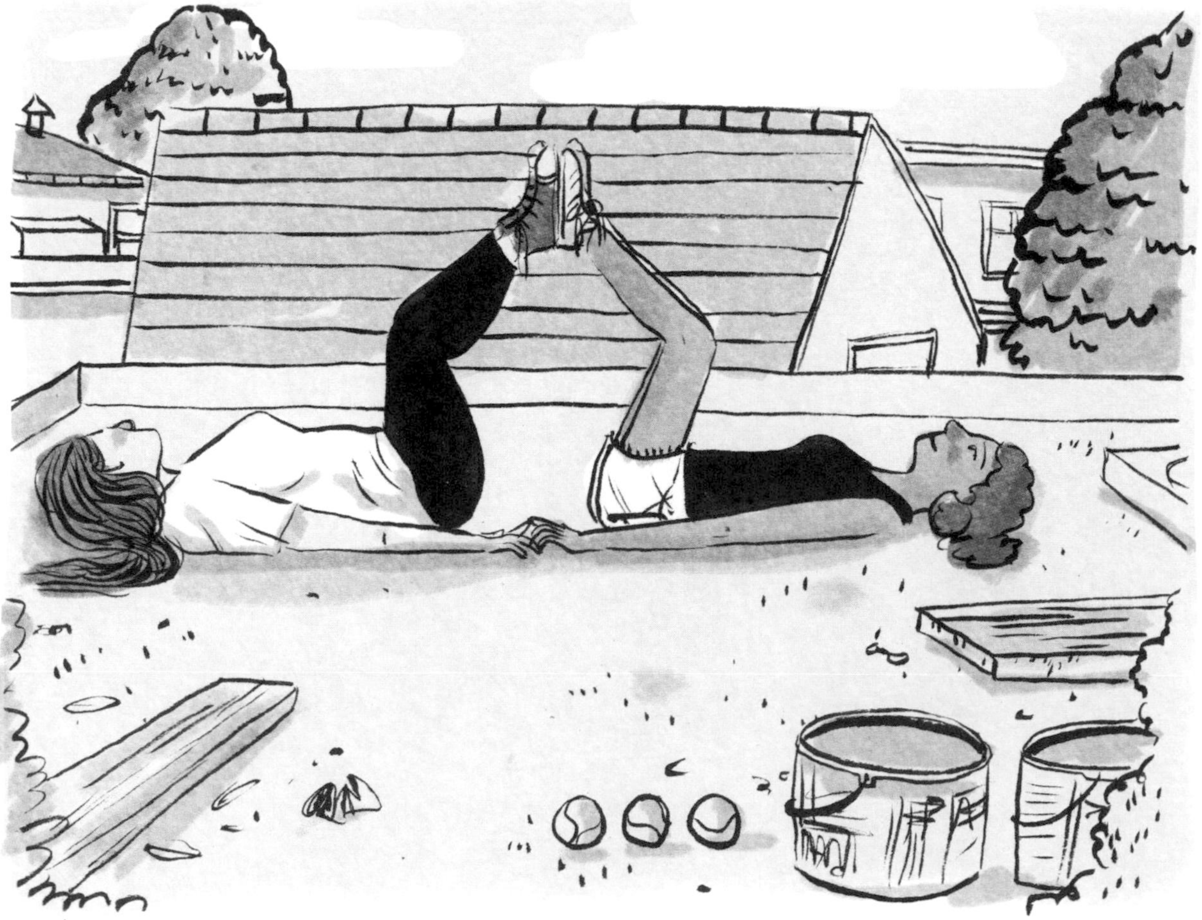

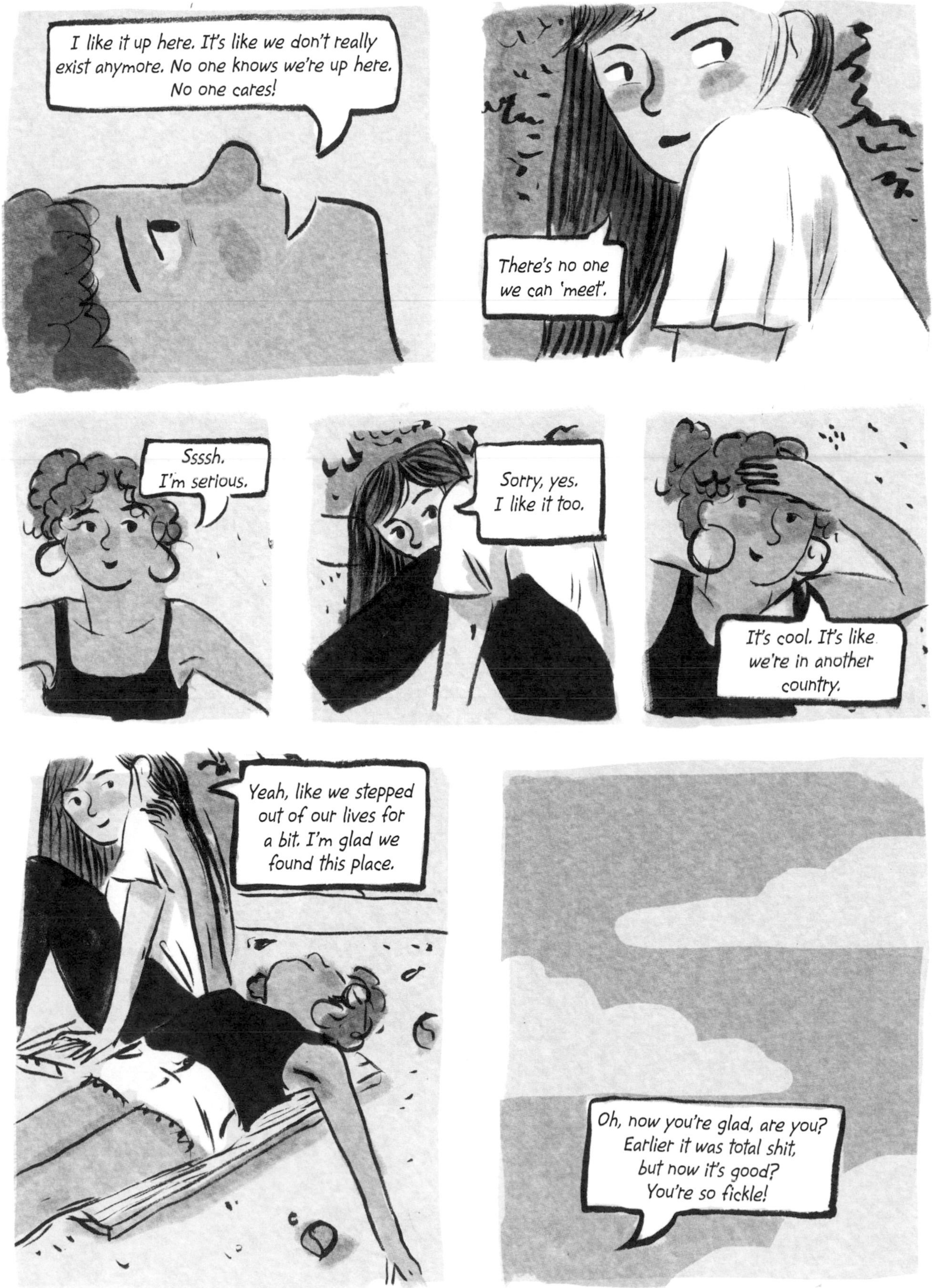

I like it up here. It's like we don't really exist anymore. No one knows we're up here. No one cares!
There's no one we can 'meet'.
Ssssh. I'm serious.
Sorry, yes. I like it too.
It's cool. It's like we're in another country.
Yeah, like we stepped out of our lives for a bit. I'm glad we found this place.
Oh, now you're glad, are you? Earlier it was total shit, but now it's good? You're so fickle!

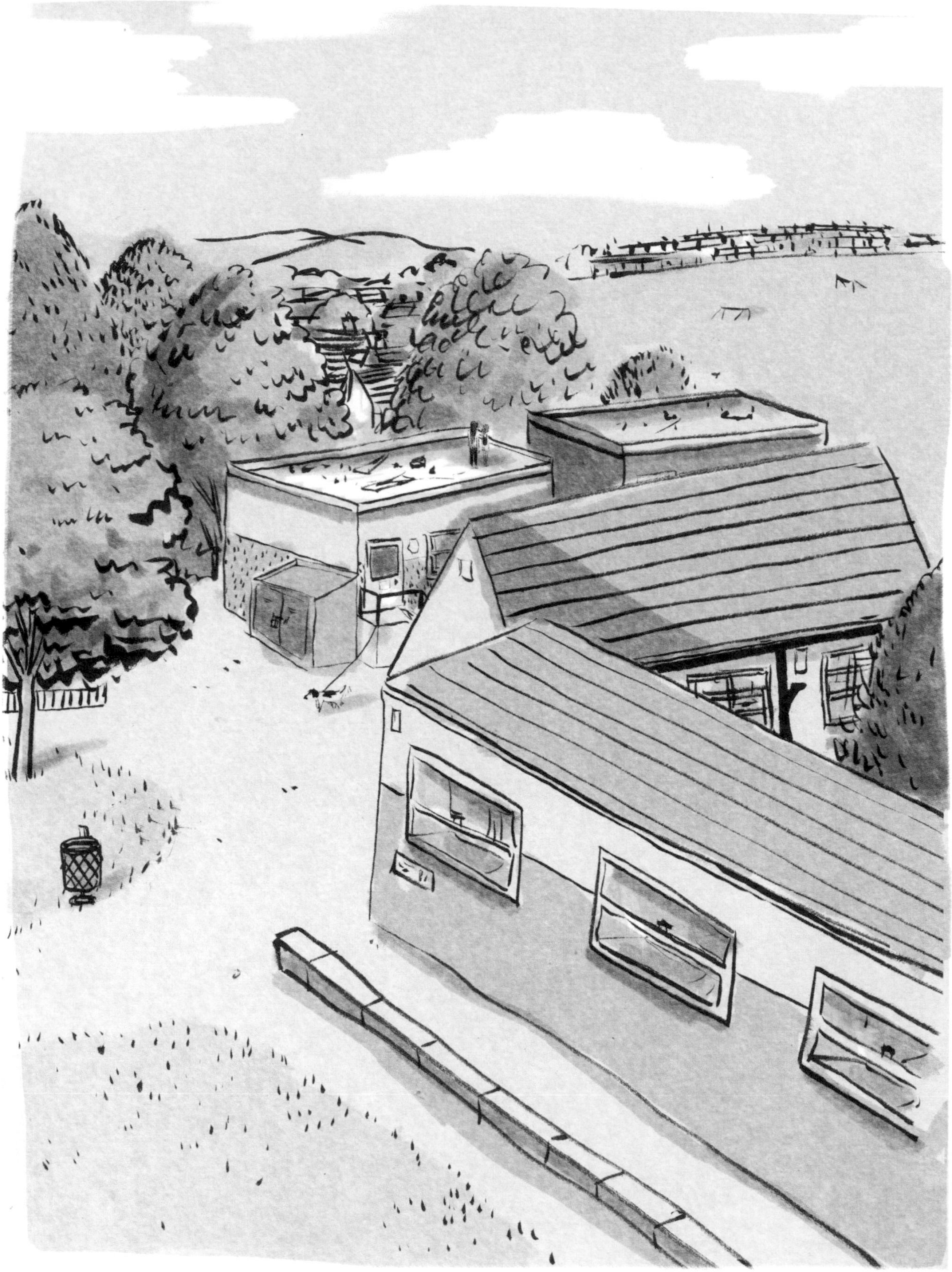

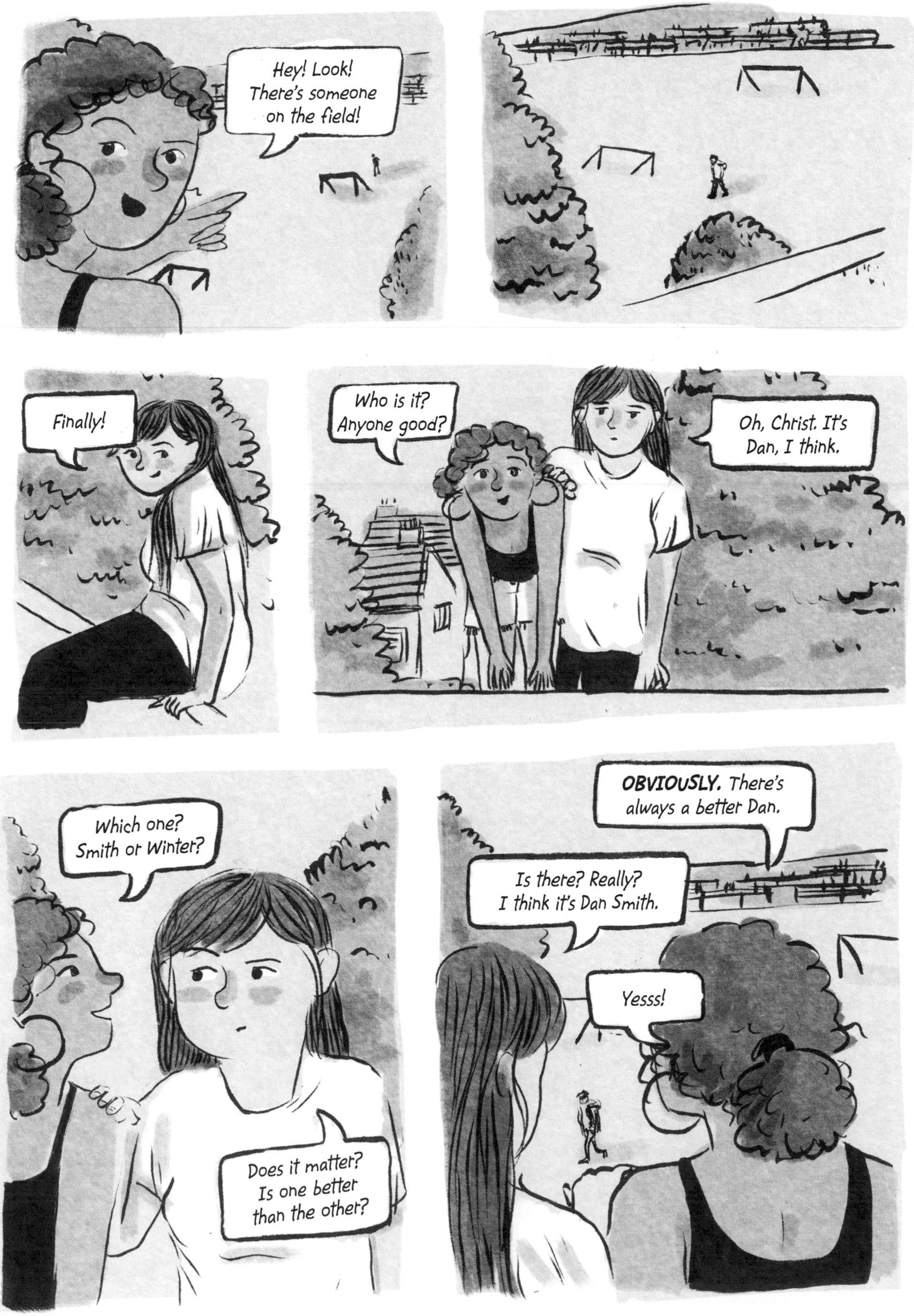
Hey! Look! There's someone on the field!
Finally!
Who is it? Anyone good?
Oh, Christ. It's Dan, I think.
Which one? Smith or Winter?
Does it matter? Is one better than the other?
OBVIOUSLY. There's always a better Dan.
Is there? Really? I think it's Dan Smith.
Yesss!

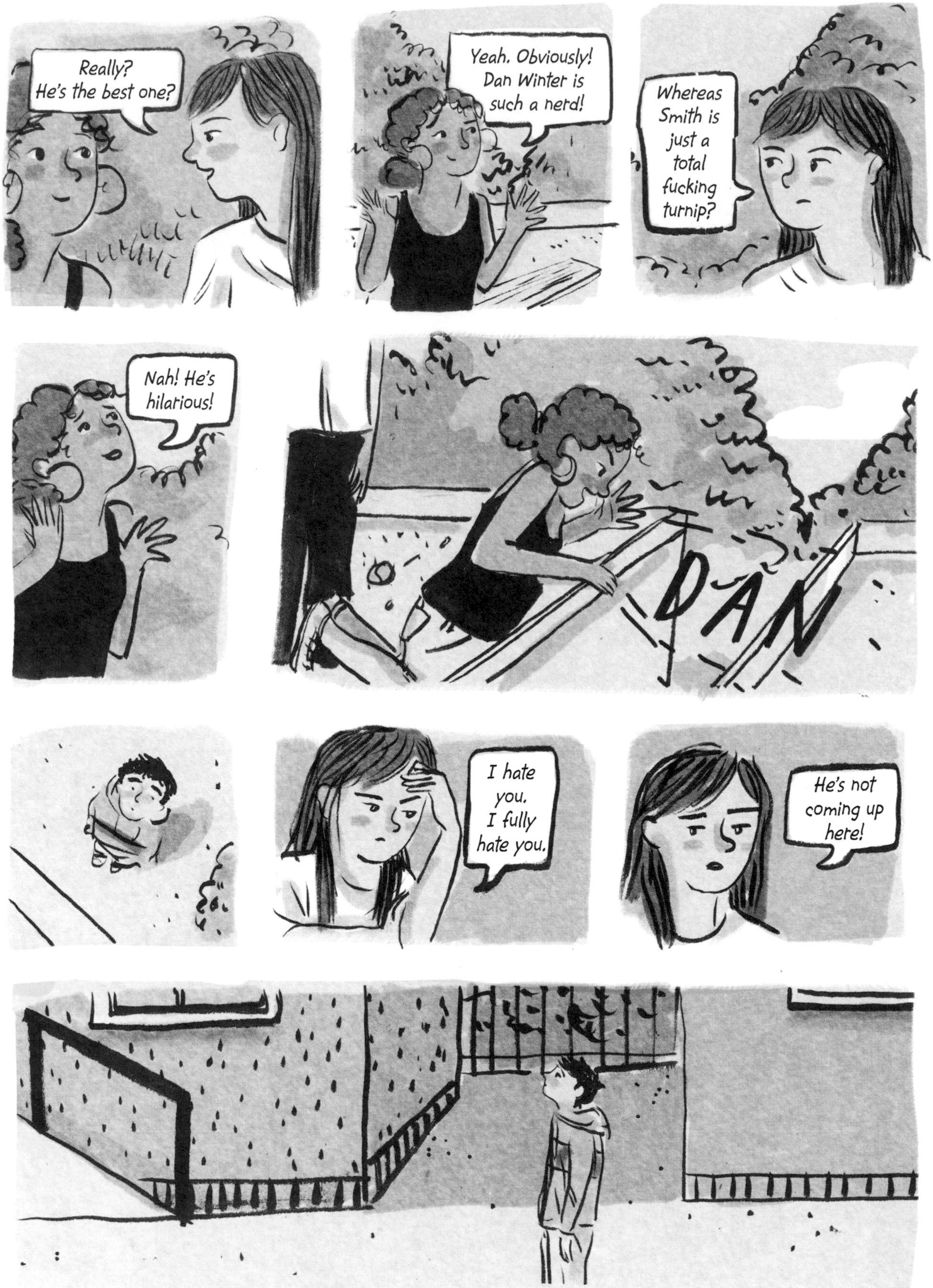
Really? He's the best one?
Yeah. Obviously! Dan Winter is such a nerd!
Whereas Smith is just a total fucking turnip?
Nah! He's hilarious!
DAN
I hate you. I fully hate you.
He's not coming up here!

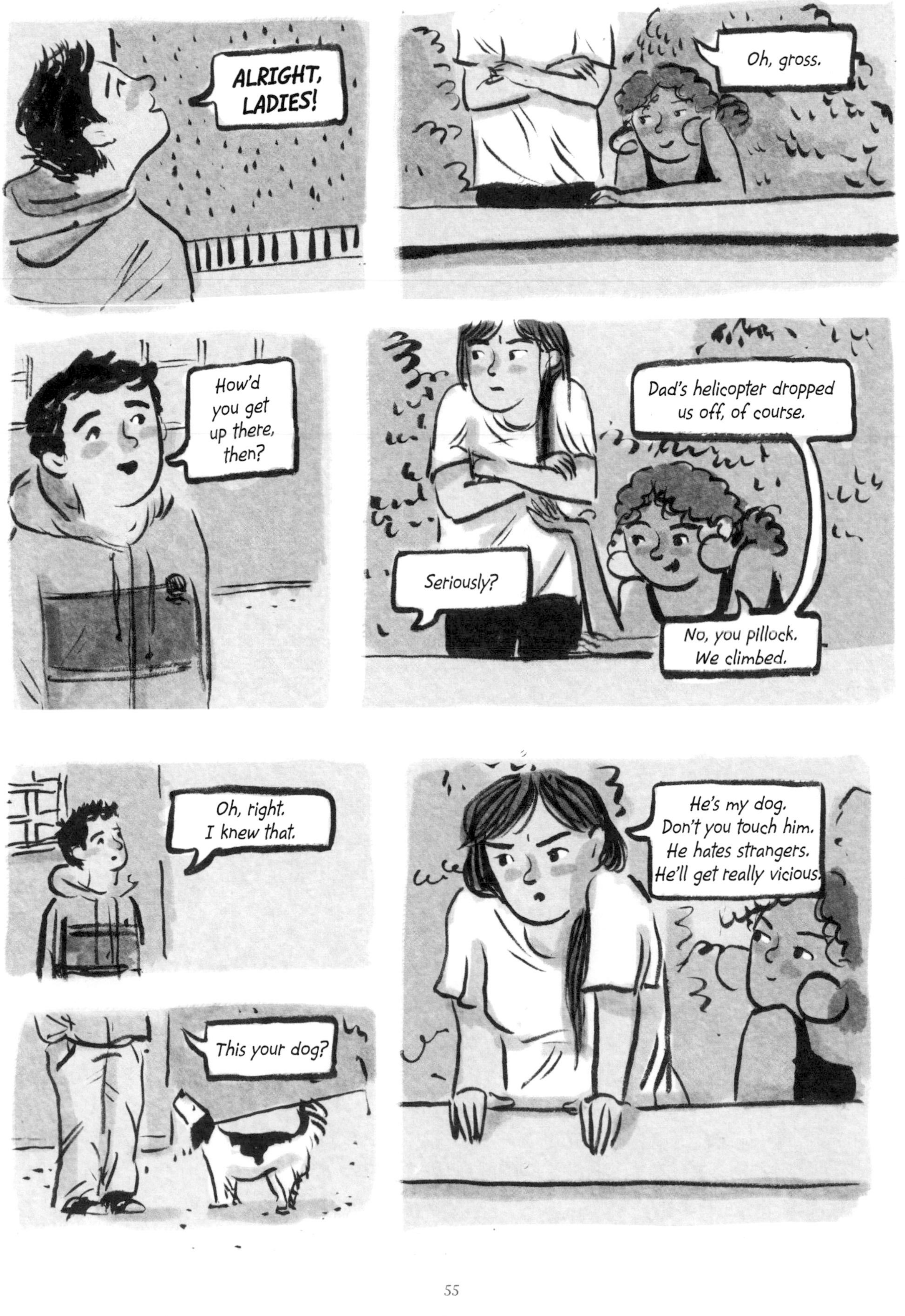

ALRIGHT, LADIES!
Oh, gross.
How'd you get up there, then?
Dad's helicopter dropped us off, of course.
Seriously?
No, you pillock. We climbed.
Oh, right. I knew that.
This your dog?
He's my dog. Don't you touch him. He hates strangers. He'll get really vicious.

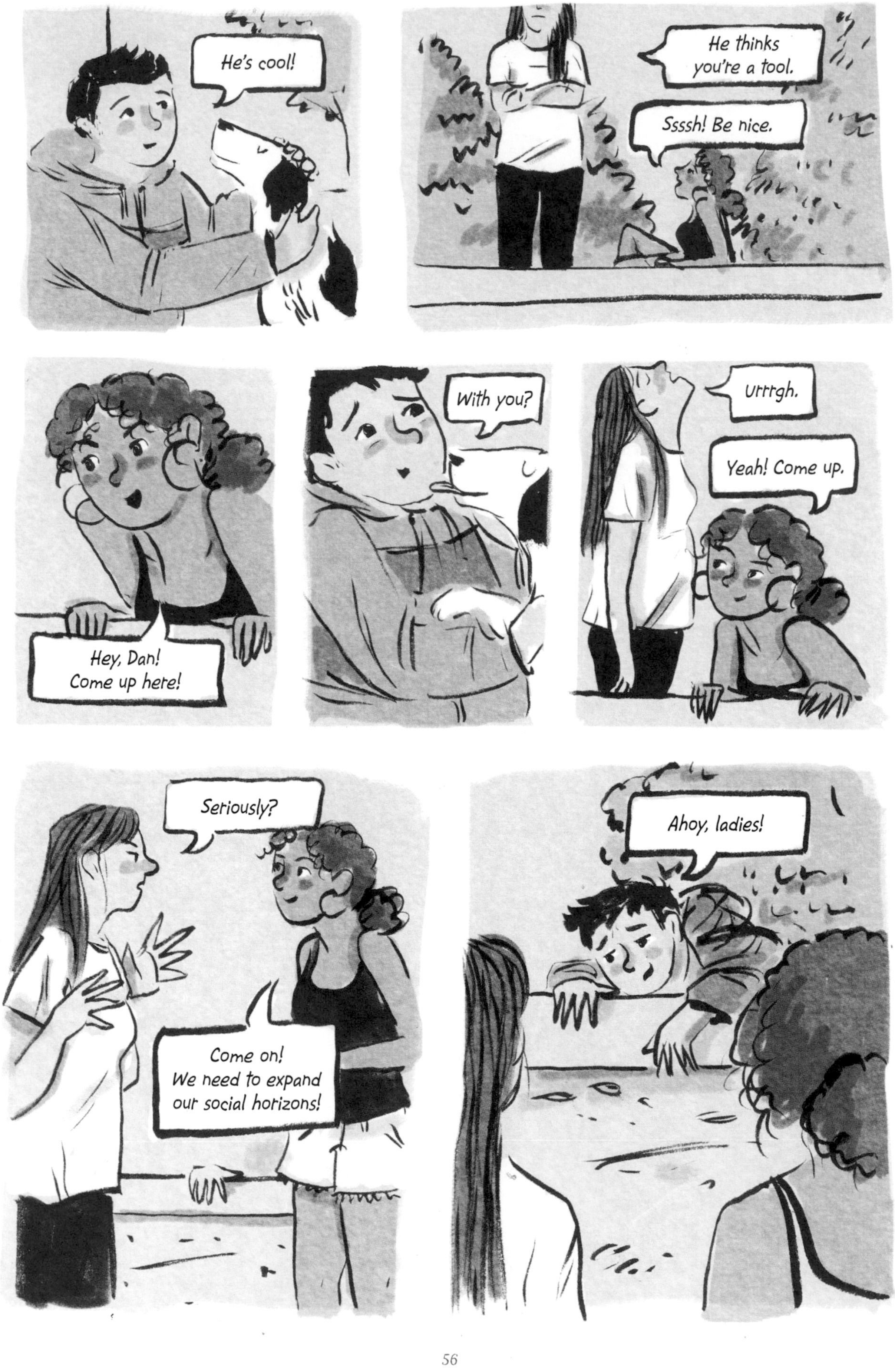
He's cool!
He thinks you're a tool.
Ssssh! Be nice.
Hey, Dan! Come up here!
With you?
Urrrgh.
Yeah! Come up.
Seriously?
Come on! We need to expand our social horizons!
Ahoy, ladies!

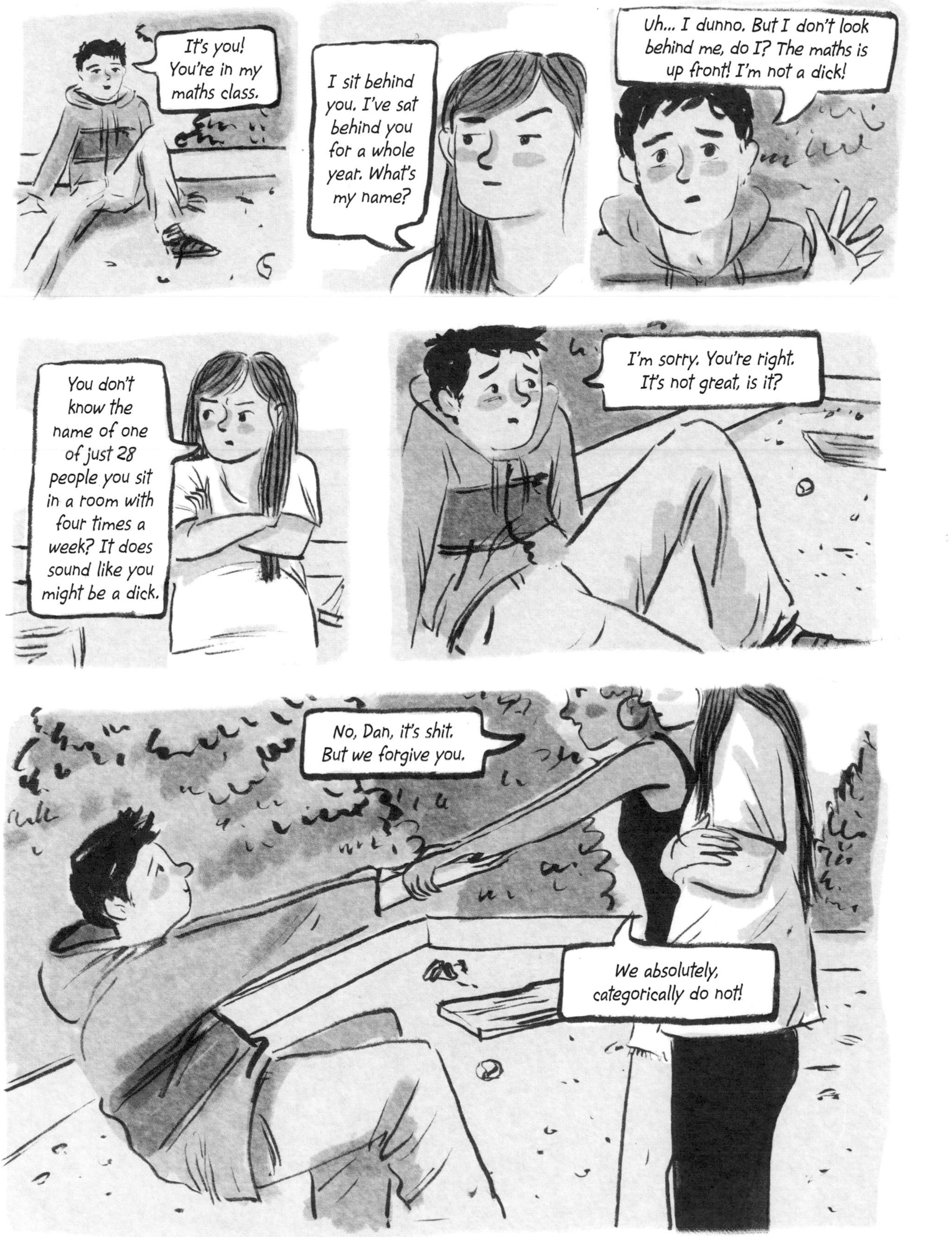
It's you! You're in my maths class.
I sit behind you. I've sat behind you for a whole year. What's my name?
Uh... I dunno. But I don't look behind me, do I? The maths is up front! I'm not a dick!
You don't know the name of one of just 28 people you sit in a room with four times a week? It does sound like you might be a dick.
I'm sorry. You're right. It's not great, is it?
No, Dan, it's shit. But we forgive you.
We absolutely, categorically do not!

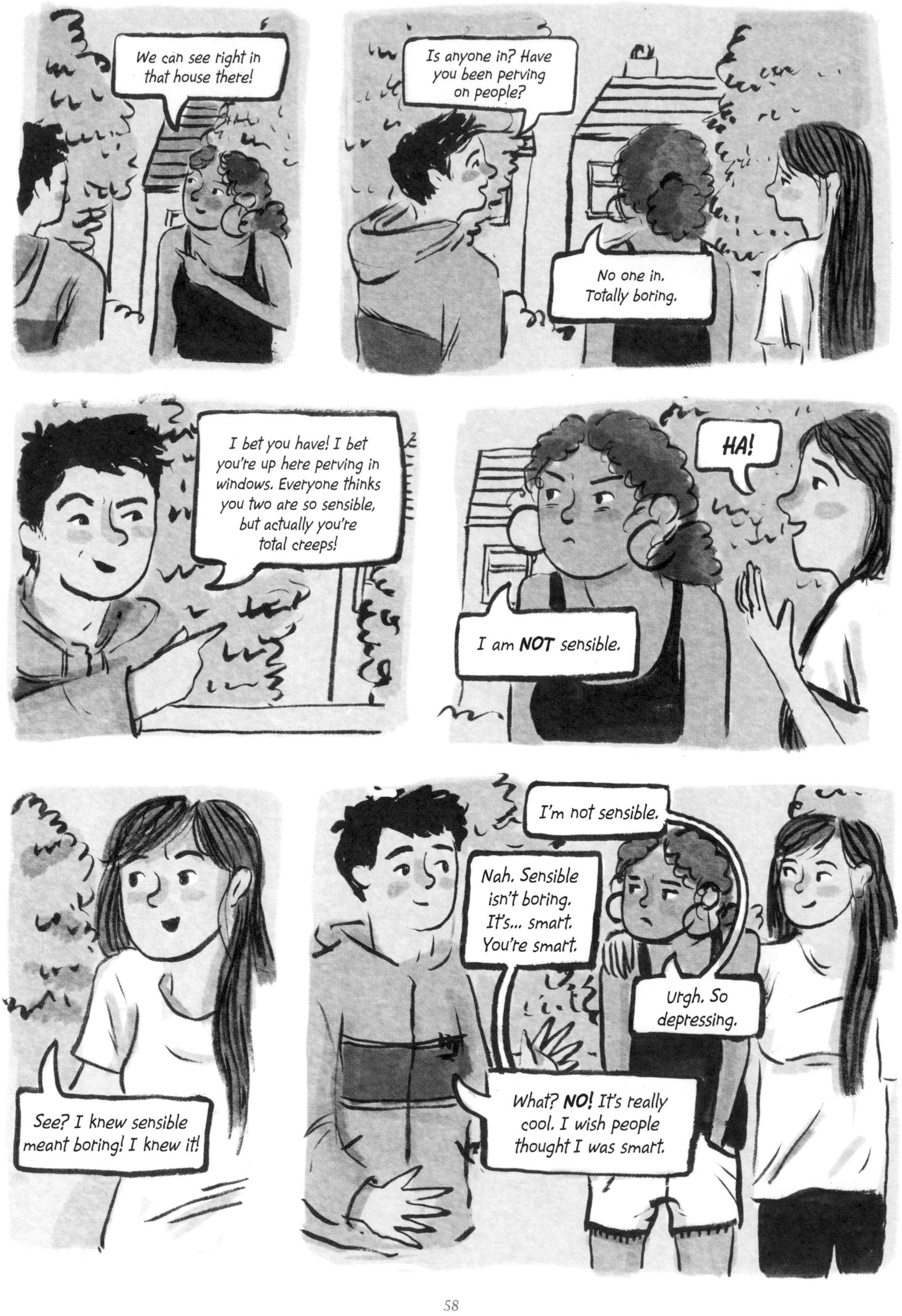
We can see right in that house there!
Is anyone in? Have you been perving on people?
No one in. Totally boring.
I bet you have! I bet you're up here perving in windows. Everyone thinks you two are so sensible, but actually you're total creeps!
HA!
I am **NOT** sensible.
See? I knew sensible meant boring! I knew it!
I'm not sensible.
Nah. Sensible isn't boring. It's... smart. You're smart.
Urgh. So depressing.
What? **NO!** It's really cool. I wish people thought I was smart.

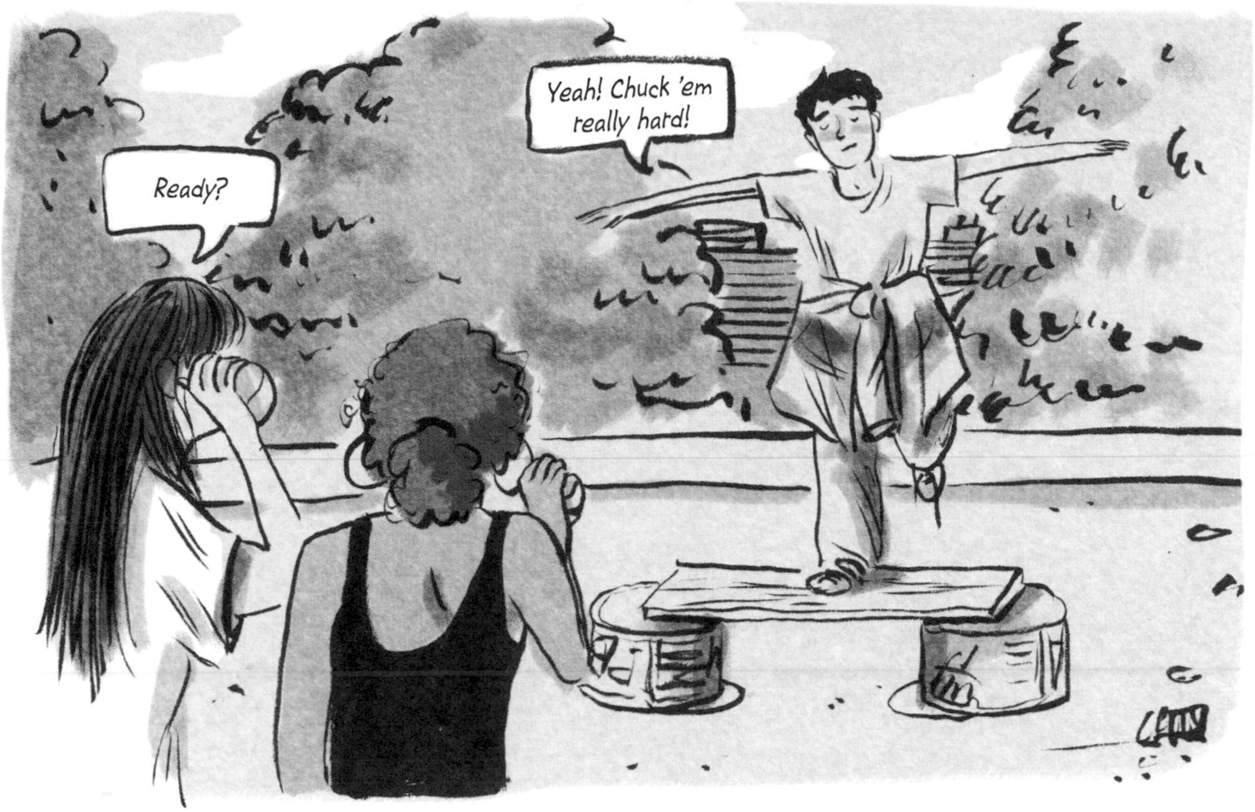
Ready?
Yeah! Chuck 'em really hard!

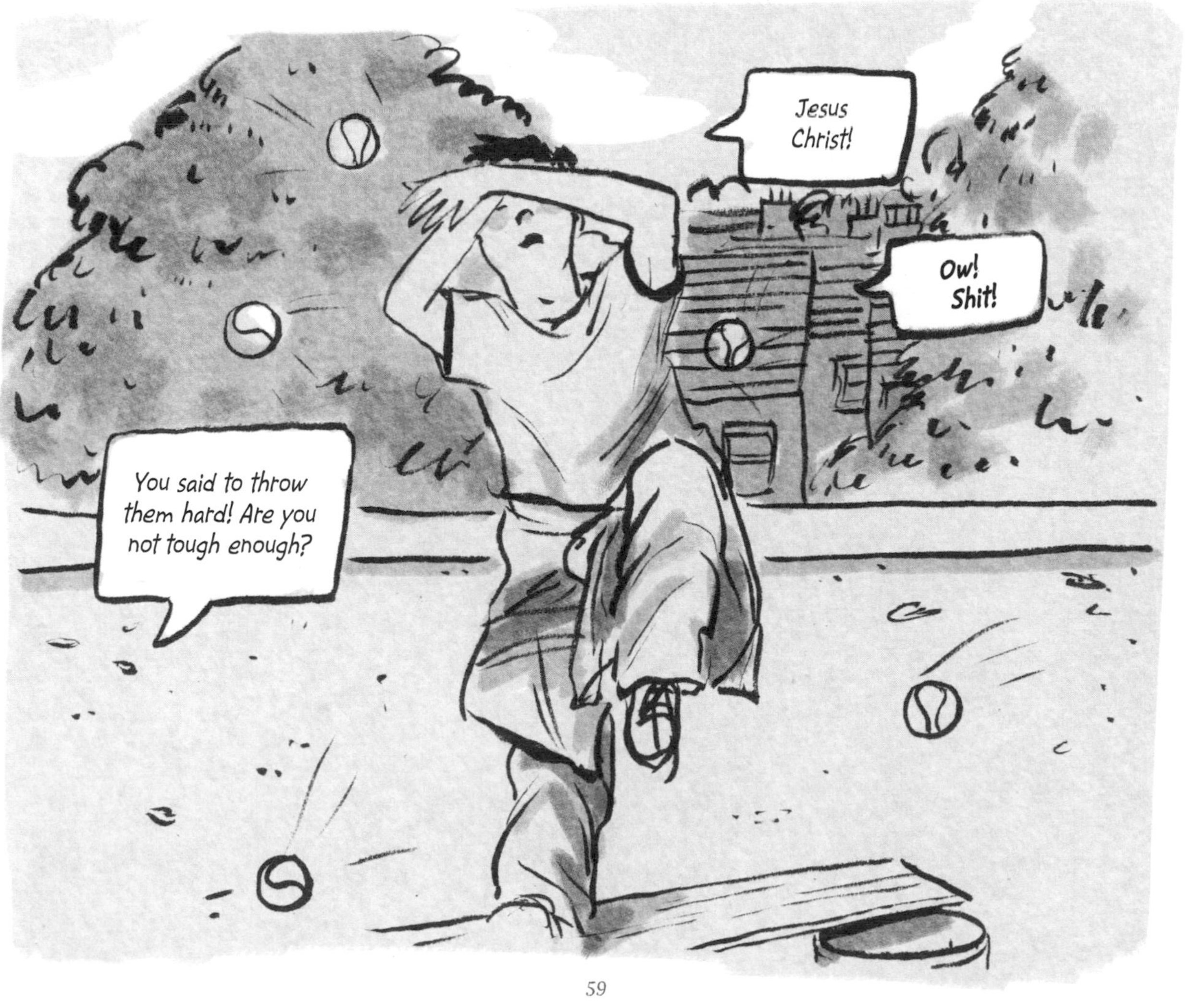
Jesus Christ!
Ow! Shit!
You said to throw them hard! Are you not tough enough?

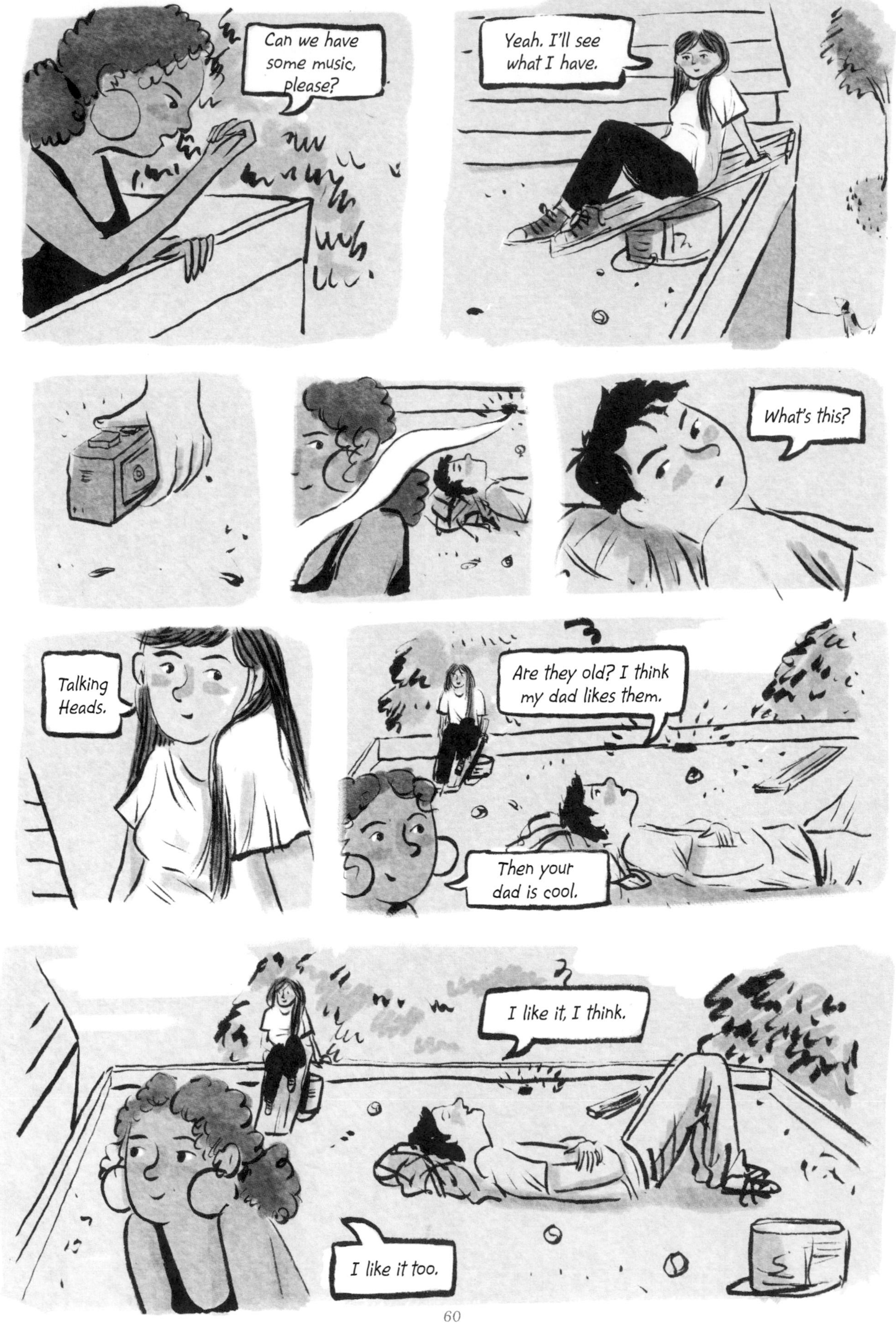
Can we have some music, please?
Yeah. I'll see what I have.
What's this?
Talking Heads.
Are they old? I think my dad likes them.
Then your dad is cool.
I like it, I think.
I like it too.

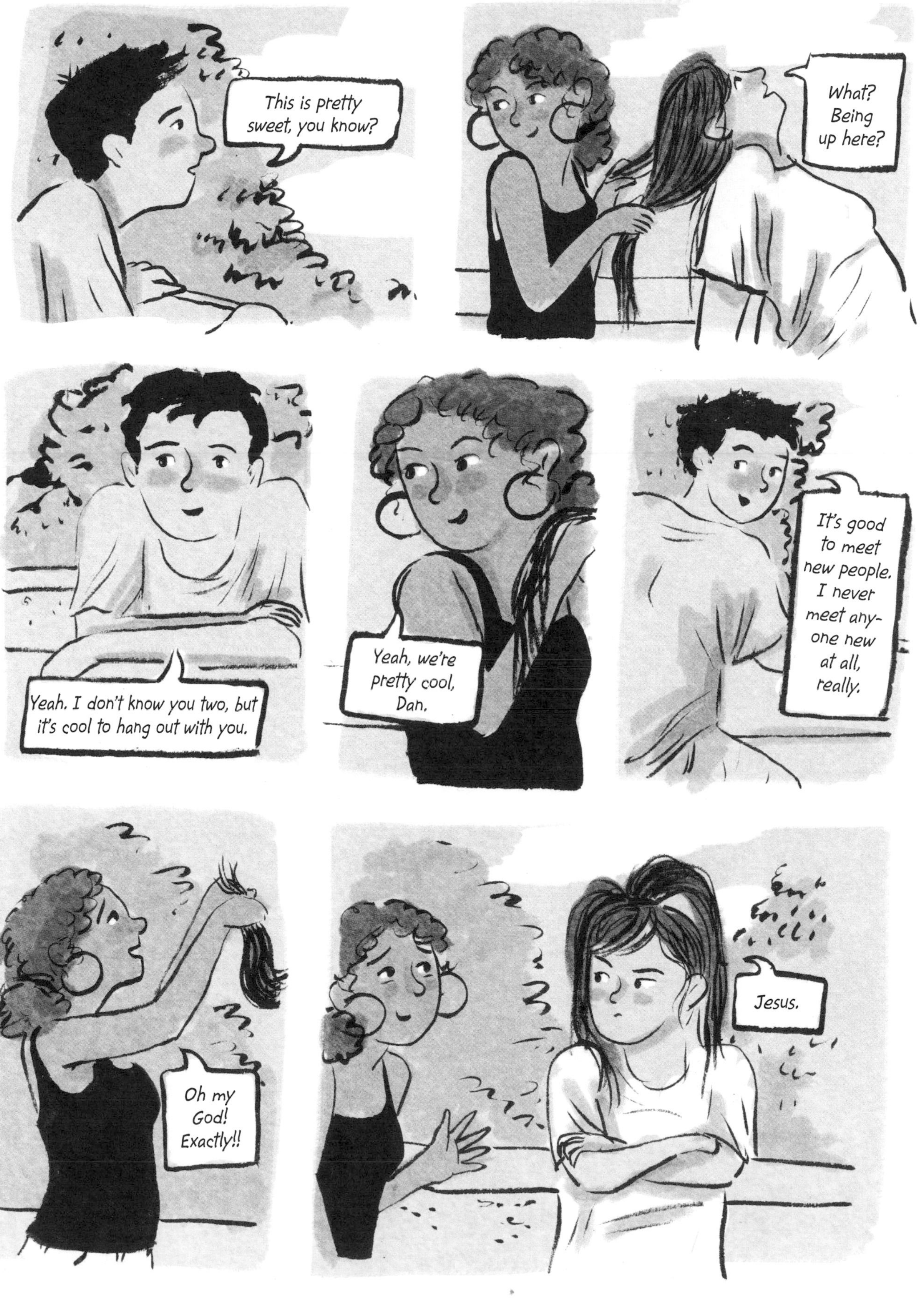
This is pretty sweet, you know?
What? Being up here?
Yeah. I don't know you two, but it's cool to hang out with you.
Yeah, we're pretty cool, Dan.
It's good to meet new people. I never meet any-one new at all, really.
Oh my God! Exactly!!
Jesus.

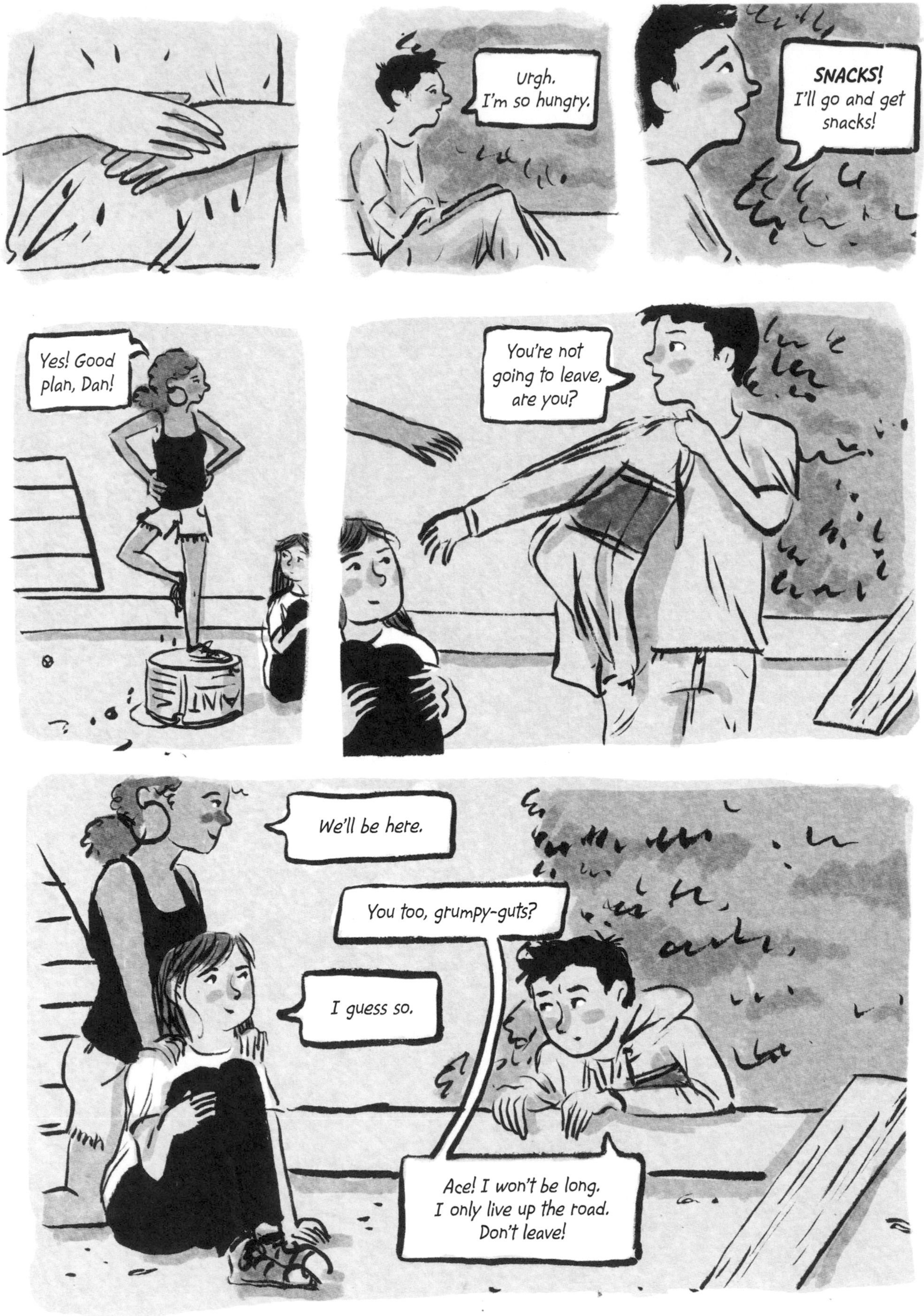
Urgh.
I'm so hungry.
SNACKS!
I'll go and get snacks!
Yes! Good plan, Dan!
You're not going to leave, are you?
We'll be here.
You too, grumpy-guts?
I guess so.
Ace! I won't be long.
I only live up the road.
Don't leave!

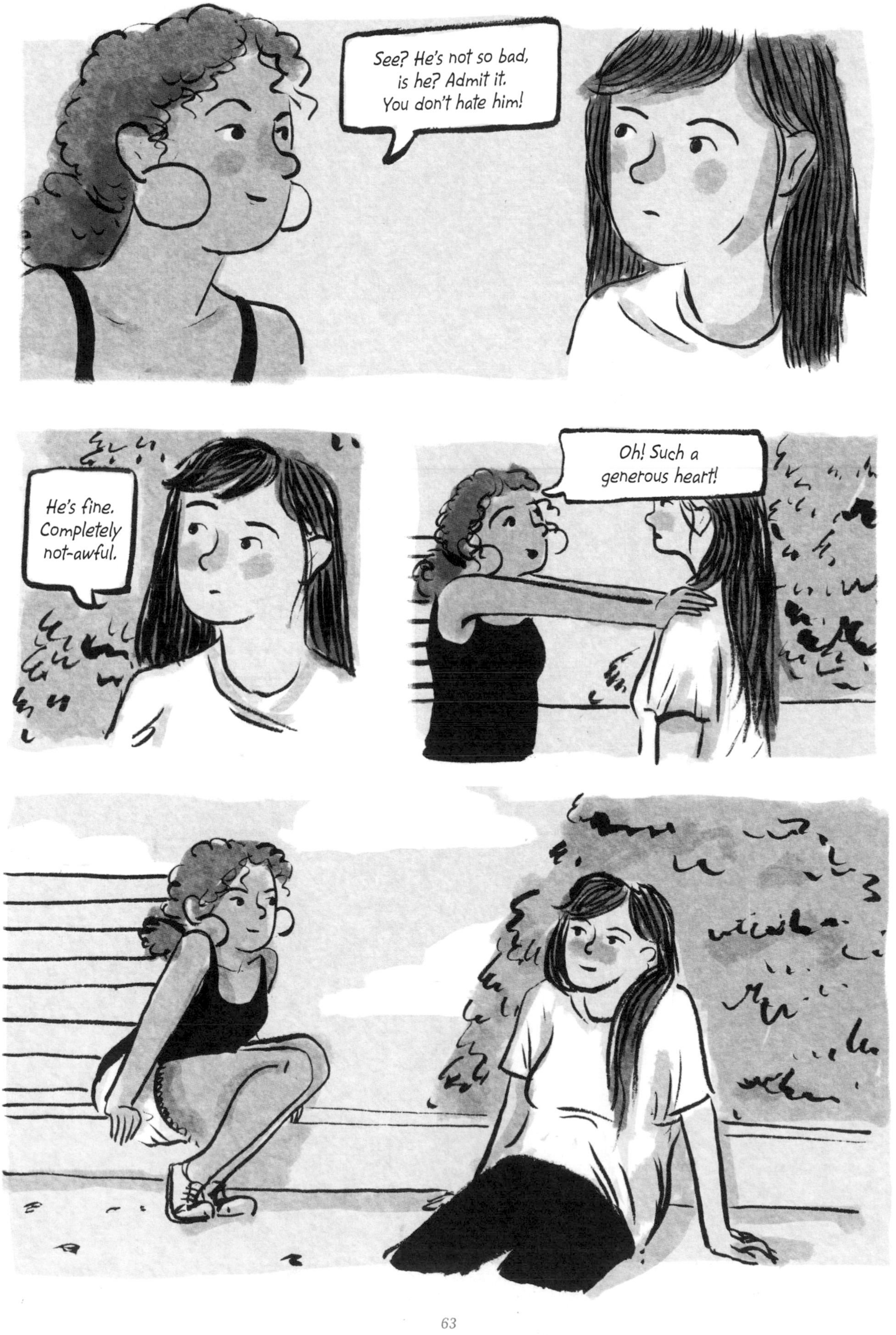
See? He's not so bad, is he? Admit it. You don't hate him!
He's fine. Completely not-awful.
Oh! Such a generous heart!

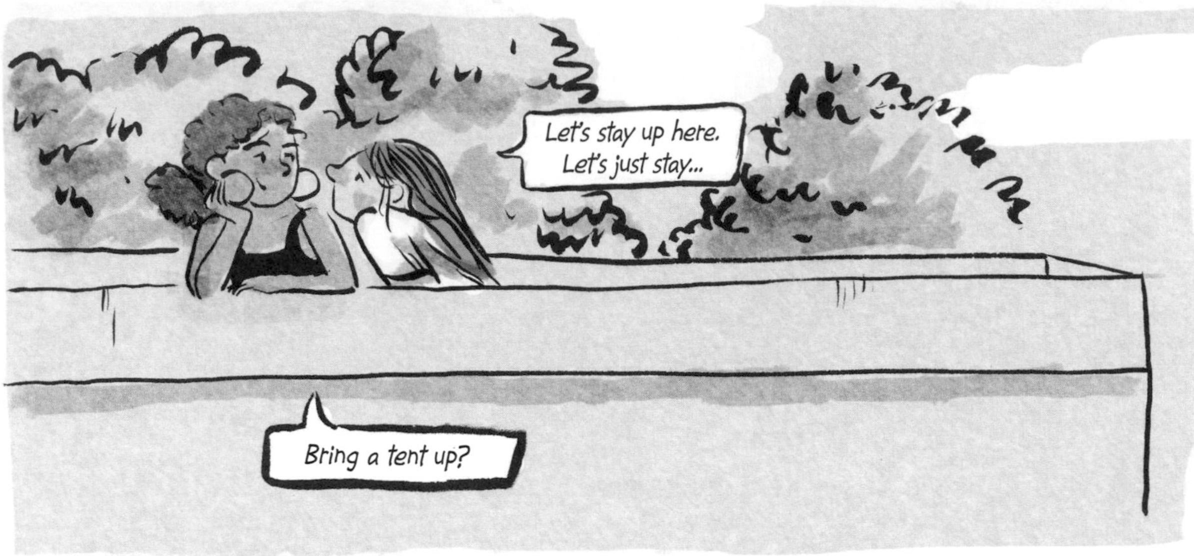
Let's stay up here.
Let's just stay...
Bring a tent up?

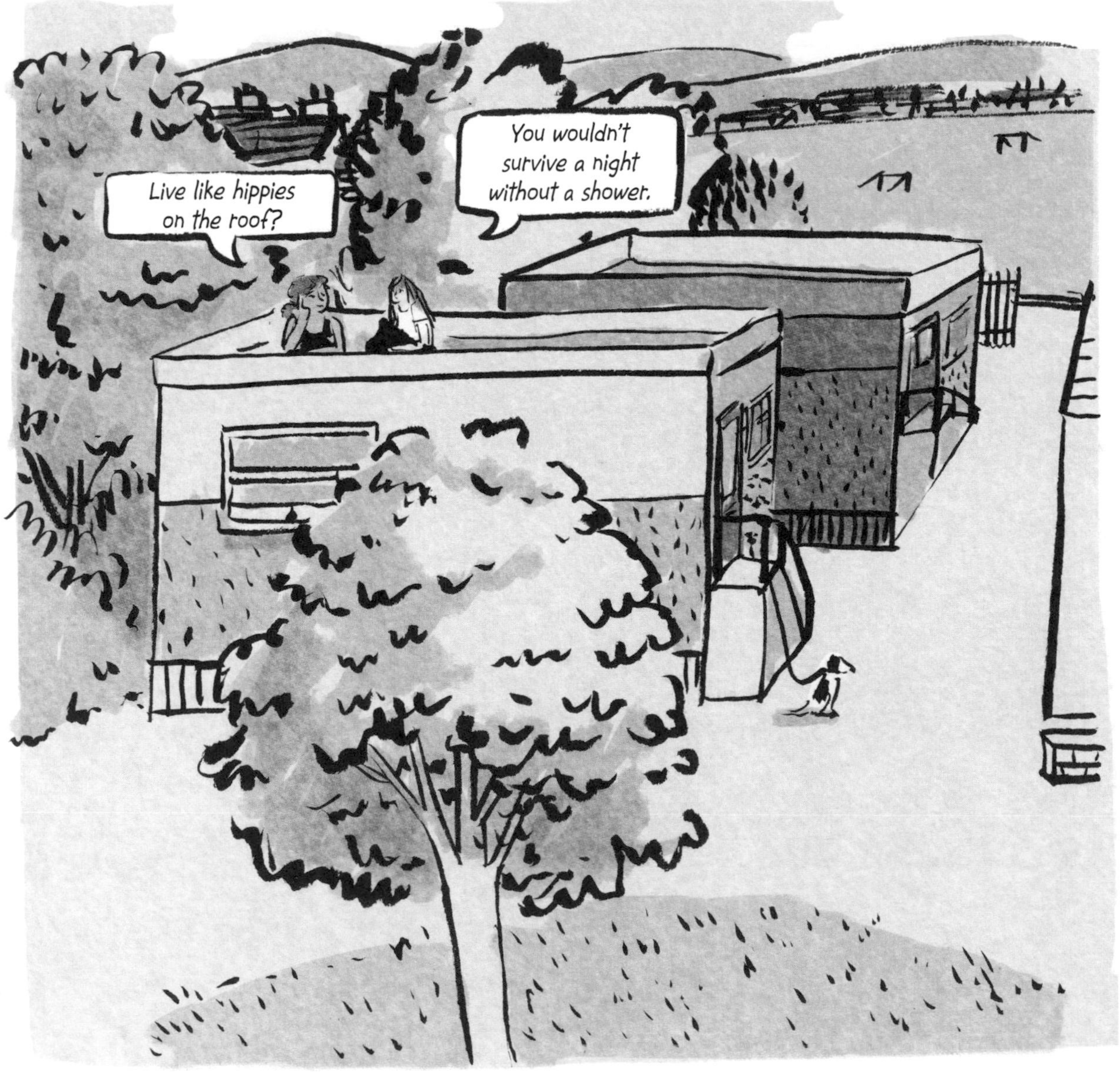
Live like hippies on the roof?
You wouldn't survive a night without a shower.

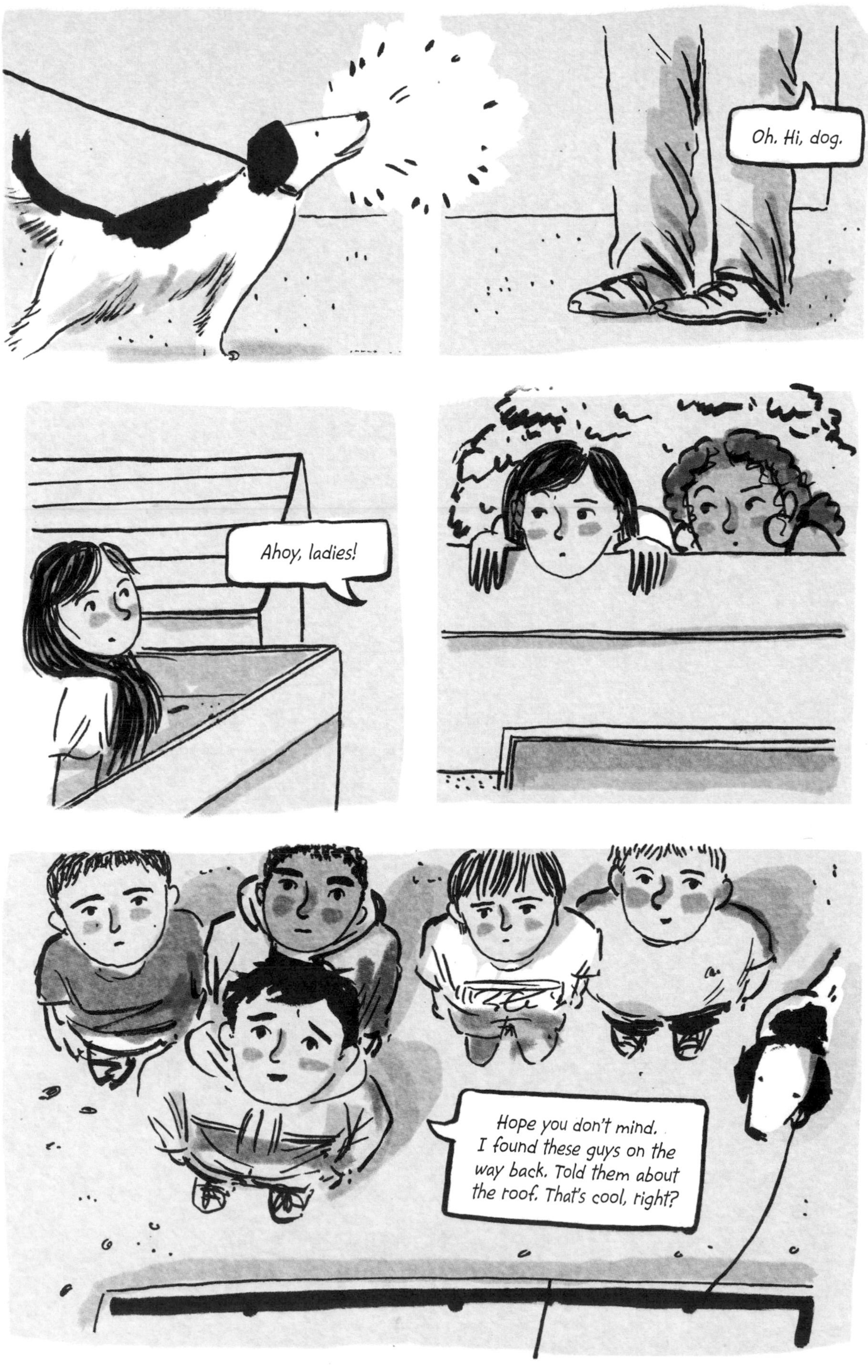
Oh. Hi, dog.
Ahoy, ladies!
Hope you don't mind. I found these guys on the way back. Told them about the roof. That's cool, right?

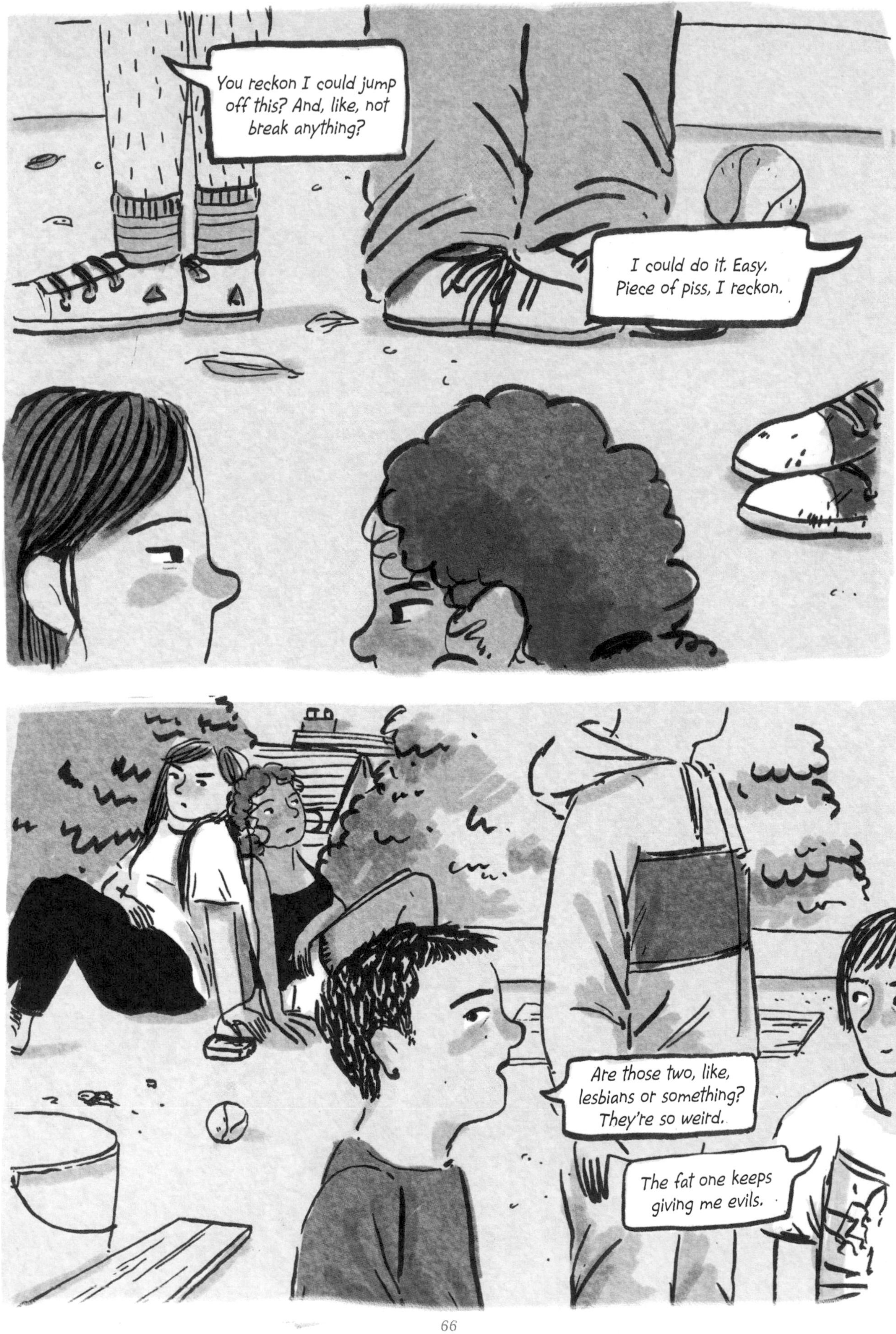
You reckon I could jump off this? And, like, not break anything?
I could do it. Easy. Piece of piss, I reckon.
Are those two, like, lesbians or something? They're so weird.
The fat one keeps giving me evils.

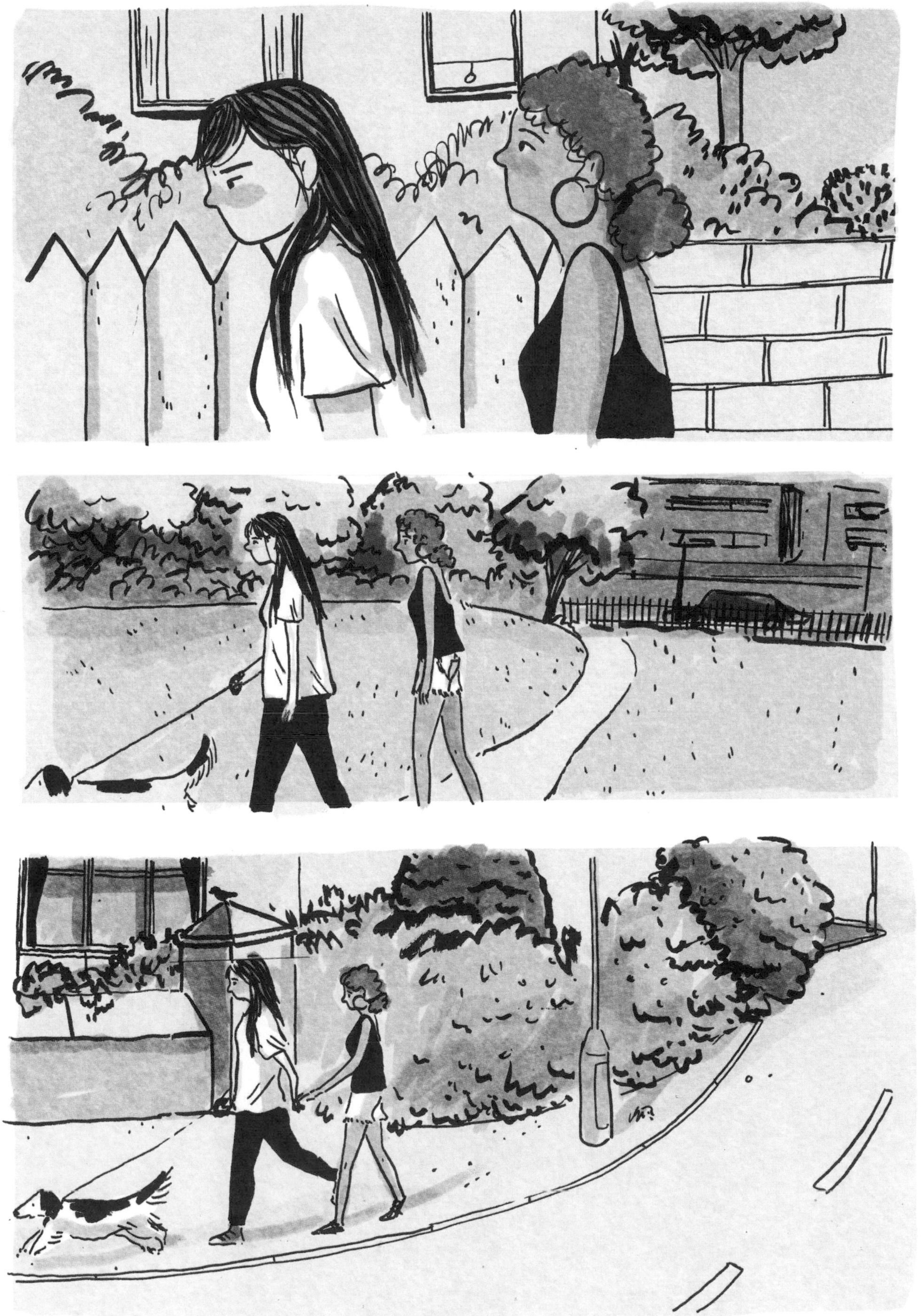

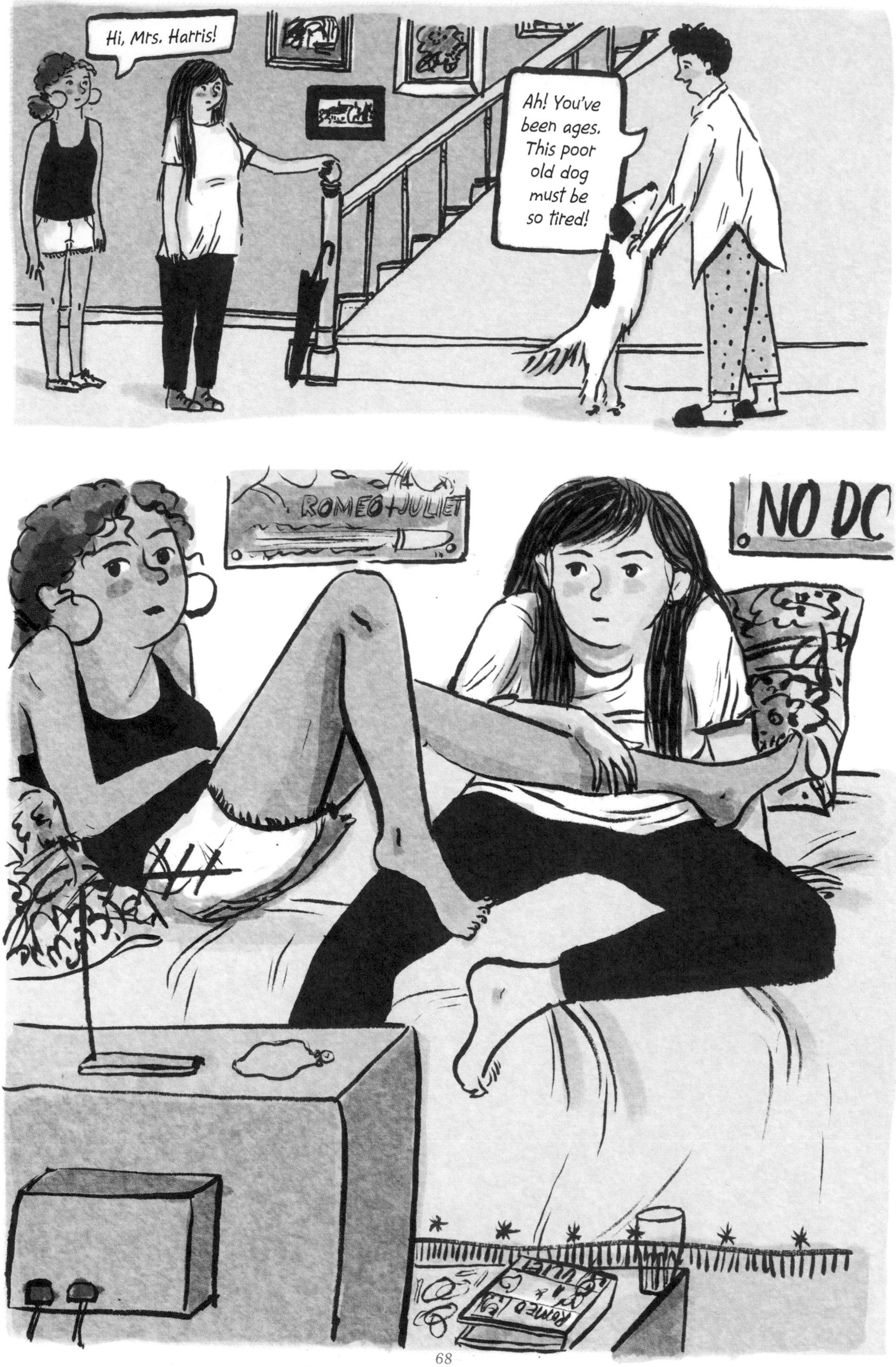
Hi, Mrs. Harris!
Ah! You've been ages. This poor old dog must be so tired!
ROMEO+JULIET
NO DC

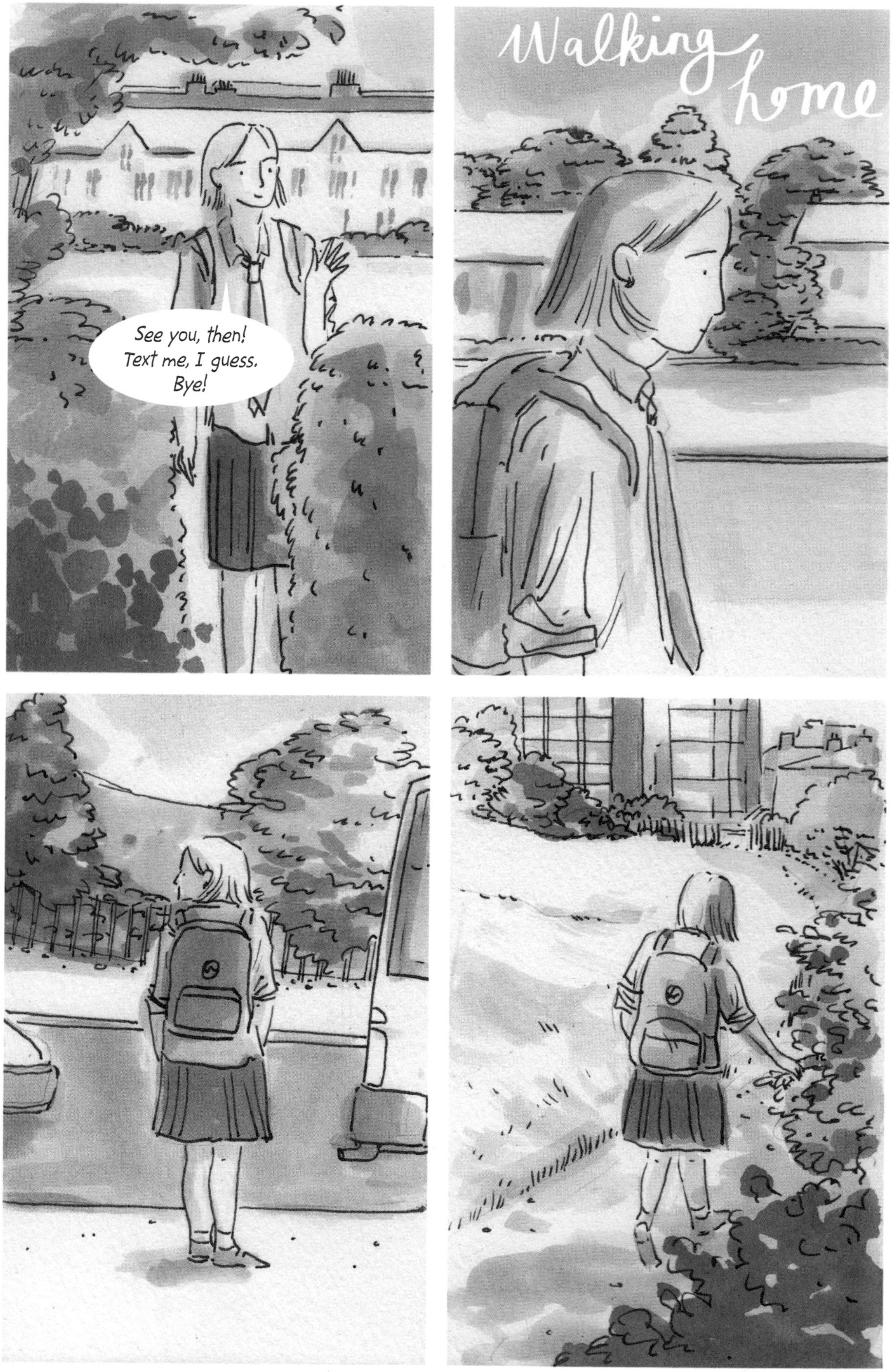
See you, then! Text me, I guess. Bye!
Walking home

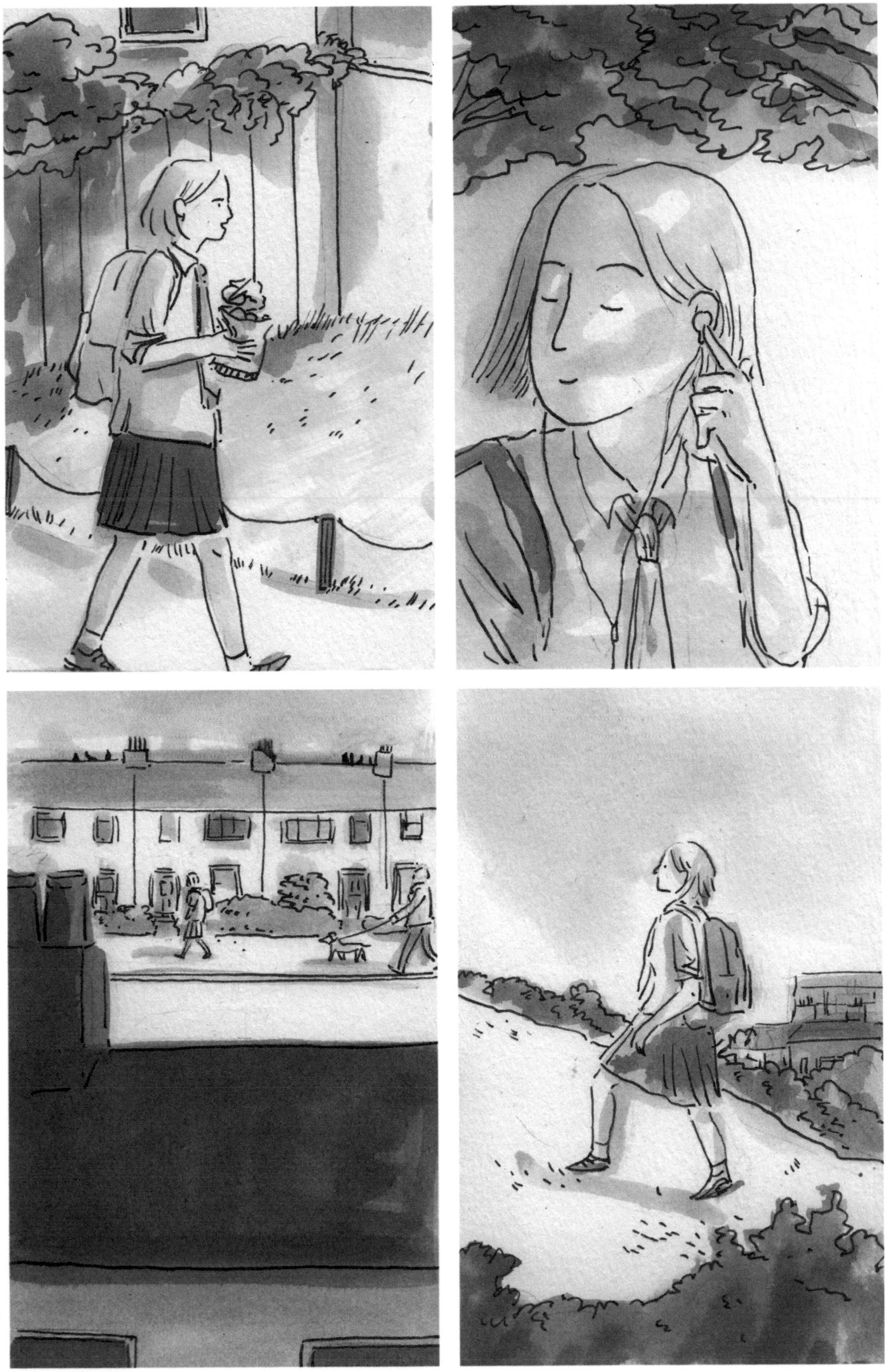

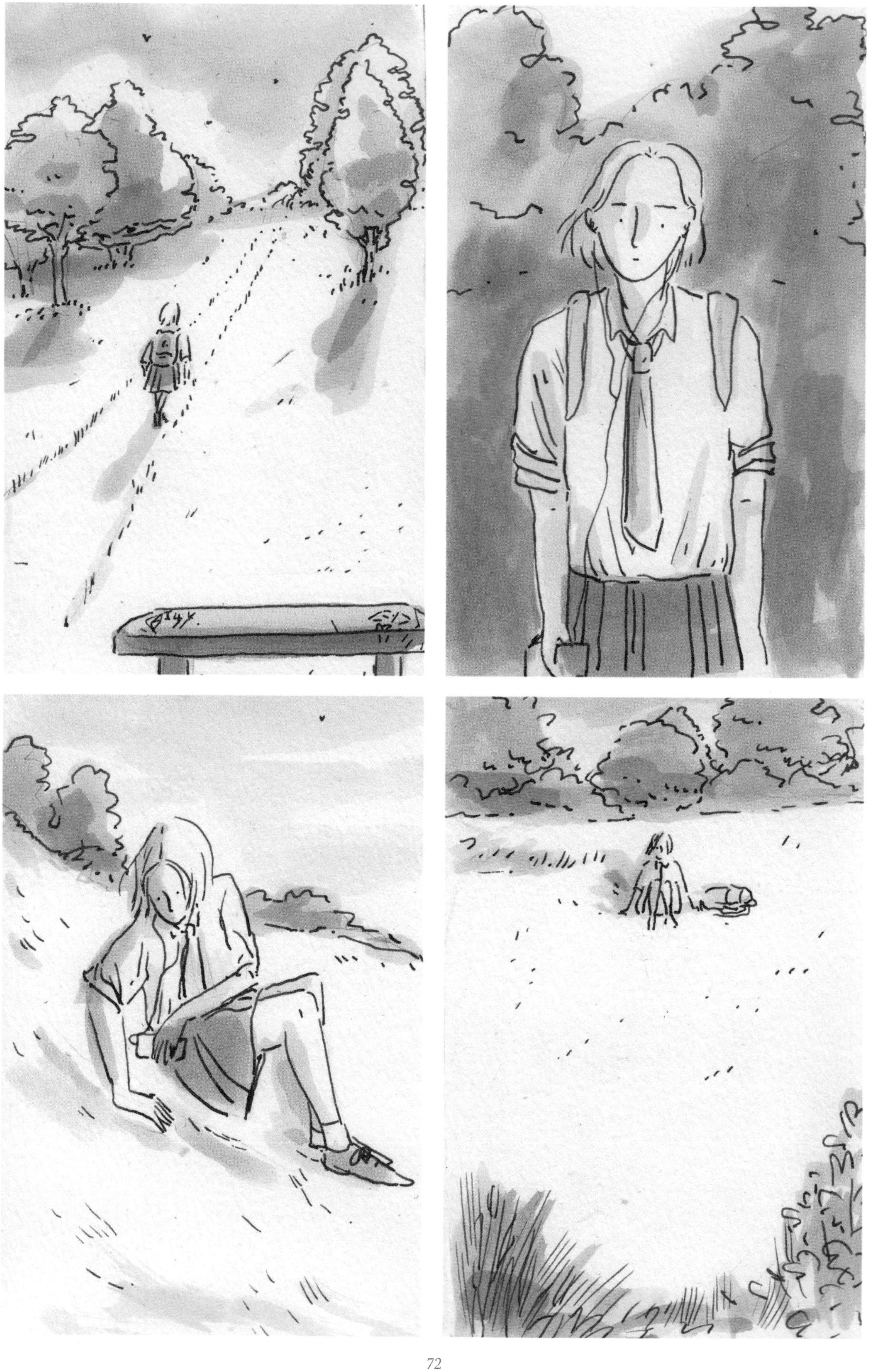

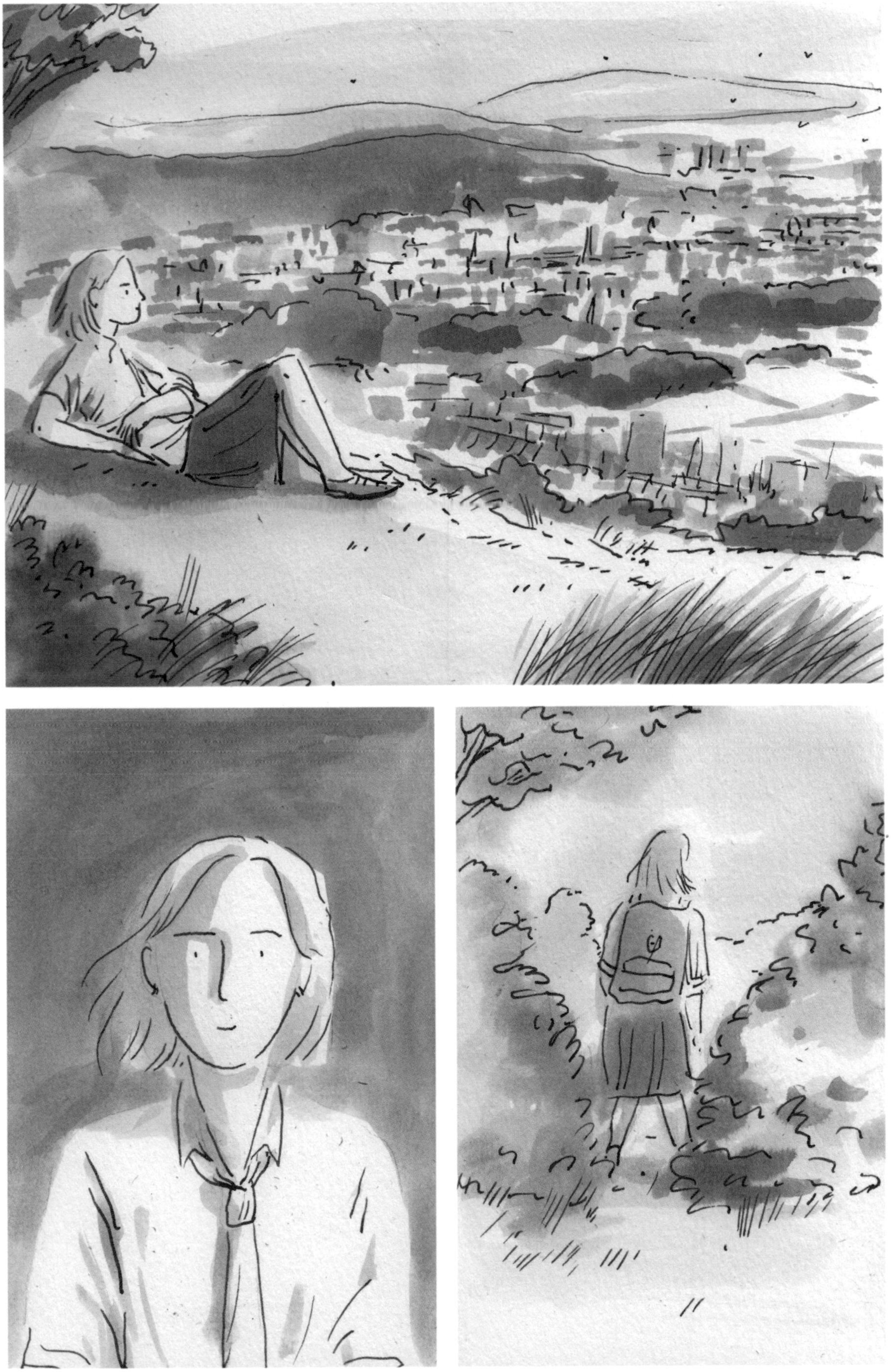

A QUICK CATCH UP

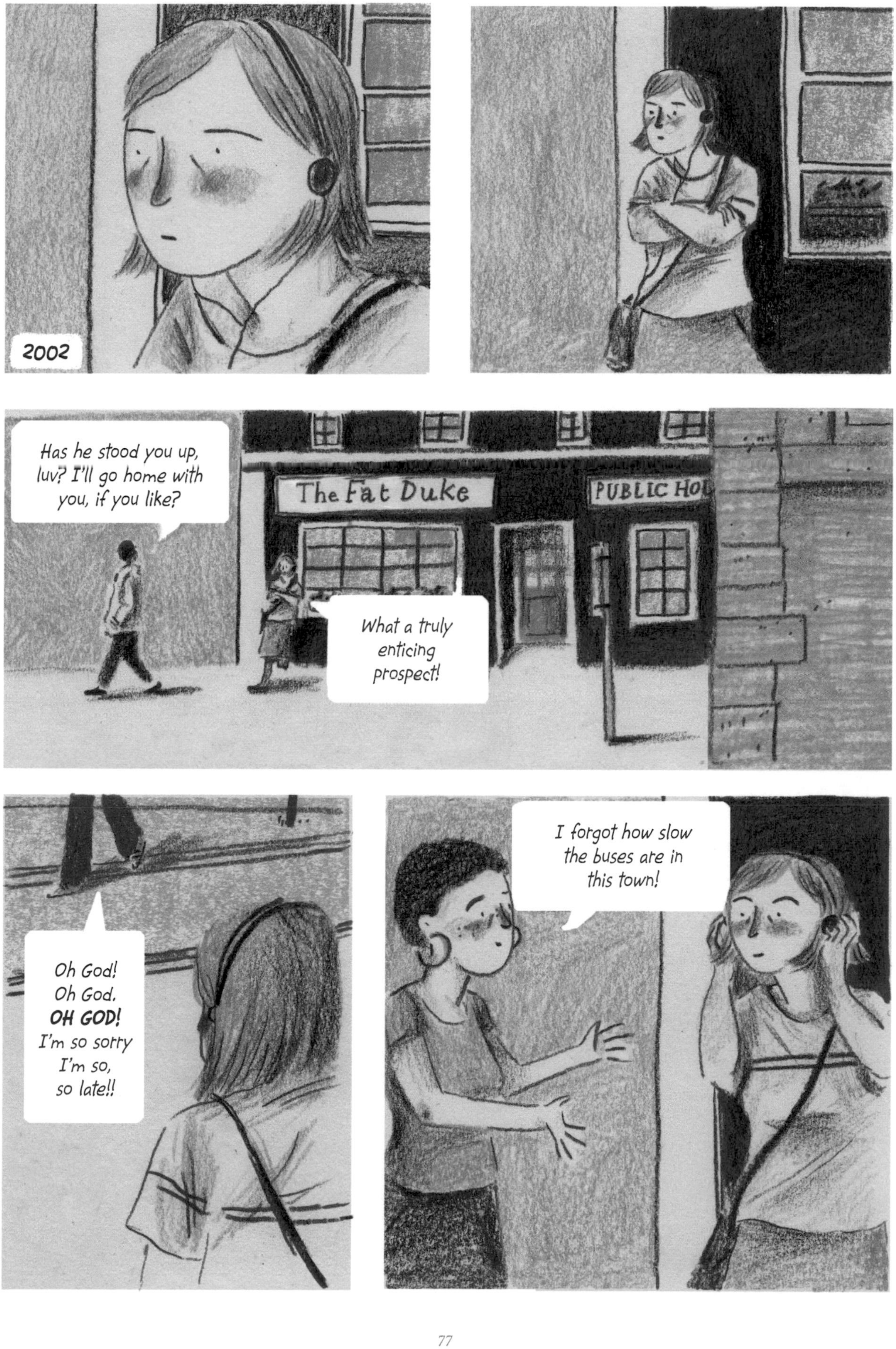
2002
Has he stood you up, luv? I'll go home with you, if you like?
The Fat Duke
PUBLIC HO
What a truly enticing prospect!
Oh God! Oh God. **OH GOD!** I'm so sorry I'm so, so late!!
I forgot how slow the buses are in this town!

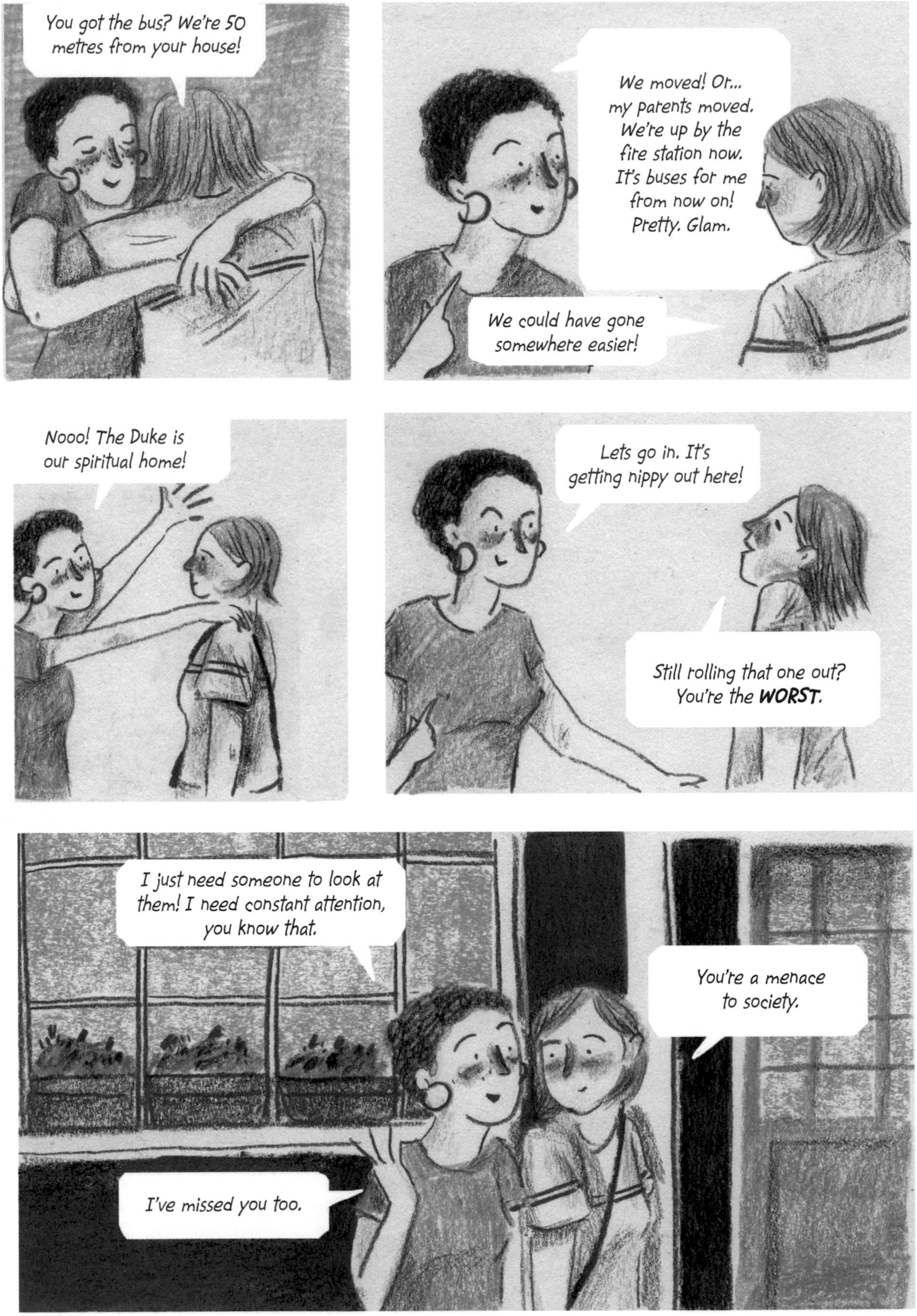
You got the bus? We're 50 metres from your house!
We moved! Or... my parents moved. We're up by the fire station now. It's buses for me from now on! Pretty. Glam.
We could have gone somewhere easier!
Nooo! The Duke is our spiritual home!
Lets go in. It's getting nippy out here!
Still rolling that one out? You're the WORST.
I just need someone to look at them! I need constant attention, you know that.
You're a menace to society.
I've missed you too.

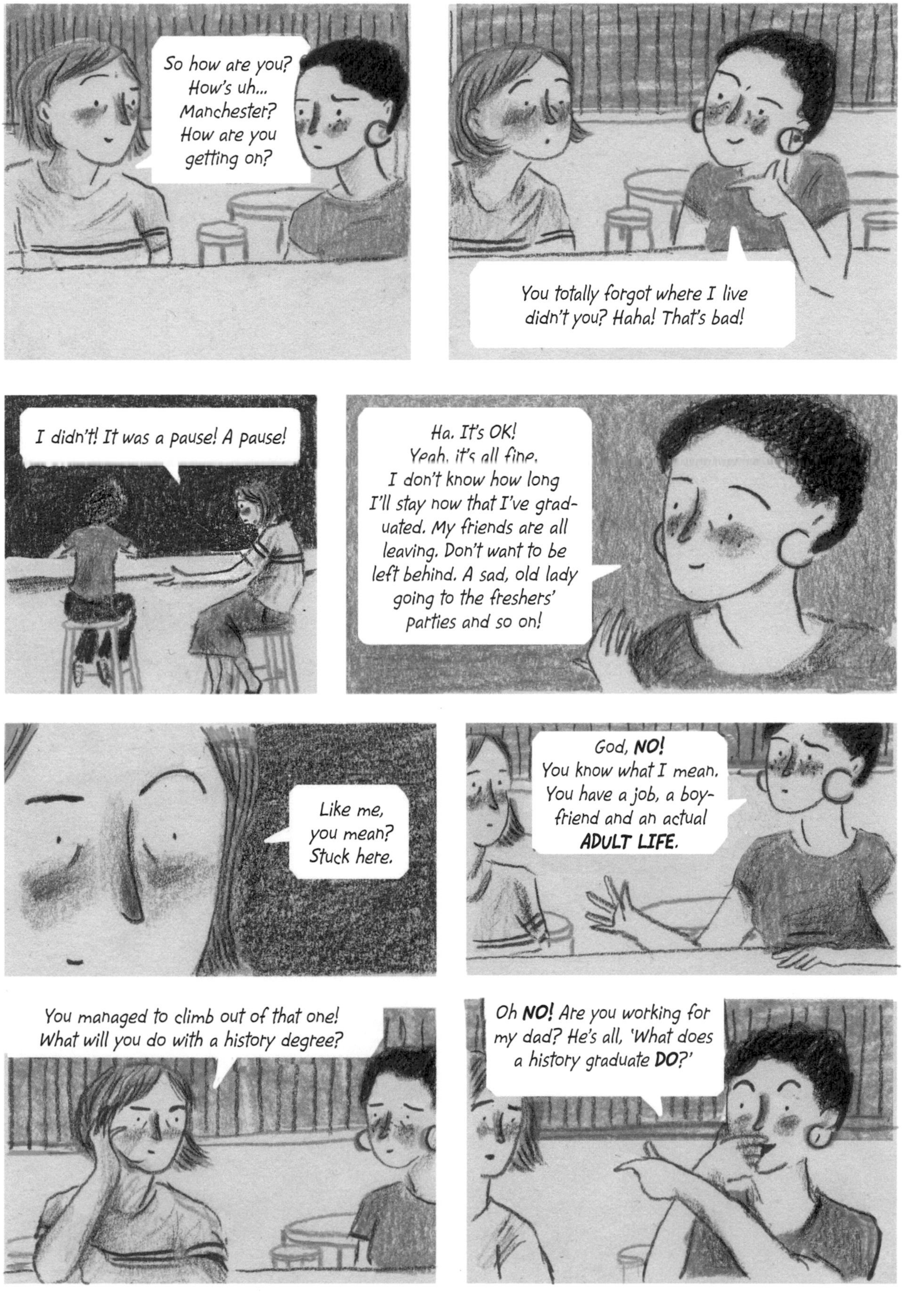
So how are you? How's uh... Manchester? How are you getting on?
You totally forgot where I live didn't you? Haha! That's bad!
I didn't! It was a pause! A pause!
Ha. It's OK! Yeah, it's all fine. I don't know how long I'll stay now that I've graduated. My friends are all leaving. Don't want to be left behind. A sad, old lady going to the freshers' parties and so on!
Like me, you mean? Stuck here.
God, **NO!** You know what I mean. You have a job, a boyfriend and an actual **ADULT LIFE**.
You managed to climb out of that one! What will you do with a history degree?
Oh **NO!** Are you working for my dad? He's all, 'What does a history graduate **DO?**'

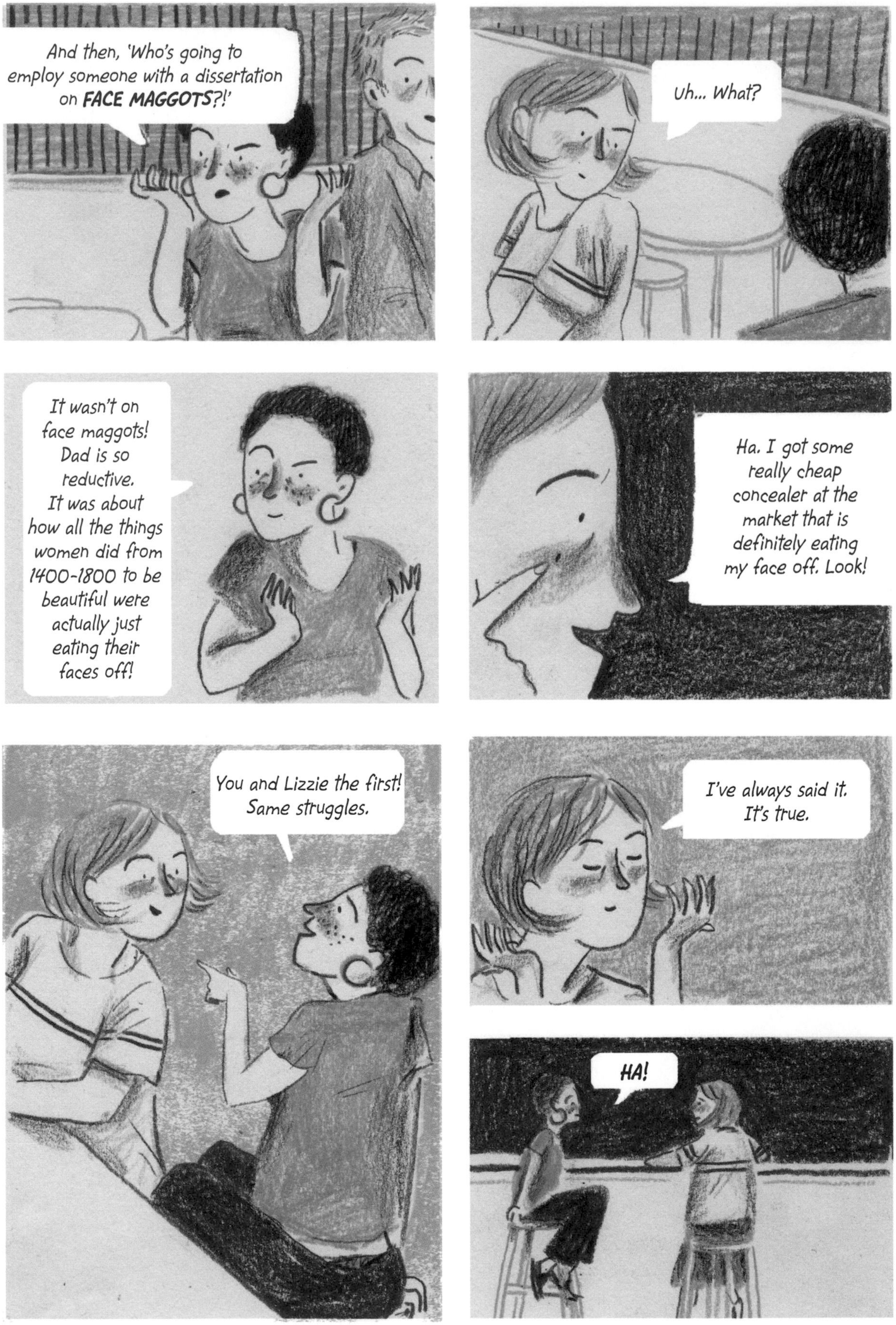
And then, 'Who's going to employ someone with a dissertation on FACE MAGGOTS?!'
Uh... What?
It wasn't on face maggots! Dad is so reductive. It was about how all the things women did from 1400-1800 to be beautiful were actually just eating their faces off!
Ha. I got some really cheap concealer at the market that is definitely eating my face off. Look!
You and Lizzie the first! Same struggles.
I've always said it. It's true.
HA!

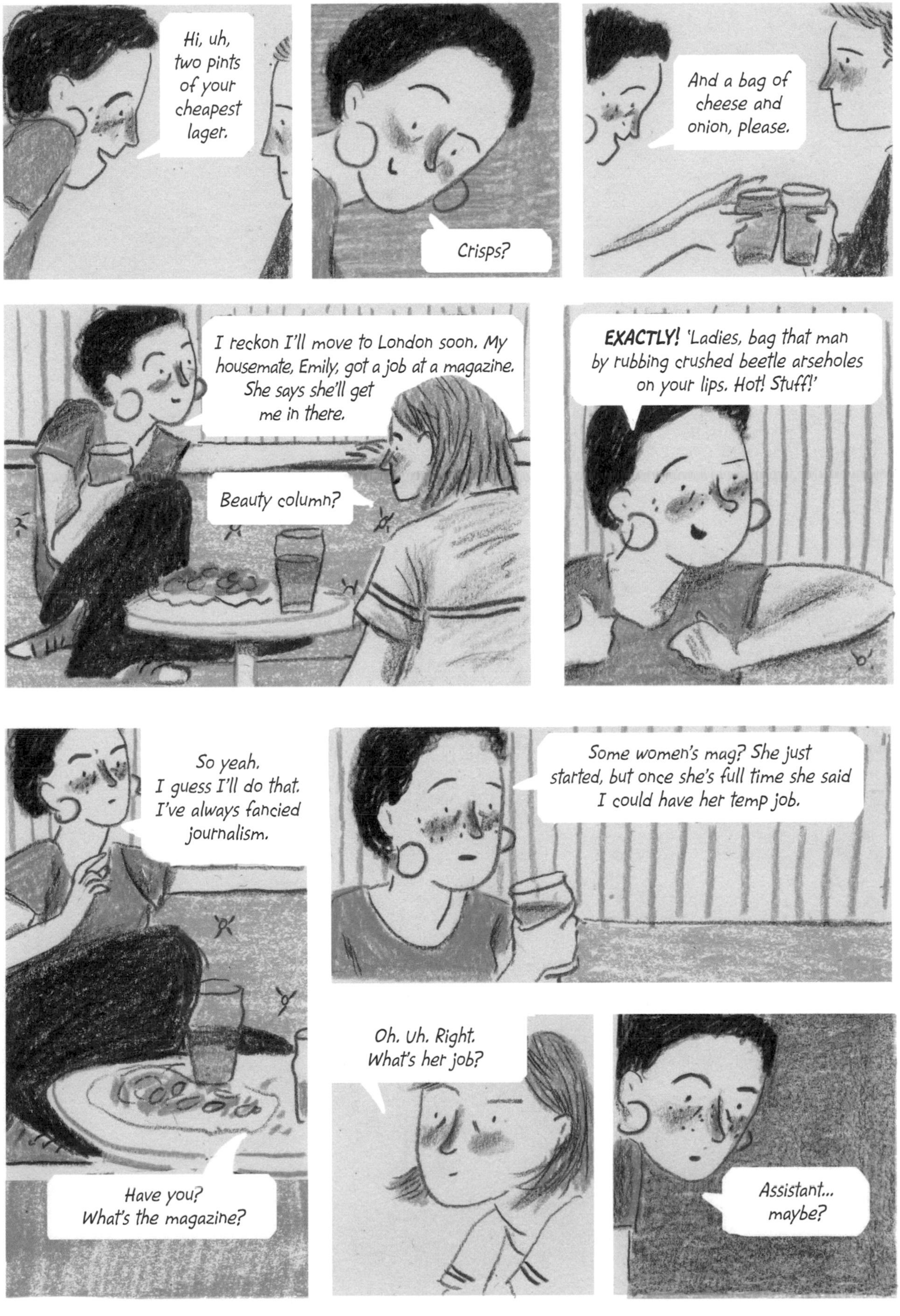
Hi, uh, two pints of your cheapest lager.
Crisps?
And a bag of cheese and onion, please.
I reckon I'll move to London soon. My housemate, Emily, got a job at a magazine. She says she'll get me in there.
Beauty column?
EXACTLY! 'Ladies, bag that man by rubbing crushed beetle arseholes on your lips. Hot! Stuff!'
So yeah. I guess I'll do that. I've always fancied journalism.
Have you? What's the magazine?
Some women's mag? She just started, but once she's full time she said I could have her temp job.
Oh. Uh. Right. What's her job?
Assistant... maybe?

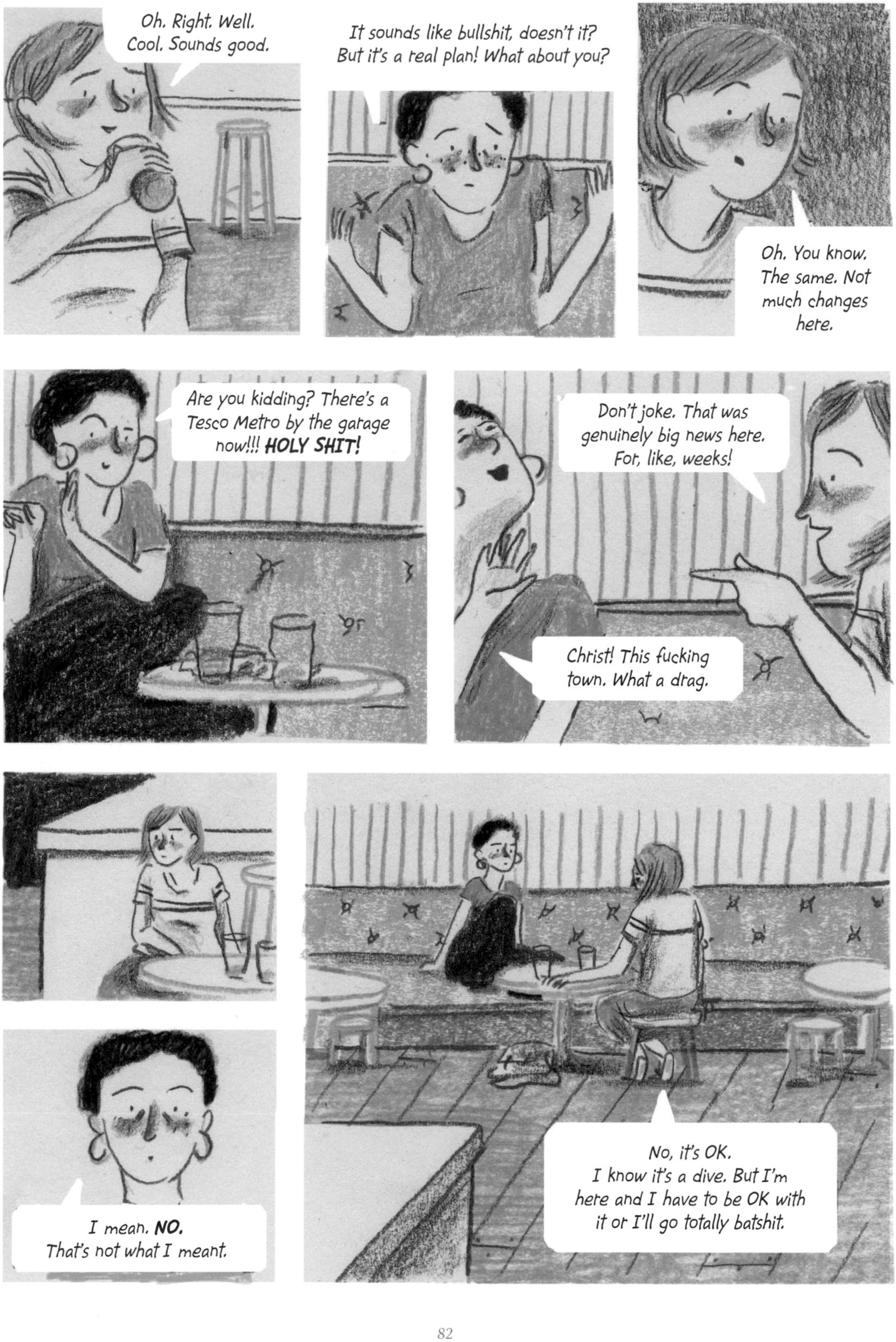

Oh. Right. Well. Cool. Sounds good.
It sounds like bullshit, doesn't it? But it's a real plan! What about you?
Oh. You know. The same. Not much changes here.
Are you kidding? There's a Tesco Metro by the garage now!!! **HOLY SHIT!**
Don't joke. That was genuinely big news here. For, like, weeks!
Christ! This fucking town. What a drag.
I mean. **NO.** That's not what I meant.
No, it's OK. I know it's a dive. But I'm here and I have to be OK with it or I'll go totally batshit.

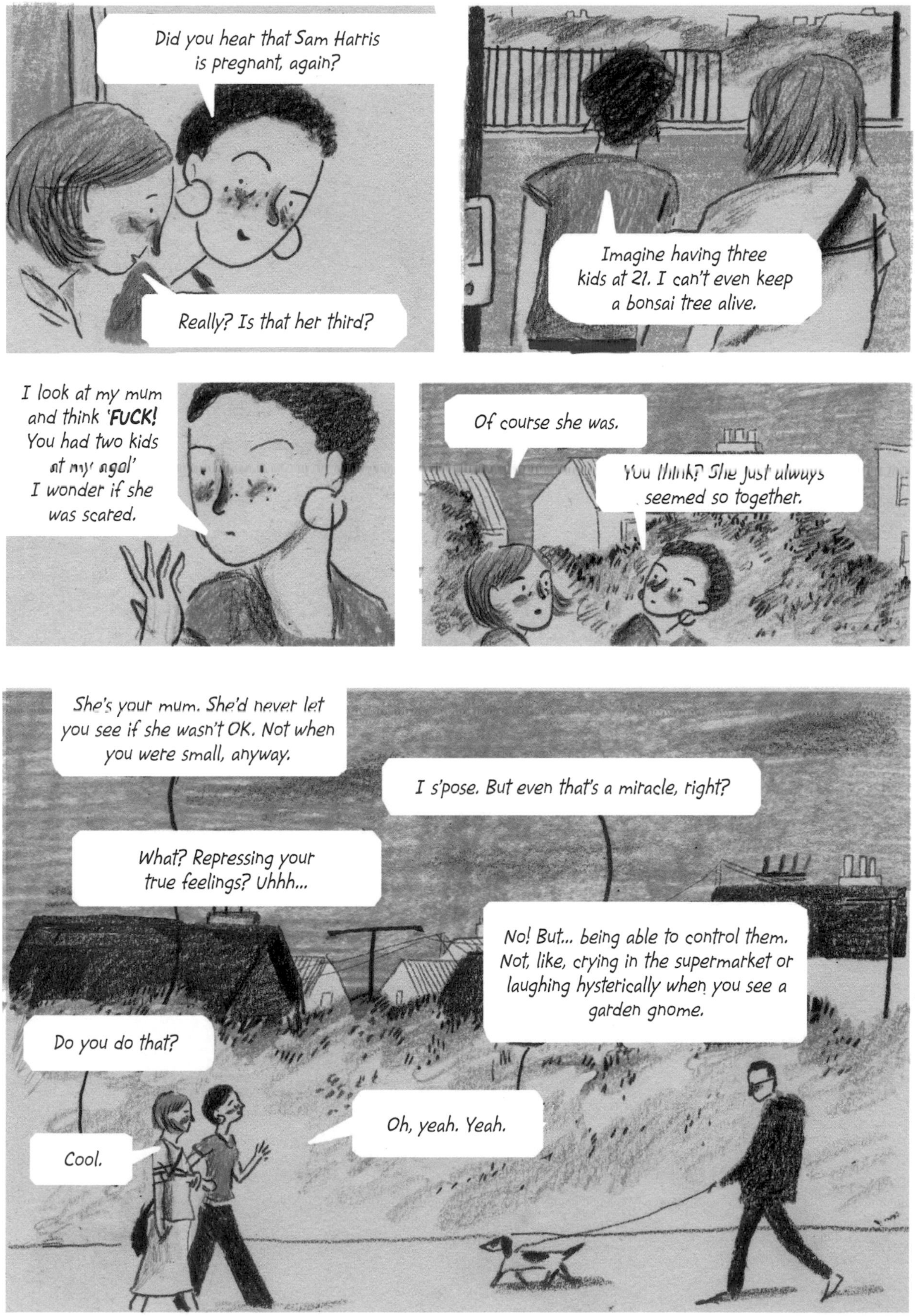
Did you hear that Sam Harris is pregnant, again?
Really? Is that her third?
Imagine having three kids at 21. I can't even keep a bonsai tree alive.
I look at my mum and think '**FUCK!** You had two kids at my age!' I wonder if she was scared.
Of course she was.
You think? She just always seemed so together.
She's your mum. She'd never let you see if she wasn't OK. Not when you were small, anyway.
I s'pose. But even that's a miracle, right?
What? Repressing your true feelings? Uhhh...
No! But... being able to control them. Not, like, crying in the supermarket or laughing hysterically when you see a garden gnome.
Do you do that?
Oh, yeah. Yeah.
Cool.

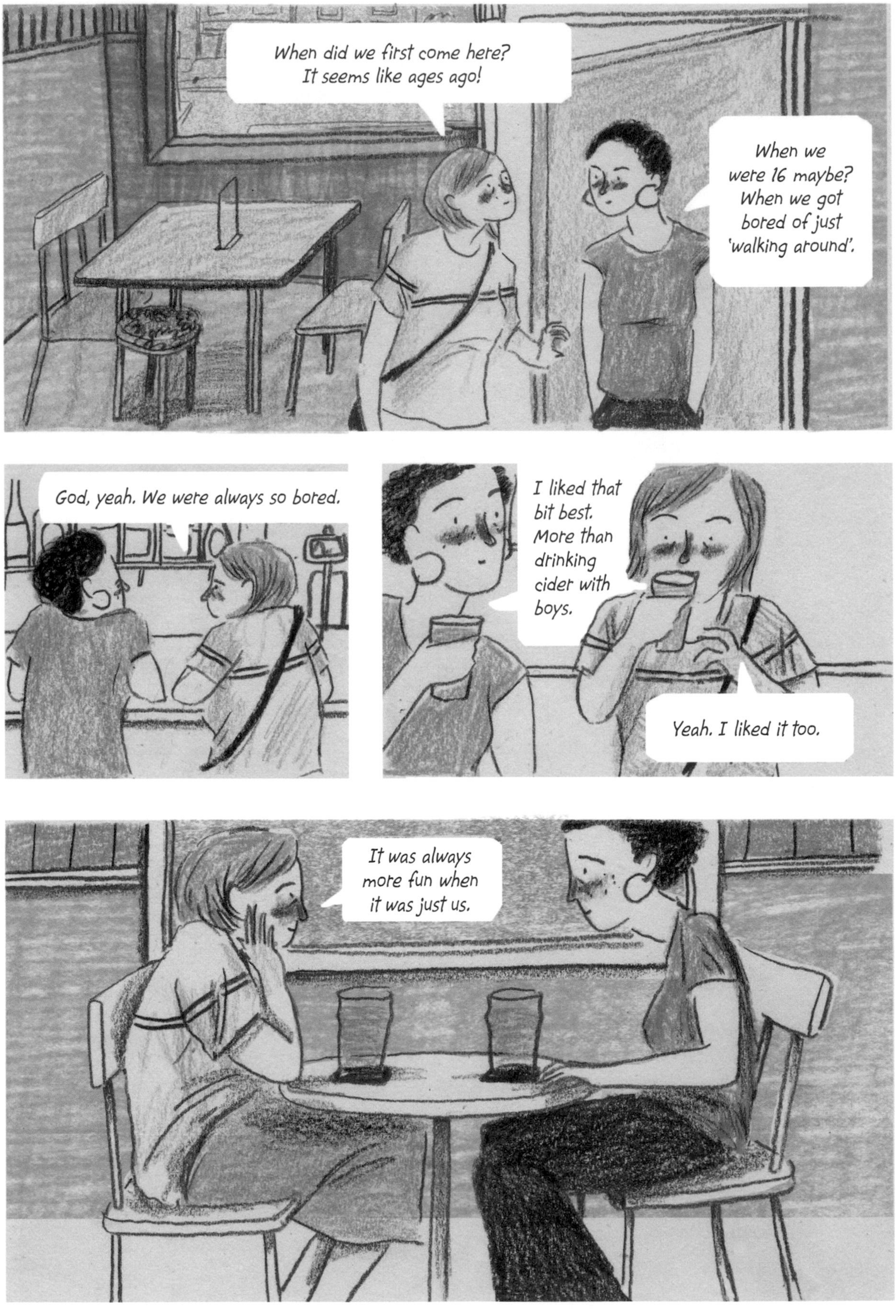
When did we first come here? It seems like ages ago!
When we were 16 maybe? When we got bored of just 'walking around'.
God, yeah. We were always so bored.
I liked that bit best. More than drinking cider with boys.
Yeah. I liked it too.
It was always more fun when it was just us.

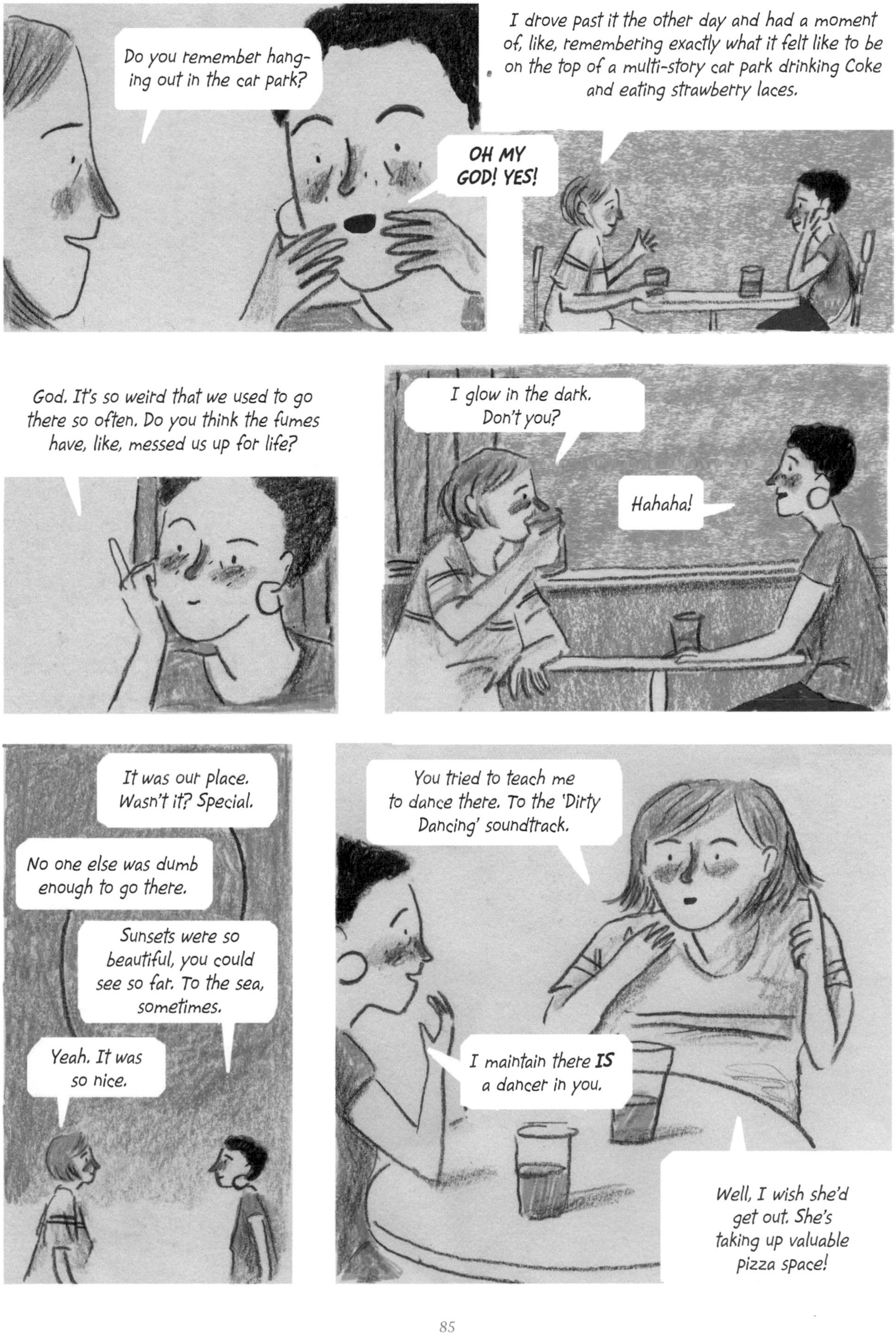
Do you remember hanging out in the car park?
OH MY GOD! YES!
I drove past it the other day and had a moment of, like, remembering exactly what it felt like to be on the top of a multi-story car park drinking Coke and eating strawberry laces.
God. It's so weird that we used to go there so often. Do you think the fumes have, like, messed us up for life?
I glow in the dark. Don't you?
Hahaha!
It was our place. Wasn't it? Special.
No one else was dumb enough to go there.
Sunsets were so beautiful, you could see so far. To the sea, sometimes.
Yeah. It was so nice.
You tried to teach me to dance there. To the 'Dirty Dancing' soundtrack.
I maintain there **IS** a dancer in you.
Well, I wish she'd get out. She's taking up valuable pizza space!

I tried to take Nick up there. When we first got together. Cos of the view. I was trying to impress him, I think.

The car park?

Yeah. Years ago.

AND? Did he ravish you there and then?

Nope.

He thought it was gross. So we went for take-away.

Ha. Of course he didn't get it!

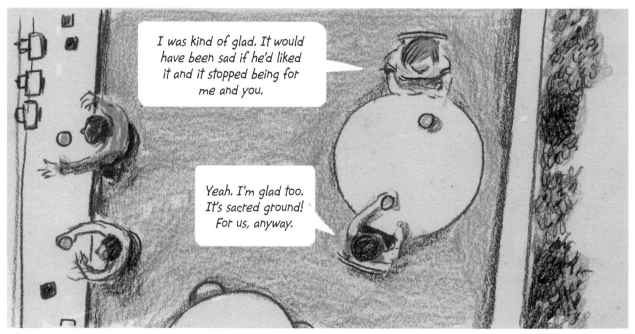

I was kind of glad. It would have been sad if he'd liked it and it stopped being for me and you.

Yeah. I'm glad too. It's sacred ground! For us, anyway.

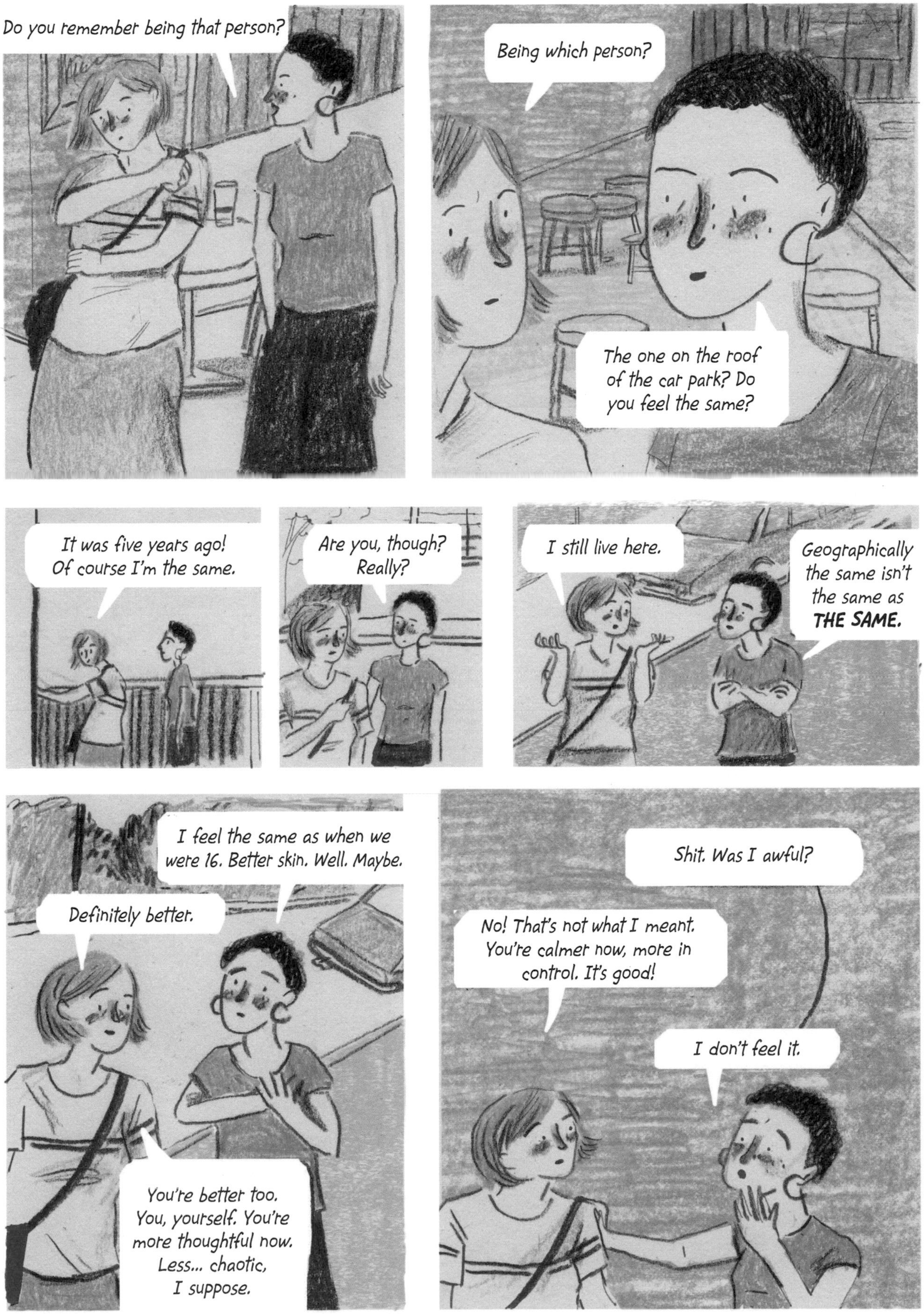
Do you remember being that person?
Being which person?
The one on the roof of the car park? Do you feel the same?
It was five years ago! Of course I'm the same.
Are you, though? Really?
I still live here.
Geographically the same isn't the same as THE SAME.
I feel the same as when we were 16. Better skin. Well. Maybe.
Definitely better.
You're better too. You, yourself. You're more thoughtful now. Less... chaotic, I suppose.
Shit. Was I awful?
No! That's not what I meant. You're calmer now, more in control. It's good!
I don't feel it.

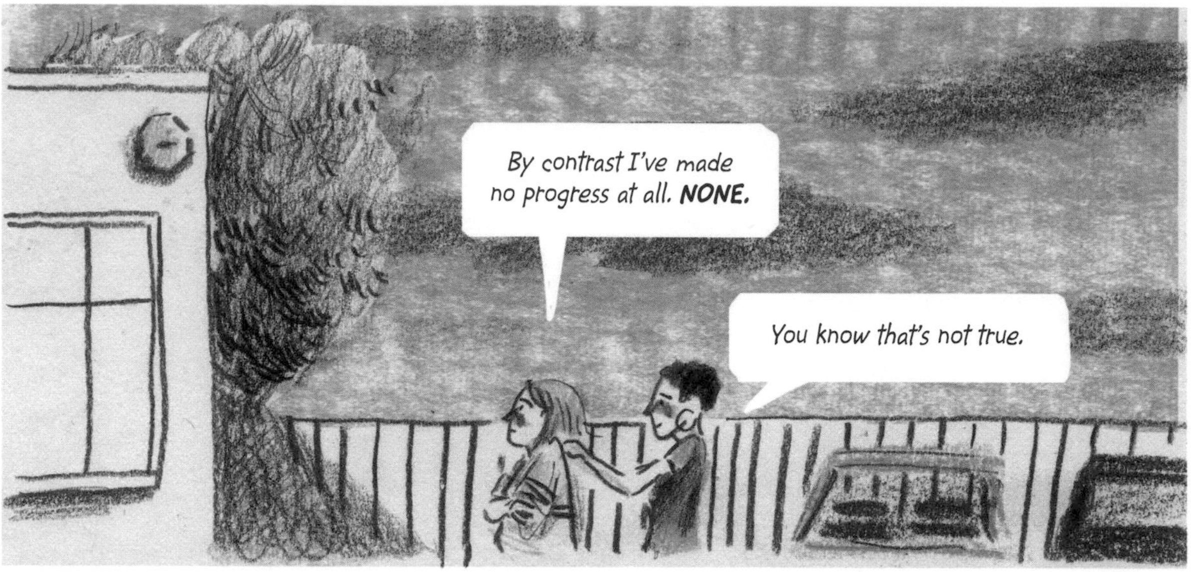
By contrast I've made no progress at all. **NONE.**
You know that's not true.

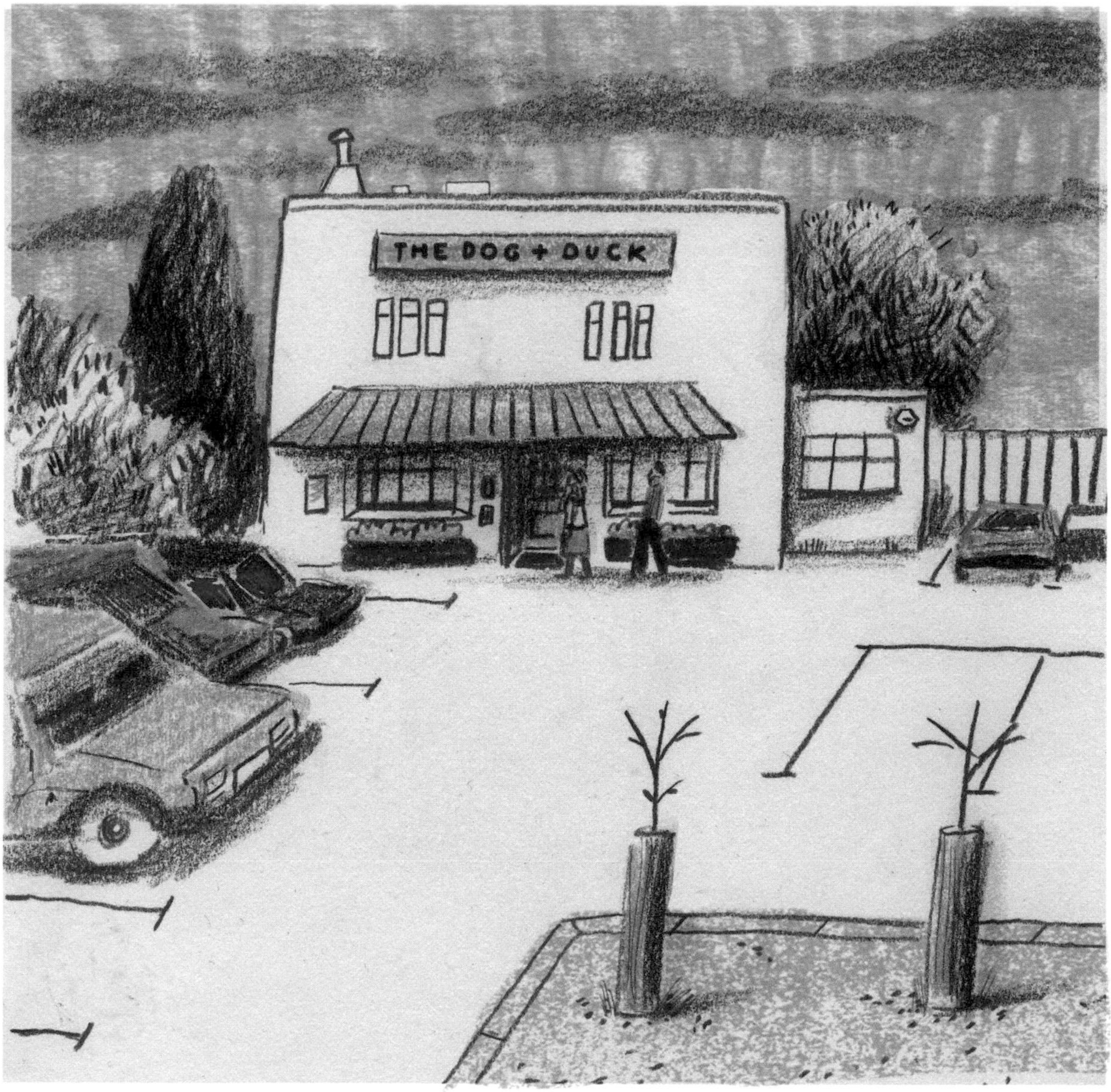
THE DOG + DUCK

Why did we stop hanging out on the holidays?

Because you stopped coming home on the holidays? And I have a full-time job?

I'd have come home more if I got to stay with you and not my mad parents.

No, you wouldn't.

Why not?

You just wouldn't. You were having too much fun.

What?

It's not that far. It'd have been easy to come back.

But you were having a good time. Why would you come back here? It's shit. I'm not accusing you of anything! It's just the truth. If university had suited me I wouldn't have come back either.

Or if Nick had done the right thing and moved with you.

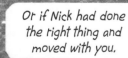

Sorry. That was unfair.

I didn't leave for Nick. I left uni cos I wasn't right for it.

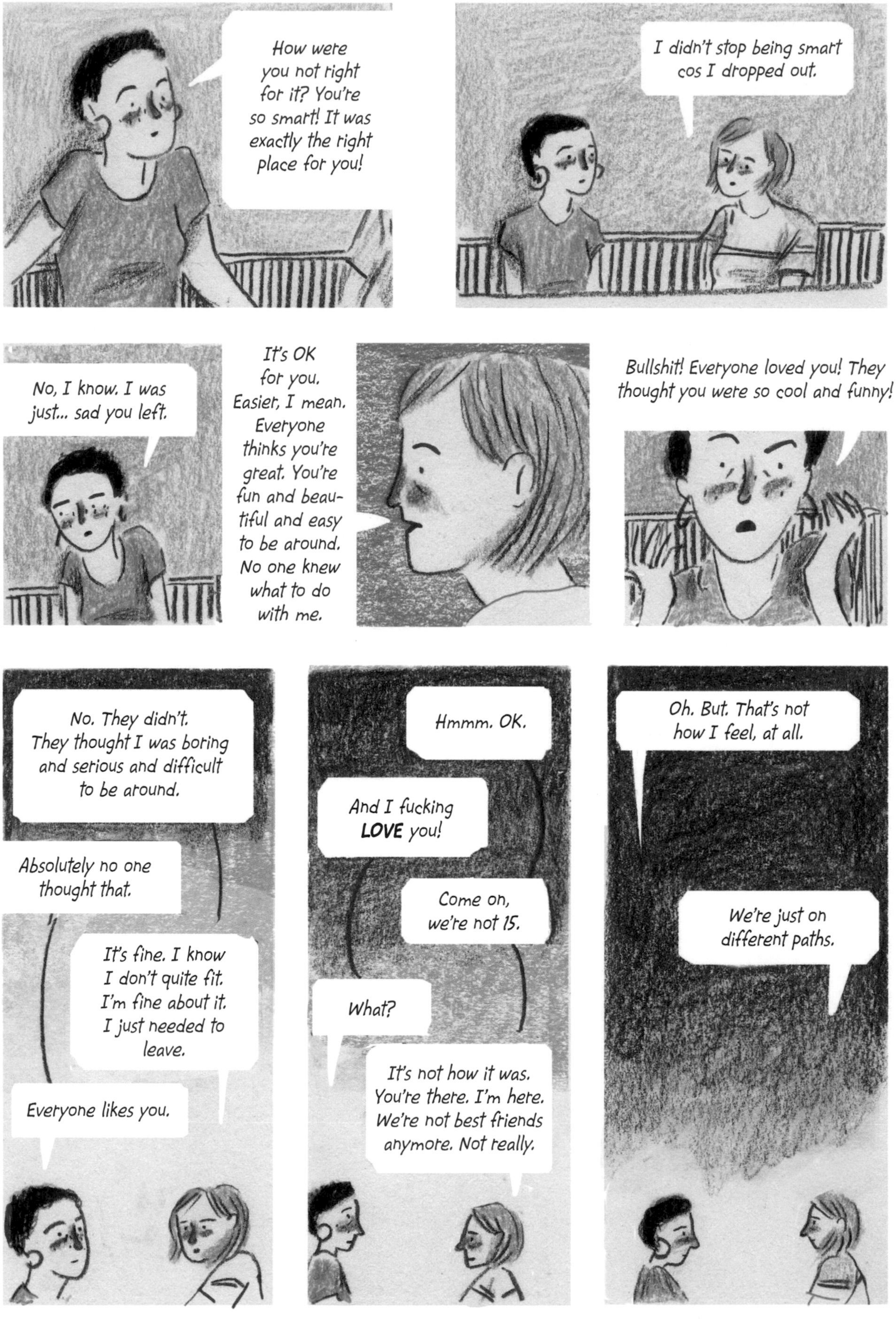
How were you not right for it? You're so smart! It was exactly the right place for you!
I didn't stop being smart cos I dropped out.
No, I know. I was just... sad you left.
It's OK for you. Easier, I mean. Everyone thinks you're great. You're fun and beau-tiful and easy to be around. No one knew what to do with me.
Bullshit! Everyone loved you! They thought you were so cool and funny!
No. They didn't. They thought I was boring and serious and difficult to be around.
Absolutely no one thought that.
It's fine. I know I don't quite fit. I'm fine about it. I just needed to leave.
Everyone likes you.
Hmmm. OK.
And I fucking LOVE you!
Come on, we're not 15.
What?
It's not how it was. You're there. I'm here. We're not best friends anymore. Not really.
Oh. But. That's not how I feel, at all.
We're just on different paths.

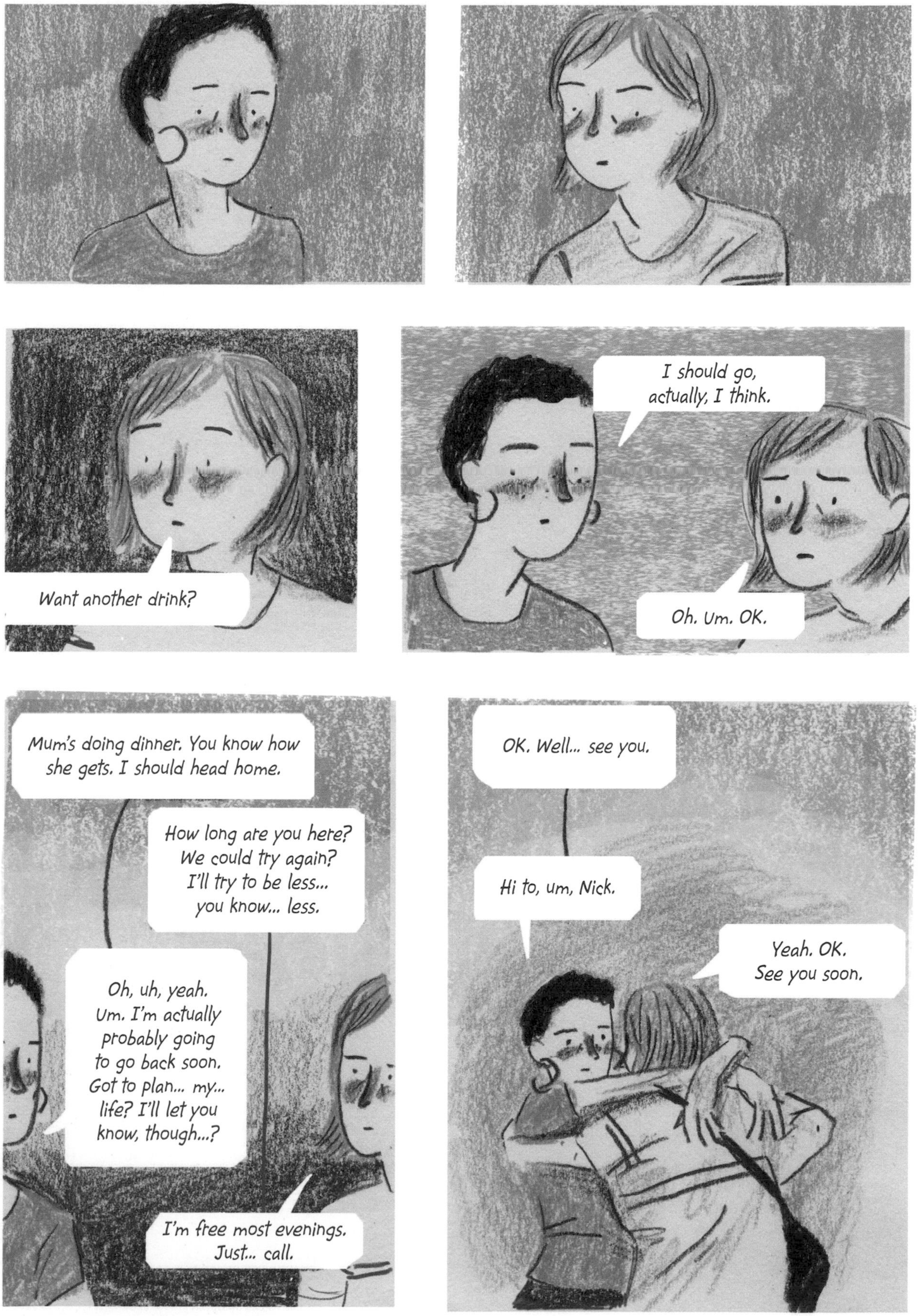
Want another drink?
I should go, actually, I think.
Oh. Um. OK.
Mum's doing dinner. You know how she gets. I should head home.
How long are you here? We could try again? I'll try to be less... you know... less.
Oh, uh, yeah. Um. I'm actually probably going to go back soon. Got to plan... my... life? I'll let you know, though...?
I'm free most evenings. Just... call.
OK. Well... see you.
Hi to, um, Nick.
Yeah. OK. See you soon.

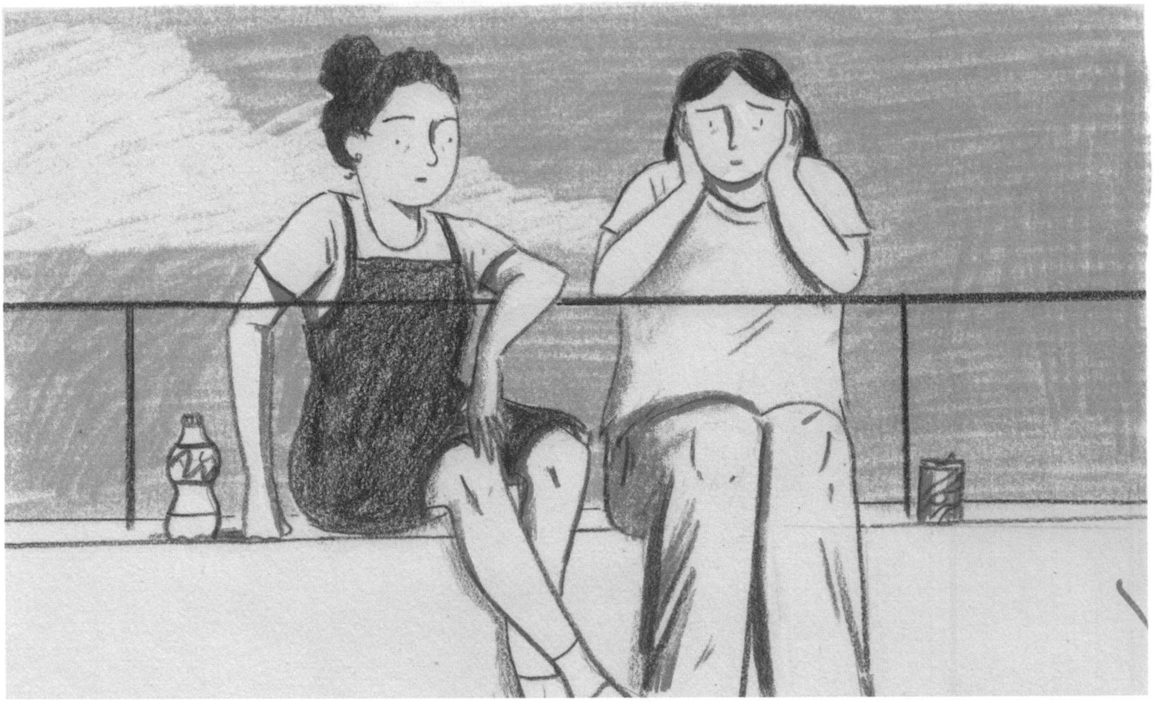

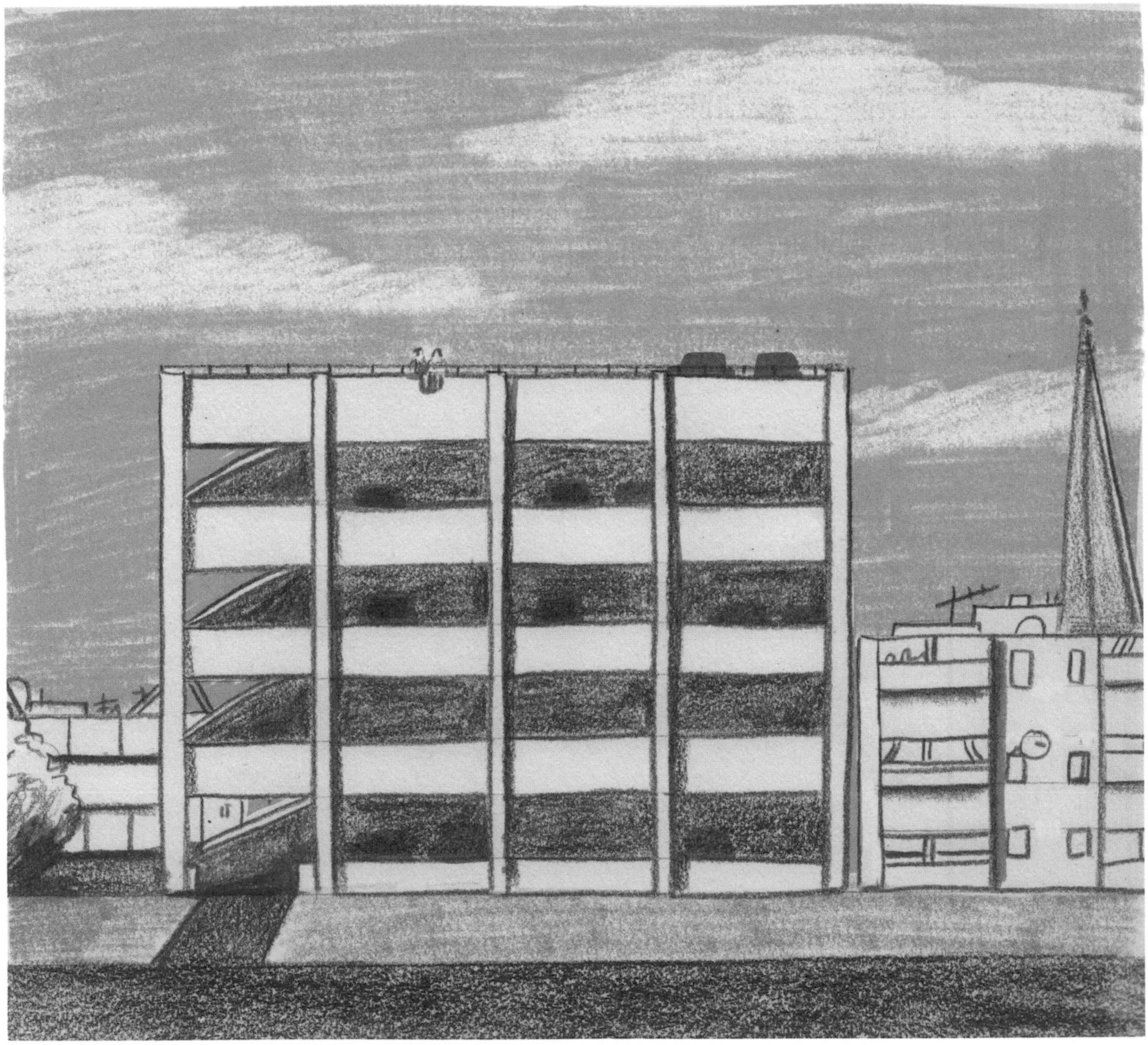

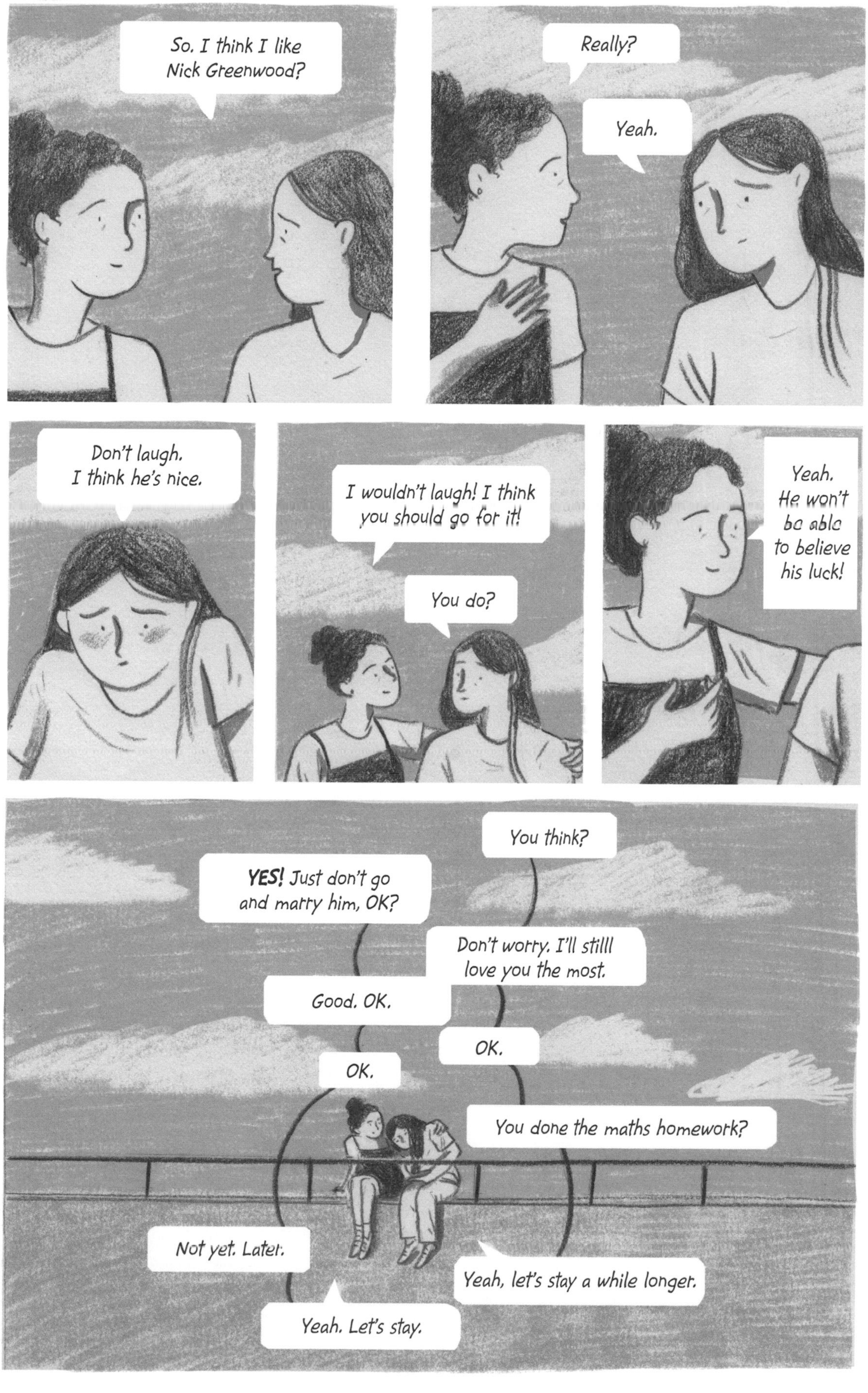

So. I think I like Nick Greenwood?
Really?
Yeah.
Don't laugh. I think he's nice.
I wouldn't laugh! I think you should go for it!
You do?
Yeah. He won't be able to believe his luck!
You think?
YES! Just don't go and marry him, OK?
Don't worry. I'll stilll love you the most.
Good. OK.
OK.
OK.
You done the maths homework?
Not yet. Later.
Yeah, let's stay a while longer.
Yeah. Let's stay.

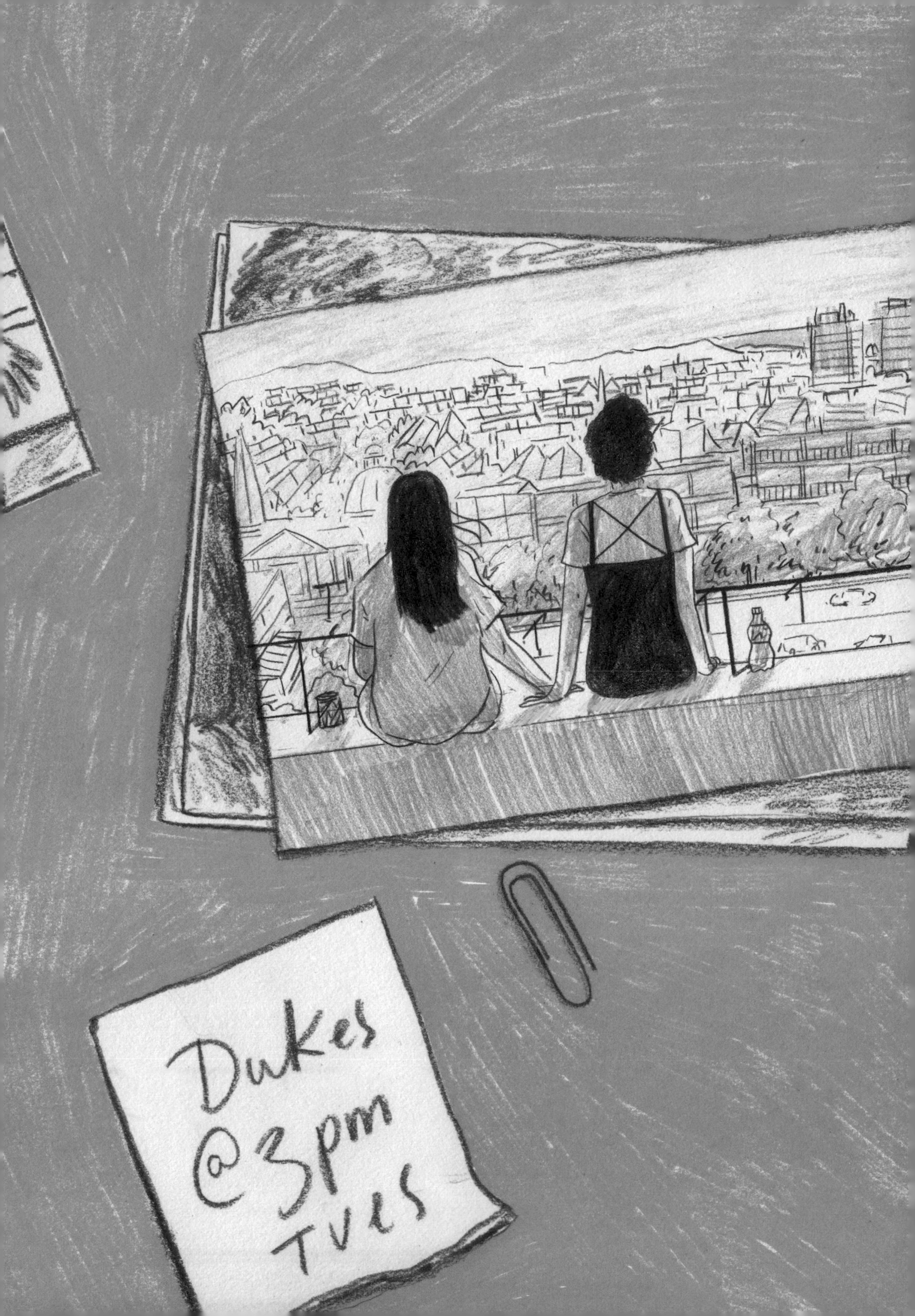
Dukes
@3pm
TUES

NO

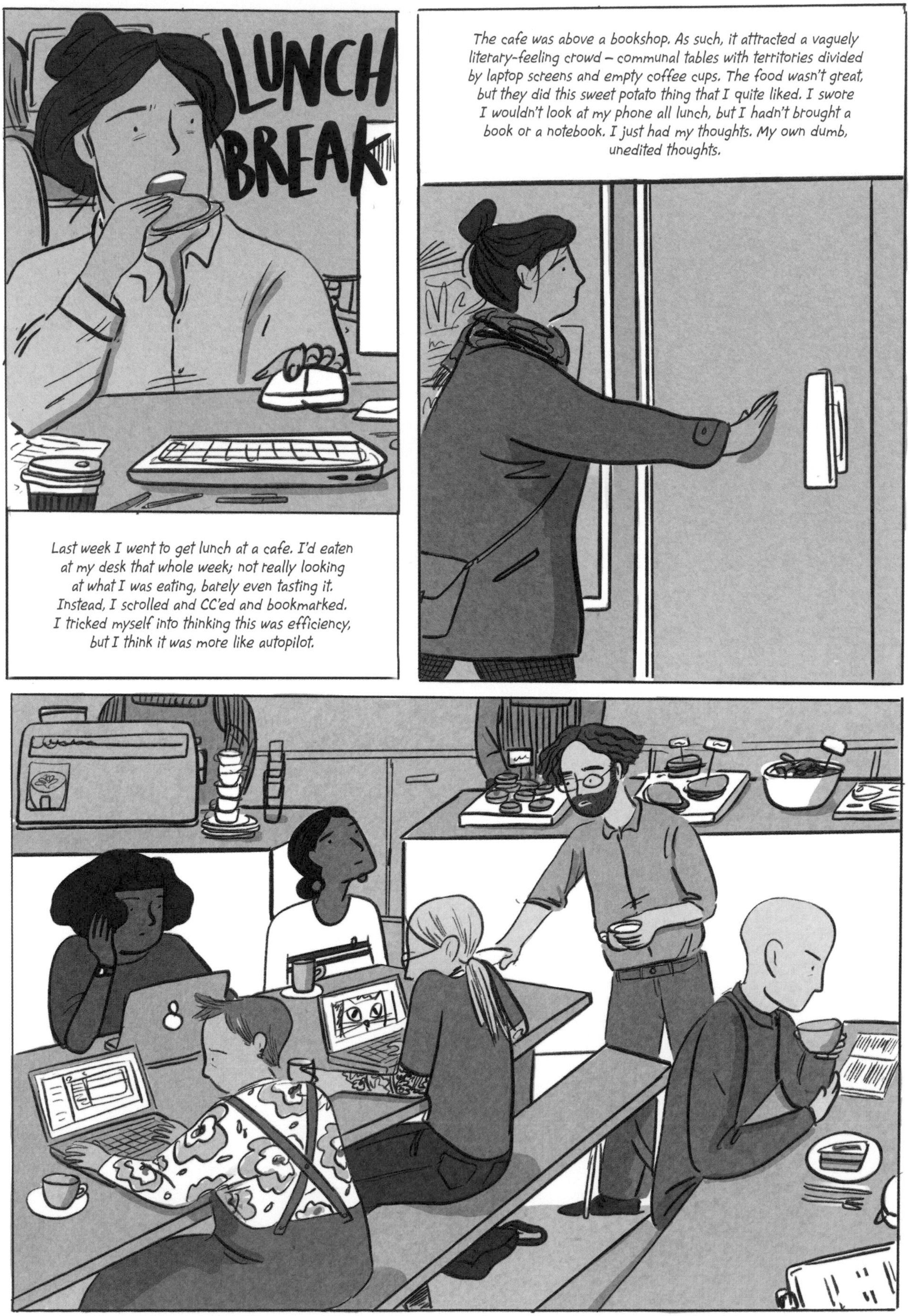
LUNCH BREAK
Last week I went to get lunch at a cafe. I'd eaten at my desk that whole week; not really looking at what I was eating, barely even tasting it. Instead, I scrolled and CC'ed and bookmarked. I tricked myself into thinking this was efficiency, but I think it was more like autopilot.
The cafe was above a bookshop. As such, it attracted a vaguely literary-feeling crowd – communal tables with territories divided by laptop screens and empty coffee cups. The food wasn't great, but they did this sweet potato thing that I quite liked. I swore I wouldn't look at my phone all lunch, but I hadn't brought a book or a notebook. I just had my thoughts. My own dumb, unedited thoughts.

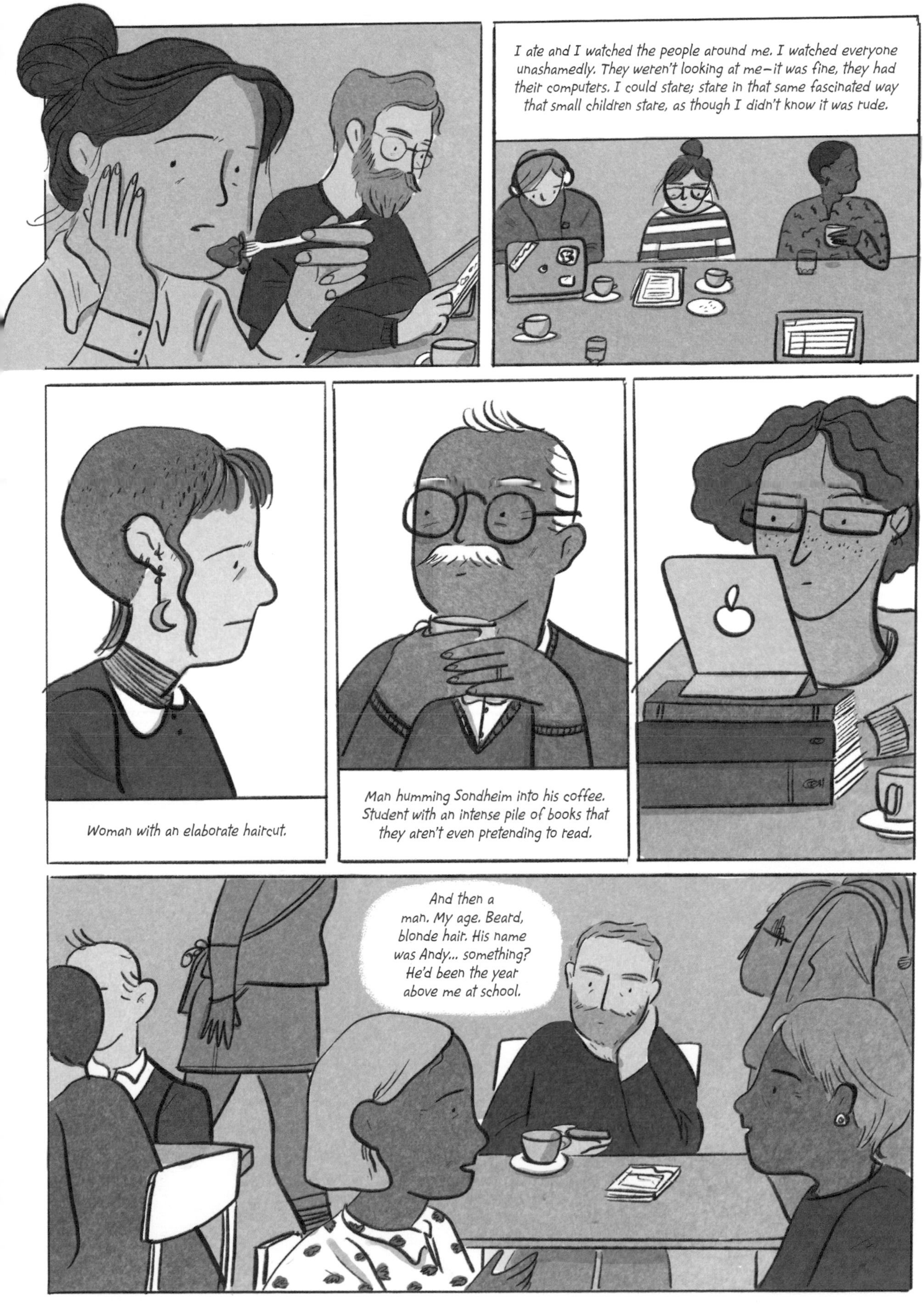
I ate and I watched the people around me. I watched everyone unashamedly. They weren't looking at me—it was fine, they had their computers. I could stare; stare in that same fascinated way that small children stare, as though I didn't know it was rude.
Woman with an elaborate haircut.
Man humming Sondheim into his coffee. Student with an intense pile of books that they aren't even pretending to read.
And then a man. My age. Beard, blonde hair. His name was Andy... something? He'd been the year above me at school.

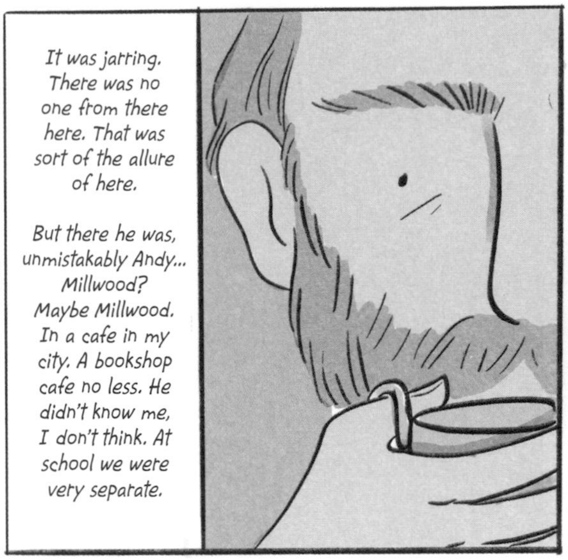
It was jarring. There was no one from there here. That was sort of the allure of here.
But there he was, unmistakably Andy... Millwood? Maybe Millwood. In a cafe in my city. A bookshop cafe no less. He didn't know me, I don't think. At school we were very separate.

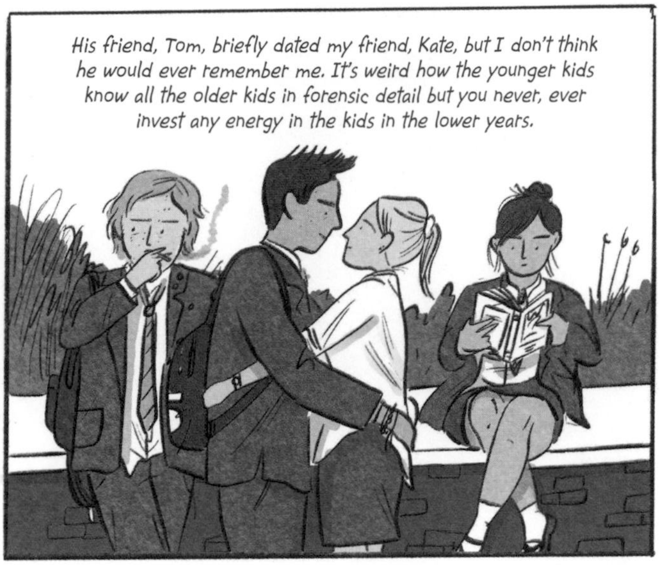
His friend, Tom, briefly dated my friend, Kate, but I don't think he would ever remember me. It's weird how the younger kids know all the older kids in forensic detail but you never, ever invest any energy in the kids in the lower years.

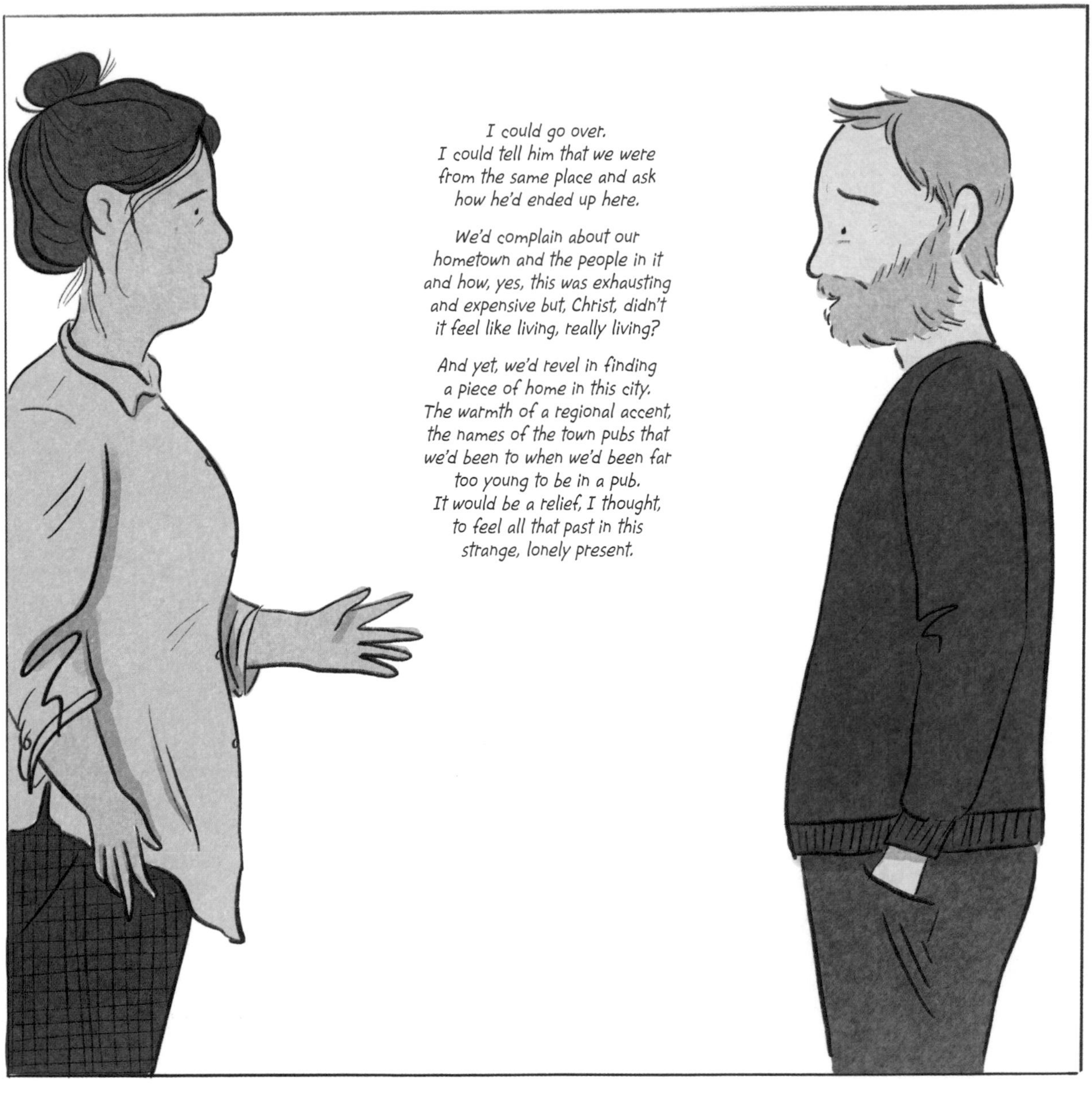
I could go over. I could tell him that we were from the same place and ask how he'd ended up here.
We'd complain about our hometown and the people in it and how, yes, this was exhausting and expensive but, Christ, didn't it feel like living, really living?
And yet, we'd revel in finding a piece of home in this city. The warmth of a regional accent, the names of the town pubs that we'd been to when we'd been far too young to be in a pub. It would be a relief, I thought, to feel all that past in this strange, lonely present.

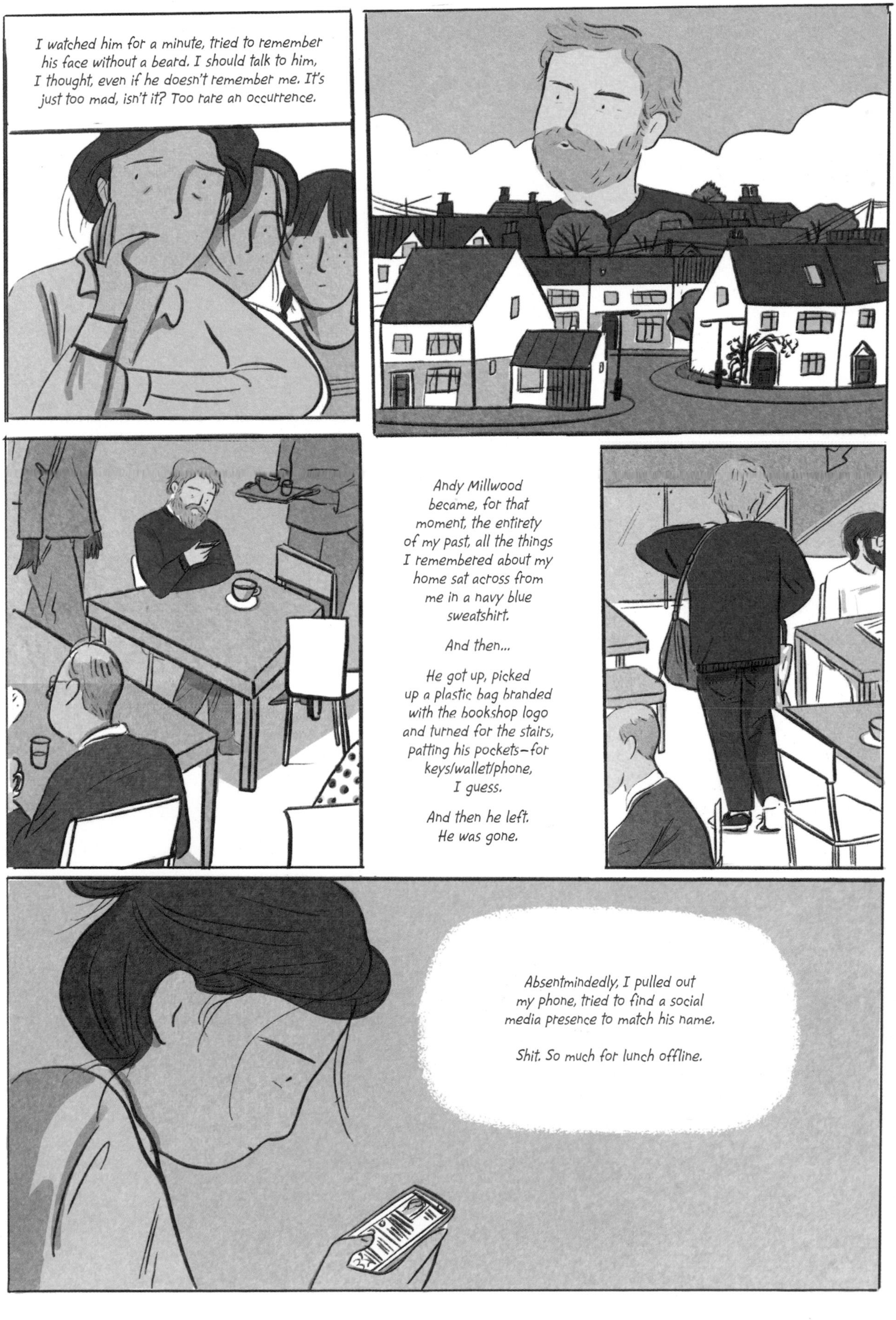

I watched him for a minute, tried to remember his face without a beard. I should talk to him, I thought, even if he doesn't remember me. It's just too mad, isn't it? Too rare an occurrence.
Andy Millwood became, for that moment, the entirety of my past, all the things I remembered about my home sat across from me in a navy blue sweatshirt.
And then...
He got up, picked up a plastic bag branded with the bookshop logo and turned for the stairs, patting his pockets—for keys/wallet/phone, I guess.
And then he left. He was gone.
Absentmindedly, I pulled out my phone, tried to find a social media presence to match his name.
Shit. So much for lunch offline.

It's not what you thought it would be

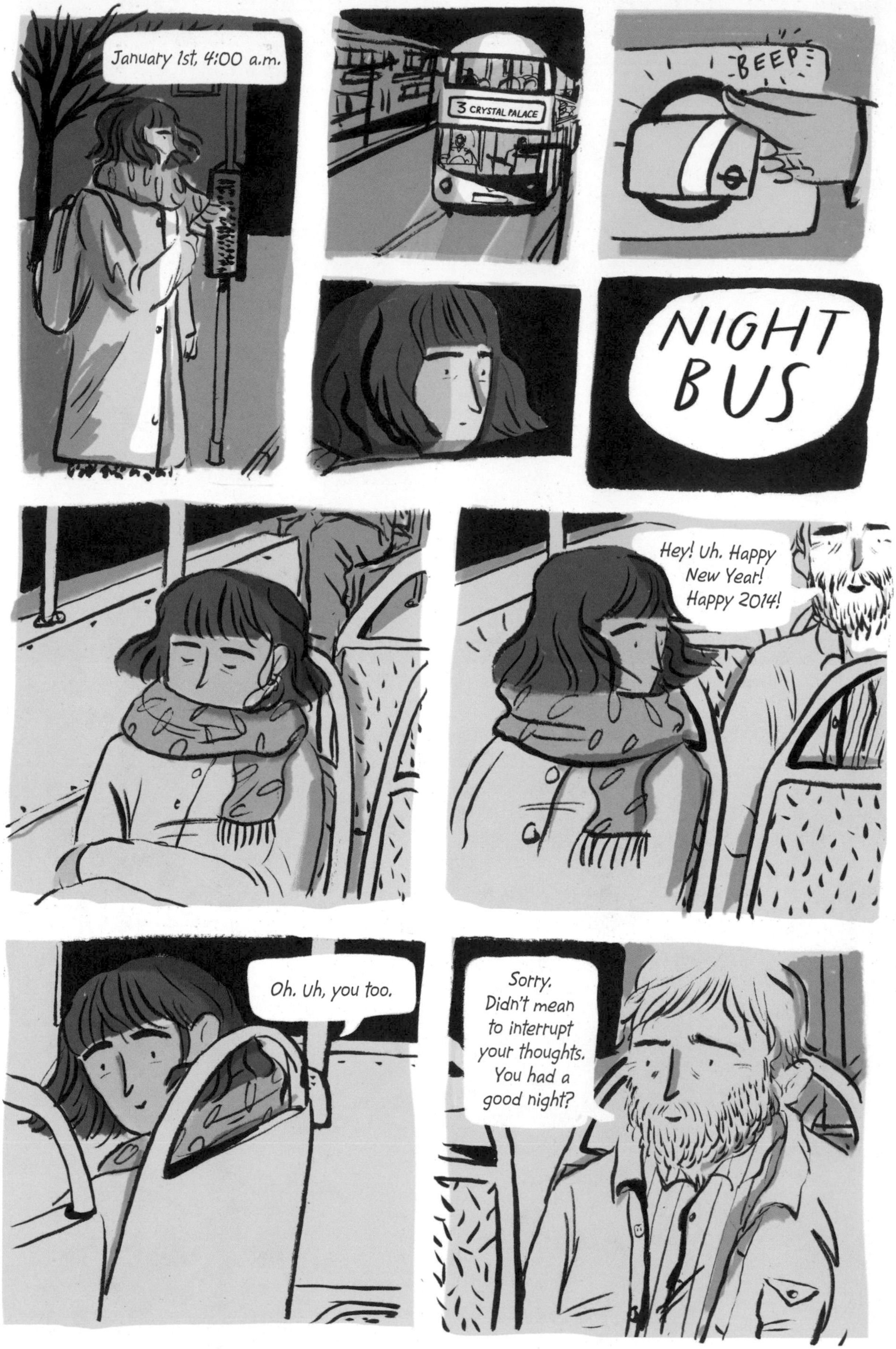

January 1st, 4:00 a.m.
3 CRYSTAL PALACE
BEEP
NIGHT BUS
Hey! Uh. Happy New Year! Happy 2014!
Oh. Uh, you too.
Sorry. Didn't mean to interrupt your thoughts. You had a good night?

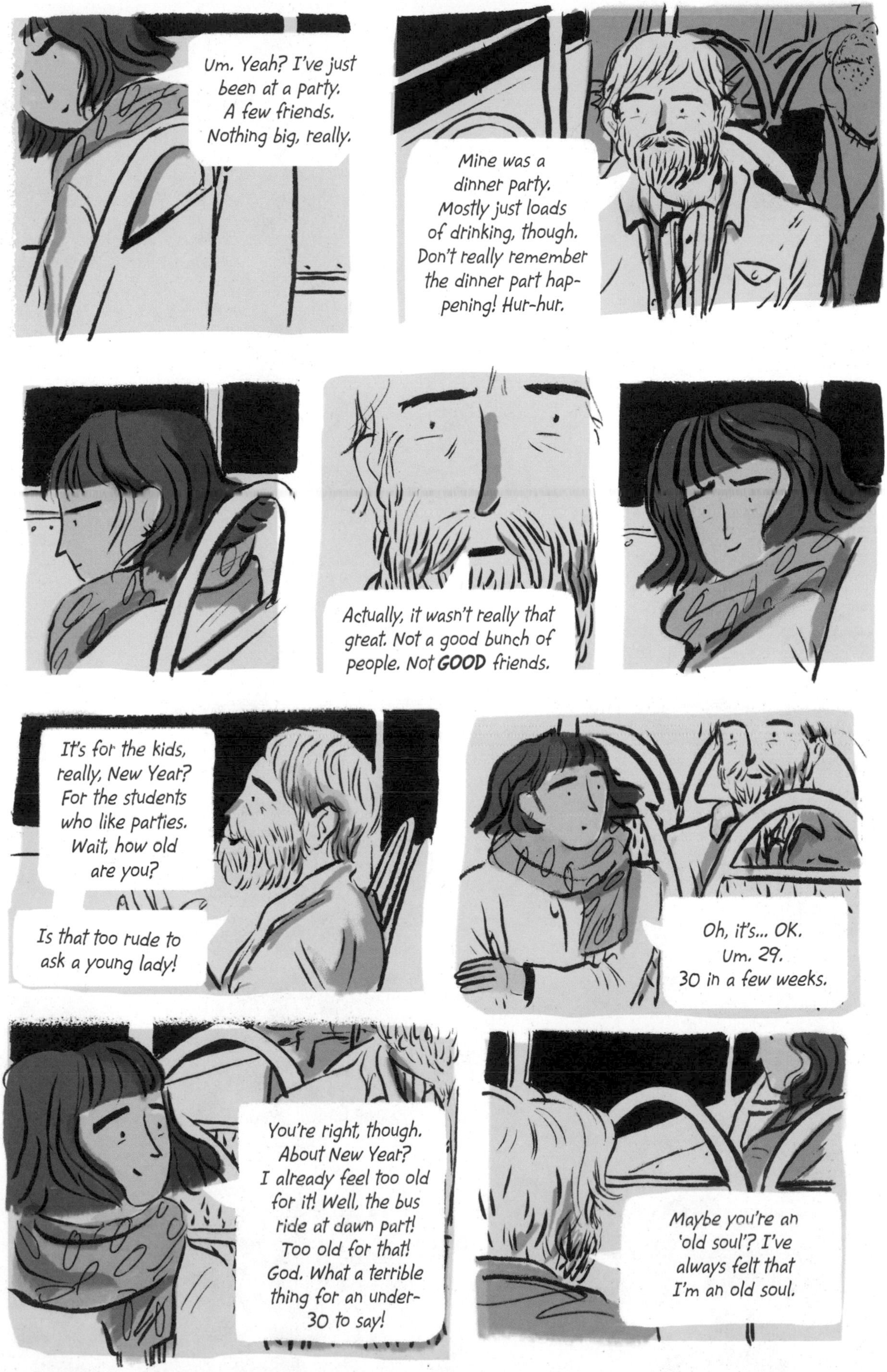
Um. Yeah? I've just been at a party. A few friends. Nothing big, really.
Mine was a dinner party. Mostly just loads of drinking, though. Don't really remember the dinner part hap-pening! Hur-hur.
Actually, it wasn't really that great. Not a good bunch of people. Not GOOD friends.
It's for the kids, really, New Year? For the students who like parties. Wait, how old are you?
Is that too rude to ask a young lady!
Oh, it's... OK. Um. 29. 30 in a few weeks.
You're right, though. About New Year? I already feel too old for it! Well, the bus ride at dawn part! Too old for that! God. What a terrible thing for an under-30 to say!
Maybe you're an 'old soul'? I've always felt that I'm an old soul.

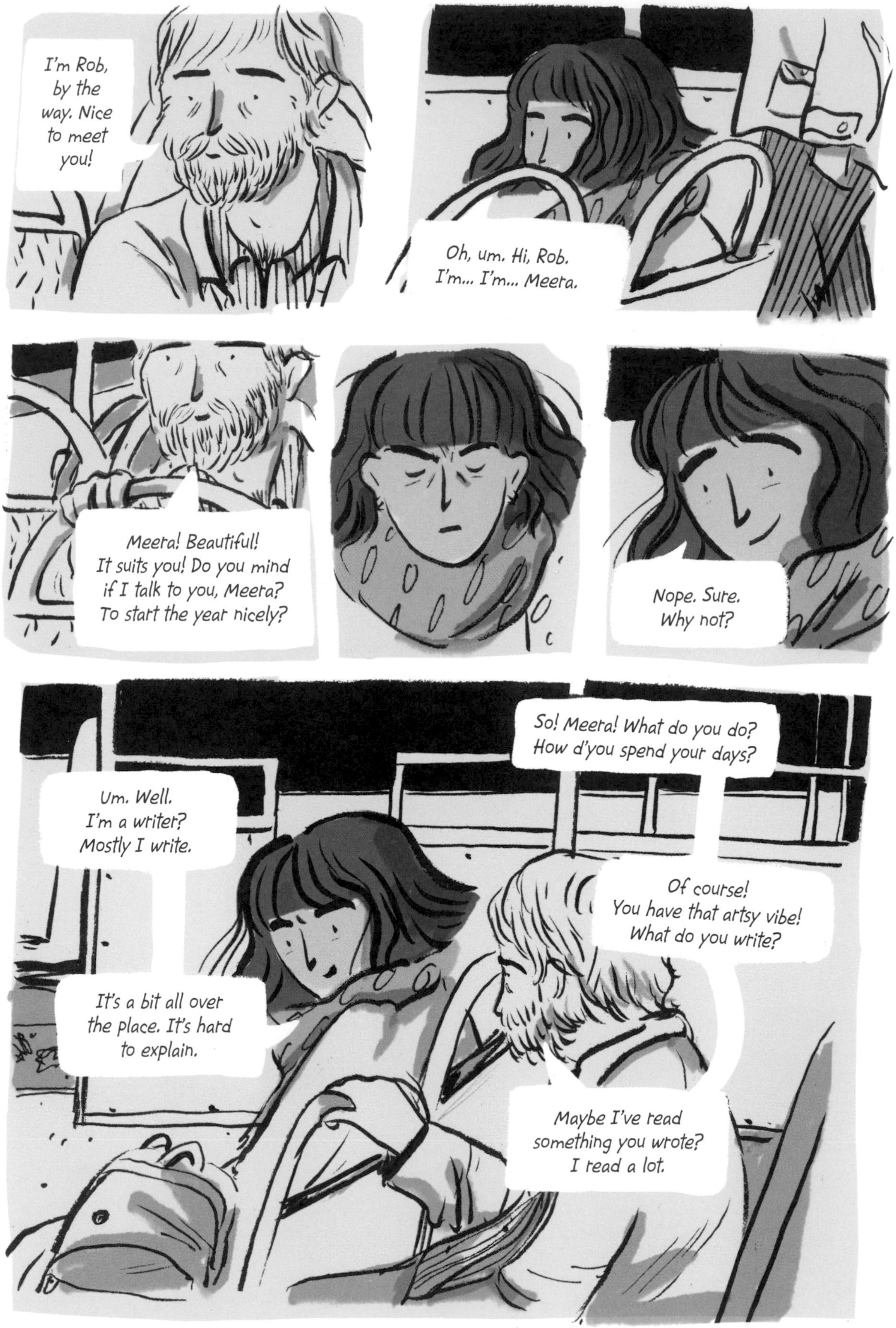
I'm Rob, by the way. Nice to meet you!
Oh, um. Hi, Rob. I'm... I'm... Meera.
Meera! Beautiful! It suits you! Do you mind if I talk to you, Meera? To start the year nicely?
Nope. Sure. Why not?
So! Meera! What do you do? How d'you spend your days?
Um. Well. I'm a writer? Mostly I write.
Of course! You have that artsy vibe! What do you write?
It's a bit all over the place. It's hard to explain.
Maybe I've read something you wrote? I read a lot.

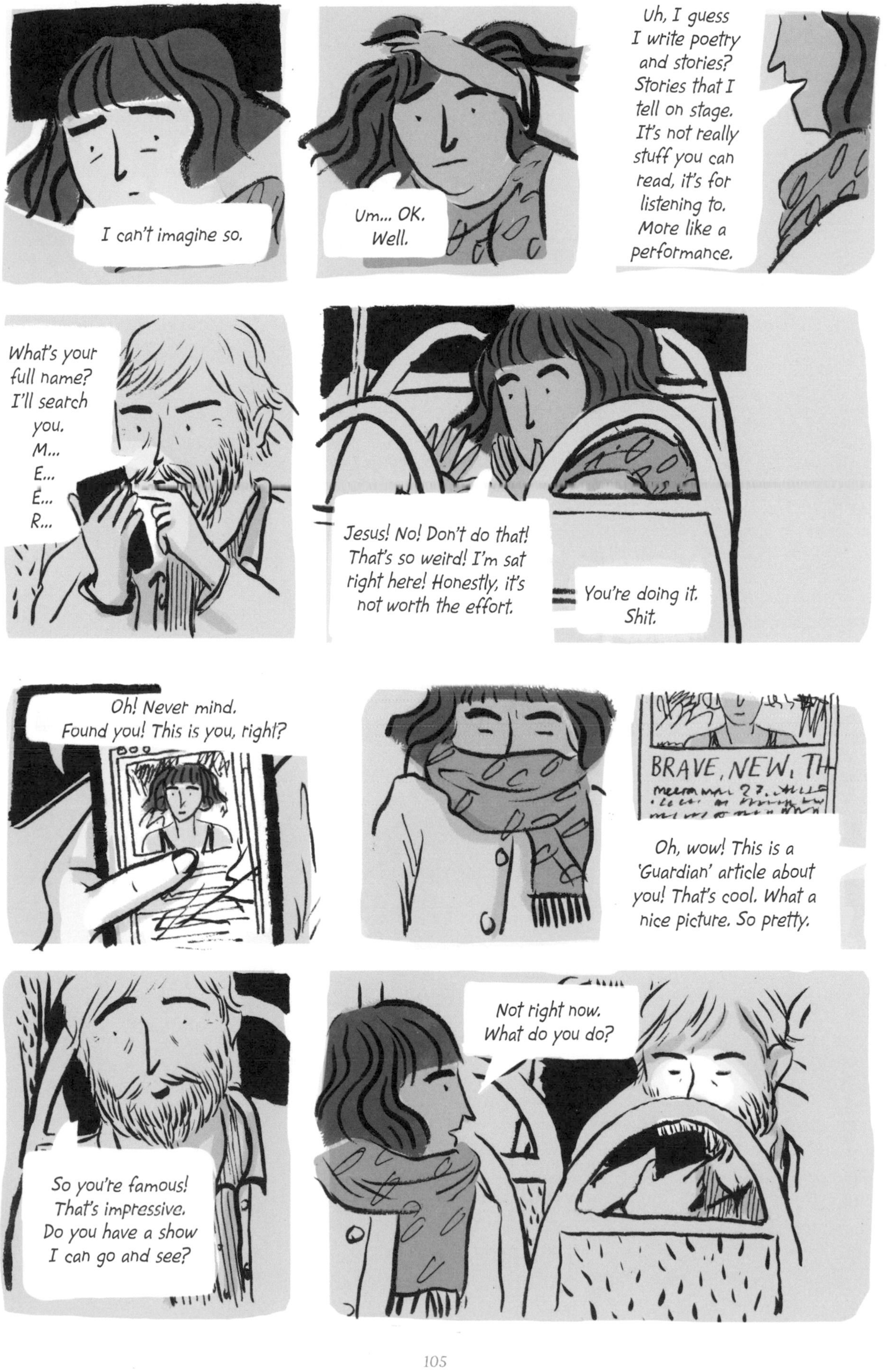
I can't imagine so.
Um... OK. Well.
Uh, I guess I write poetry and stories? Stories that I tell on stage. It's not really stuff you can read, it's for listening to. More like a performance.
What's your full name? I'll search you. M... E... E... R...
Jesus! No! Don't do that! That's so weird! I'm sat right here! Honestly, it's not worth the effort.
You're doing it. Shit.
Oh! Never mind. Found you! This is you, right?
BRAVE, NEW, TH
Oh, wow! This is a 'Guardian' article about you! That's cool. What a nice picture. So pretty.
So you're famous! That's impressive. Do you have a show I can go and see?
Not right now. What do you do?

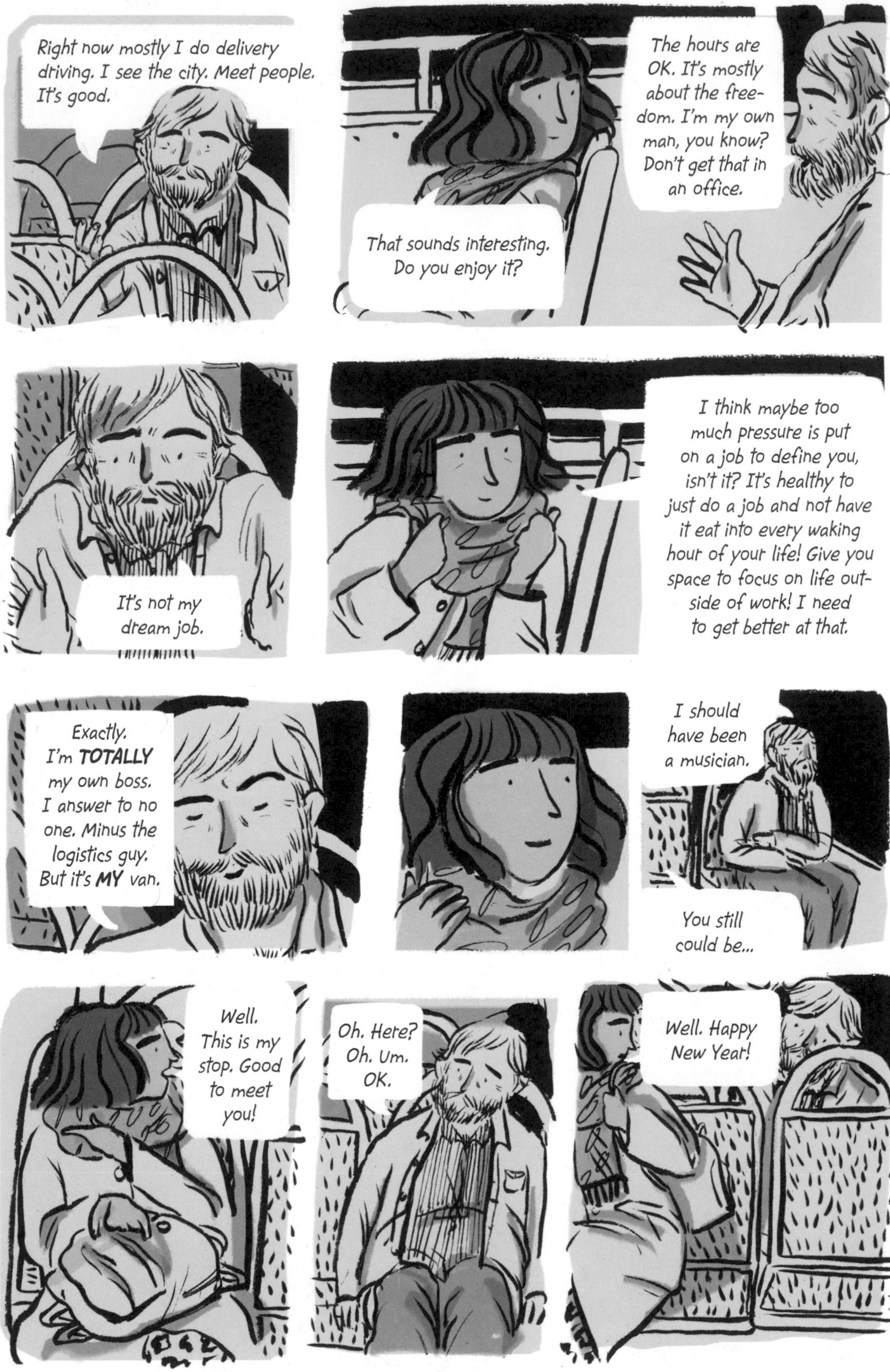

Right now mostly I do delivery driving. I see the city. Meet people. It's good.
That sounds interesting. Do you enjoy it?
The hours are OK. It's mostly about the free-dom. I'm my own man, you know? Don't get that in an office.
It's not my dream job.
I think maybe too much pressure is put on a job to define you, isn't it? It's healthy to just do a job and not have it eat into every waking hour of your life! Give you space to focus on life out-side of work! I need to get better at that.
Exactly. I'm **TOTALLY** my own boss. I answer to no one. Minus the logistics guy. But it's **MY** van.
I should have been a musician.
You still could be...
Well. This is my stop. Good to meet you!
Oh. Here? Oh. Um. OK.
Well. Happy New Year!

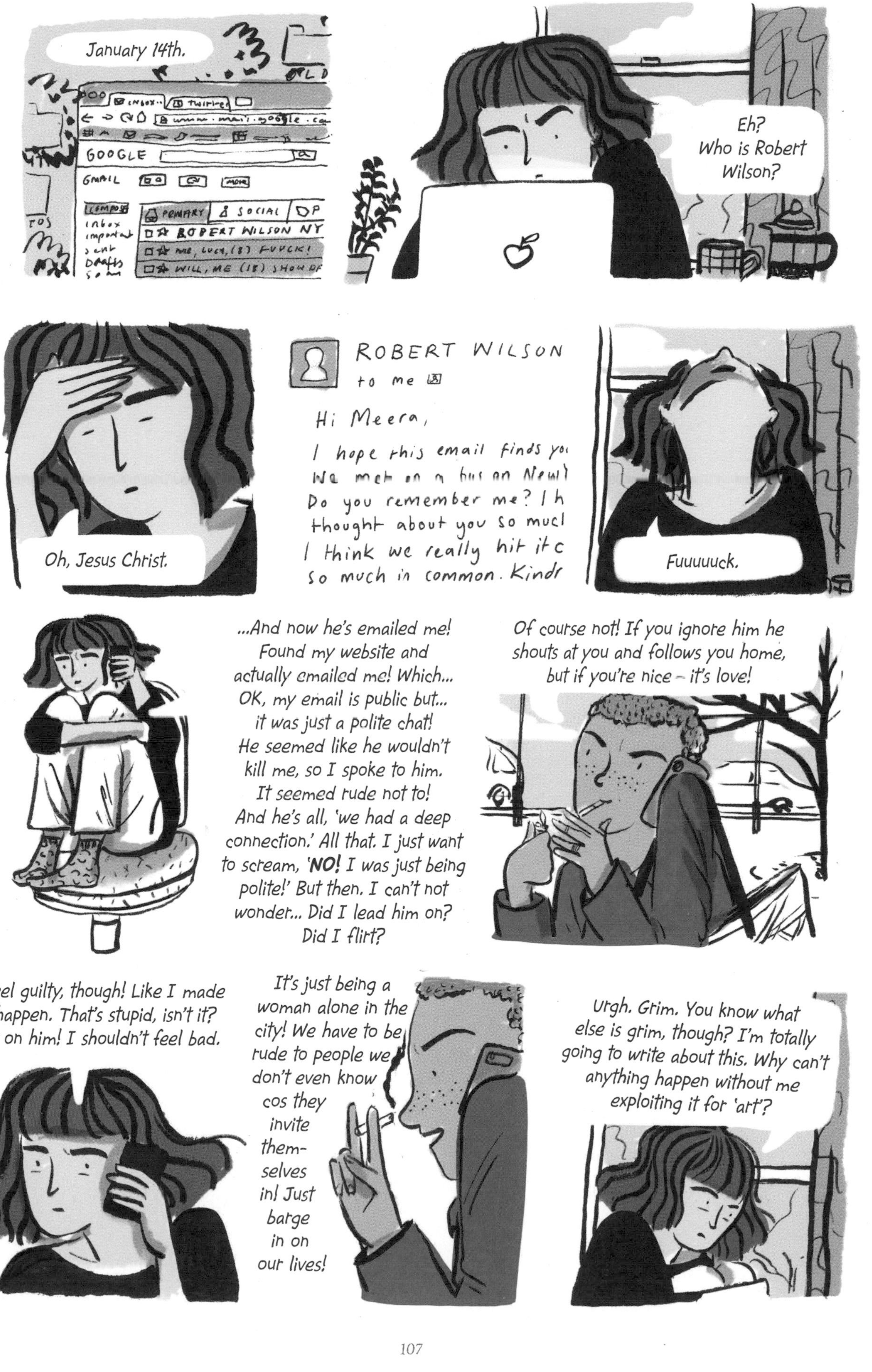
January 14th.
GOOGLE
GMAIL
ROBERT WILSON NY
Eh? Who is Robert Wilson?
Oh, Jesus Christ.
ROBERT WILSON
to me
Hi Meera,
I hope this email finds yo
We met on a bus on New
Do you remember me? I h
thought about you so muc
I think we really hit it c
so much in common. Kind
Fuuuuuck.
...And now he's emailed me! Found my website and actually emailed me! Which... OK, my email is public but... it was just a polite chat! He seemed like he wouldn't kill me, so I spoke to him. It seemed rude not to! And he's all, 'we had a deep connection.' All that. I just want to scream, '**NO!** I was just being polite!' But then. I can't not wonder... Did I lead him on? Did I flirt?
Of course not! If you ignore him he shouts at you and follows you home, but if you're nice – it's love!
I feel guilty, though! Like I made it happen. That's stupid, isn't it? It's on him! I shouldn't feel bad.
It's just being a woman alone in the city! We have to be rude to people we don't even know cos they invite them-selves in! Just barge in on our lives!
Urgh. Grim. You know what else is grim, though? I'm totally going to write about this. Why can't anything happen without me exploiting it for 'art'?

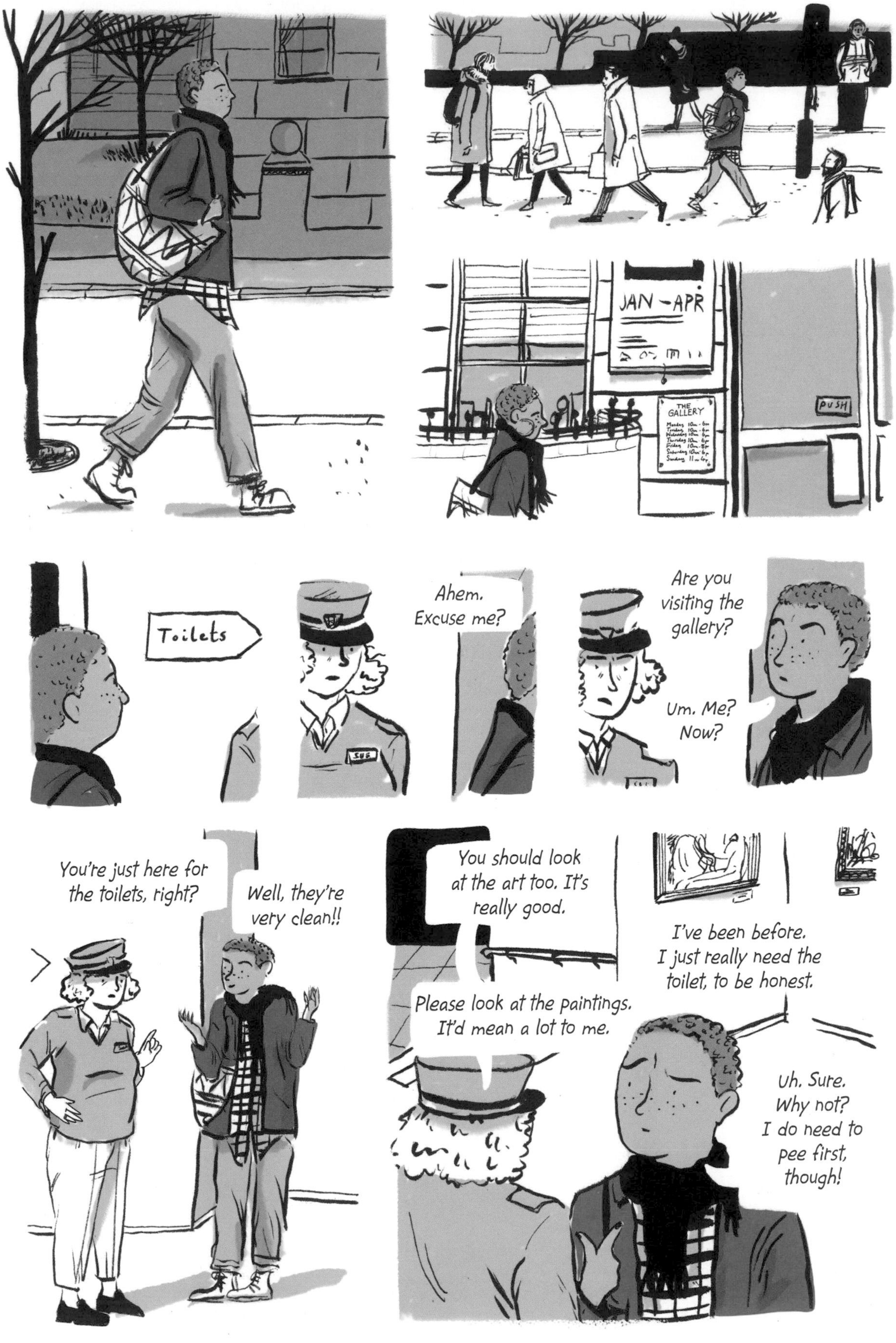
JAN - APR
THE GALLERY
PUSH
Toilets
Ahem. Excuse me?
Are you visiting the gallery?
Um. Me? Now?
You're just here for the toilets, right?
Well, they're very clean!!
You should look at the art too. It's really good.
I've been before. I just really need the toilet, to be honest.
Please look at the paintings. It'd mean a lot to me.
Uh. Sure. Why not? I do need to pee first, though!

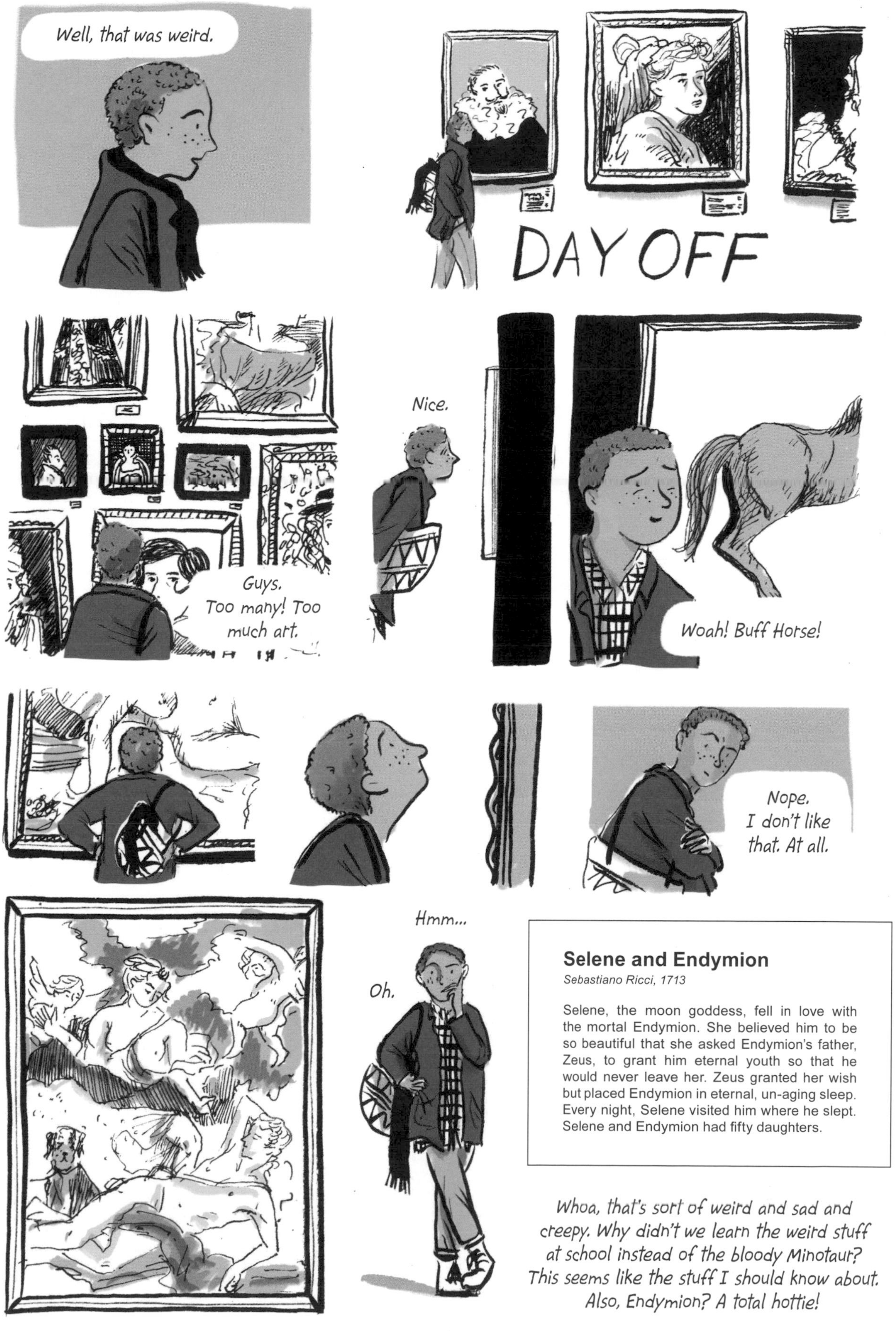
Well, that was weird.
DAY OFF
Guys. Too many! Too much art.
Nice.
Woah! Buff Horse!
Nope. I don't like that. At all.
Hmm...
Oh.
Selene and Endymion
Sebastiano Ricci, 1713
Selene, the moon goddess, fell in love with the mortal Endymion. She believed him to be so beautiful that she asked Endymion's father, Zeus, to grant him eternal youth so that he would never leave her. Zeus granted her wish but placed Endymion in eternal, un-aging sleep. Every night, Selene visited him where he slept. Selene and Endymion had fifty daughters.
Whoa, that's sort of weird and sad and creepy. Why didn't we learn the weird stuff at school instead of the bloody Minotaur? This seems like the stuff I should know about. Also, Endymion? A total hottie!

I should know that stuff. Mythology and so on. I don't know anything.

Ah, sunshine! Welcome, freckles!

Alright, Sexy?

Oh my! What an intriguing alleyway!

GREEK MYTHOLO
I love this stuff! My favorite is Daphne. Her dad turned her into a tree because Apollo fancied her. Typical dads!
THE GARD
A PLAY
BOOKS
Ha! Oh God, poor lass! I don't know mythology but I thought I'd learn, in the name of masturbatory self-improvement!
Masturbatory self-improvement? Urgh.
Oh I want to
COF
take you home. I want
You want a coffee?
COFFE
Ah, you're OK. Just the song, thanks.
children. And you might be my girl
I wonder what I look like here, now. I wonder if I look like I know what I'm doing. Like I have a plan.

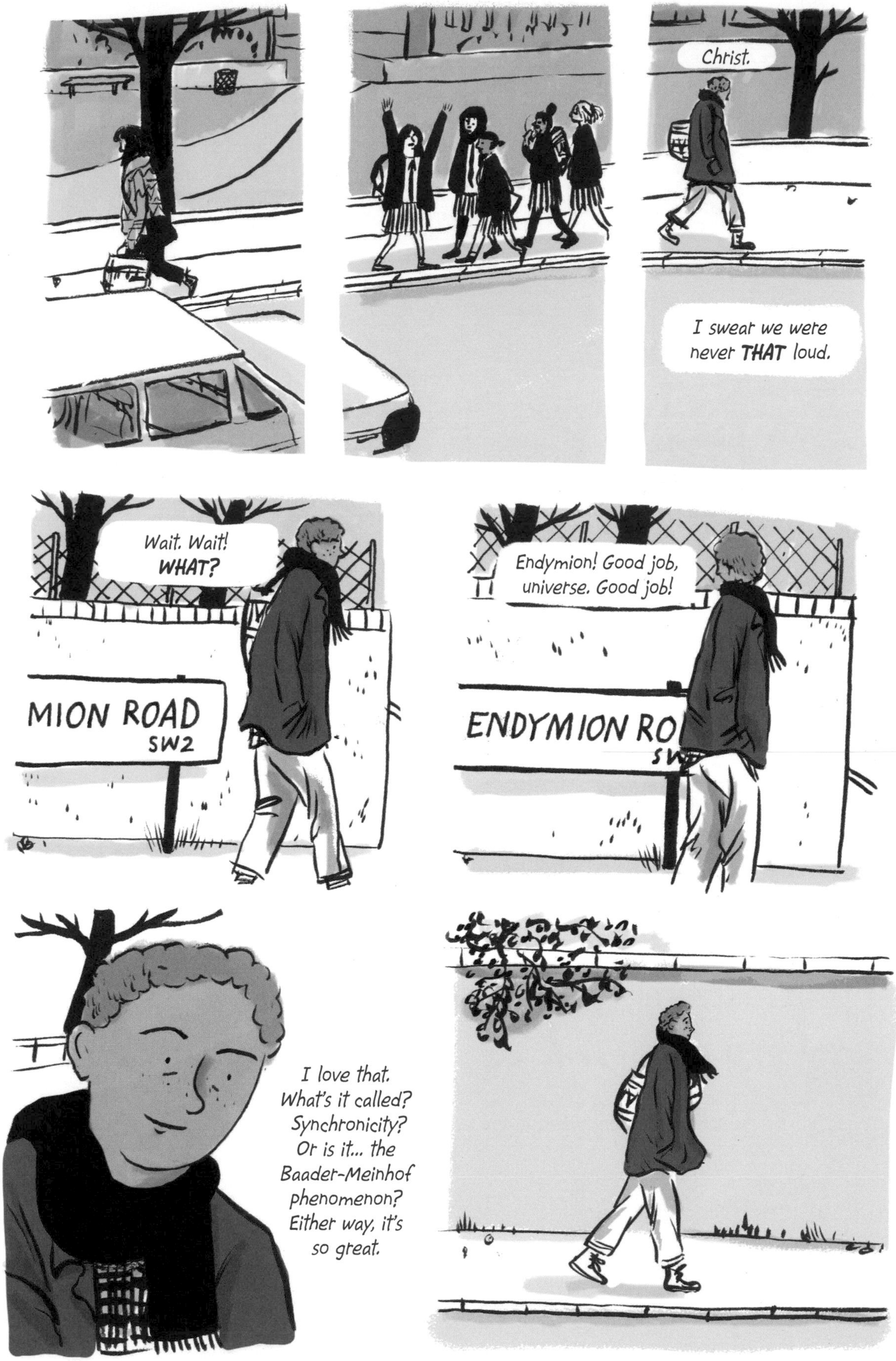
Christ.
I swear we were never THAT loud.
Wait. Wait! WHAT?
MION ROAD SW2
Endymion! Good job, universe. Good job!
ENDYMION RO
I love that. What's it called? Synchronicity? Or is it... the Baader-Meinhof phenomenon? Either way, it's so great.

WOAH, it's hot in here!

I see you two **LEGENDS** saved me the stool. Cheers!

How was the day off?

Sort of glorious?

I mean... not actually glorious. But pretty good as days go.

Can I talk like a dick just for a sec?

Do you think about, like, being a young-ish woman walking alone in the city? Ever? Not strictly in terms of, uh, vulnerability, but just... what it feels like?

I want to be good at being on my own, but when I'm out I try so hard to be unobtrusive that I'm not doing things as I really want to do them. Besides, it's sort of impossible to be unobtrusive as a woman, because other people make us visible, right? They watch us! They comment on us. I think I'm invisible, and then—'alright, sexy.'

And I don't think I **TRY** to shrink away, I'm not a shrinker! But I do think I try to stay out of the way—and it's shit! So today I tried to have a day where I saw everything at my own speed. And first thing, a security guard forced me to look at art! So weird. But there was this painting of 'Selene'.

And she loved Endymion and wanted to love him forever, so Zeus cast him into perpetual sleep.

And she just watches him. Only somehow they have kids too so clearly... she was doing some stuff. But it was interesting to me cos, like, she was looking at **HIM**. And all the other classical women were being raped by Zeus or turned into swans.

113

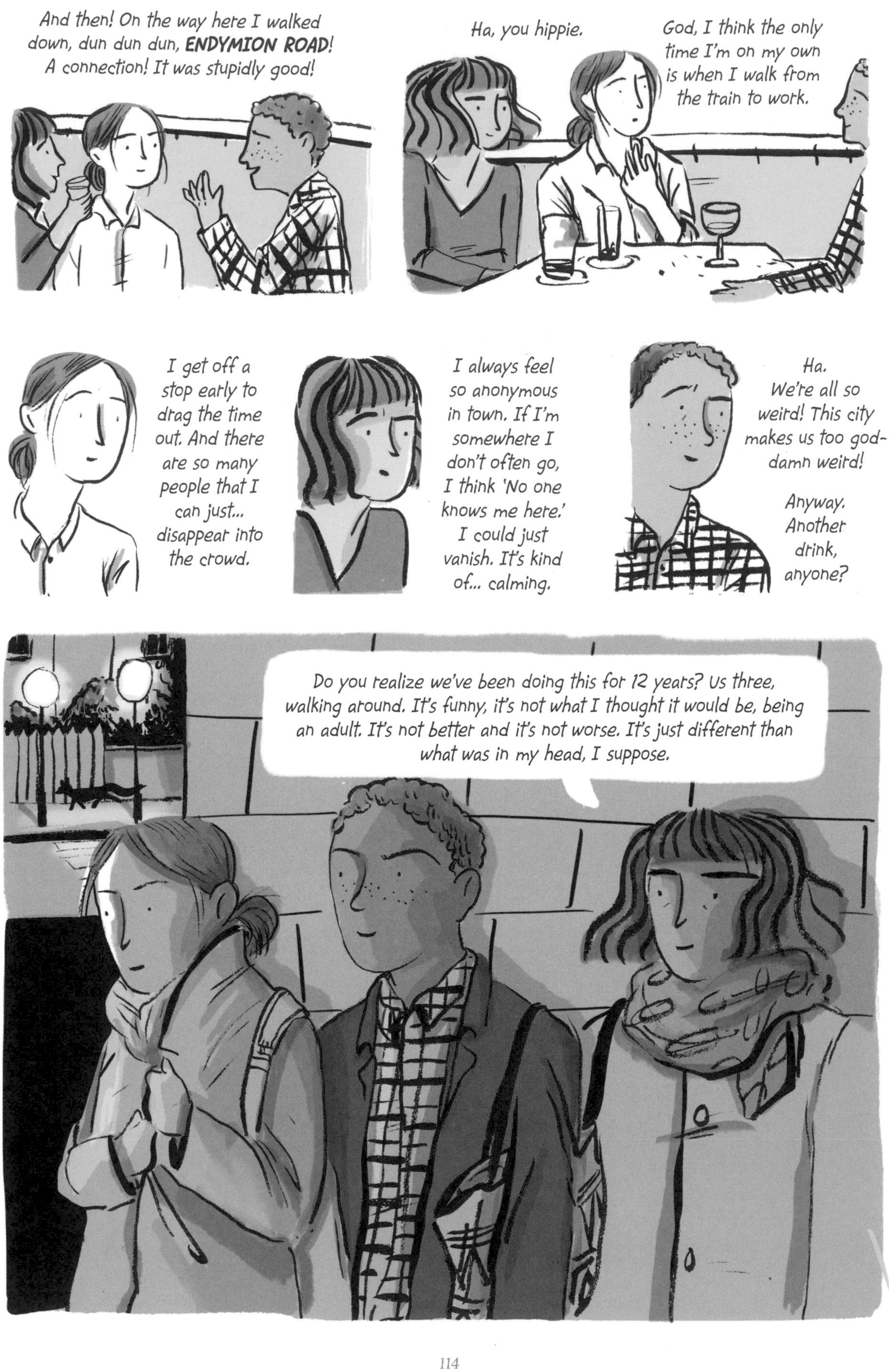
And then! On the way here I walked down, dun dun dun, **ENDYMION ROAD**! A connection! It was stupidly good!
Ha, you hippie.
God, I think the only time I'm on my own is when I walk from the train to work.
I get off a stop early to drag the time out. And there are so many people that I can just... disappear into the crowd.
I always feel so anonymous in town. If I'm somewhere I don't often go, I think 'No one knows me here.' I could just vanish. It's kind of... calming.
Ha. We're all so weird! This city makes us too god-damn weird!
Anyway. Another drink, anyone?
Do you realize we've been doing this for 12 years? Us three, walking around. It's funny, it's not what I thought it would be, being an adult. It's not better and it's not worse. It's just different than what was in my head, I suppose.

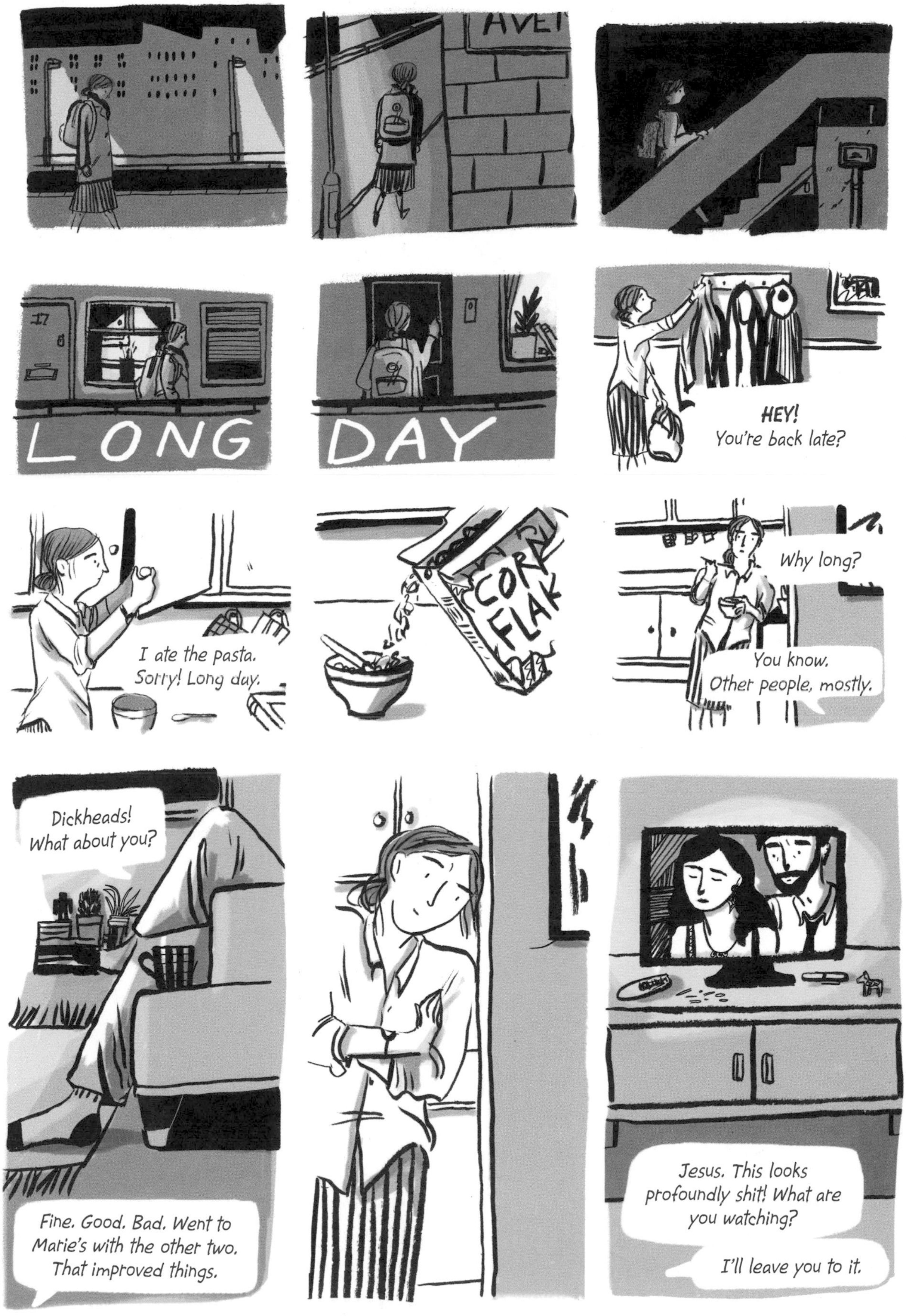
LONG DAY
HEY!
You're back late?
I ate the pasta.
Sorry! Long day.
CORN FLAK
Why long?
You know.
Other people, mostly.
Dickheads!
What about you?
Fine. Good. Bad. Went to Marie's with the other two. That improved things.
Jesus. This looks profoundly shit! What are you watching?
I'll leave you to it.

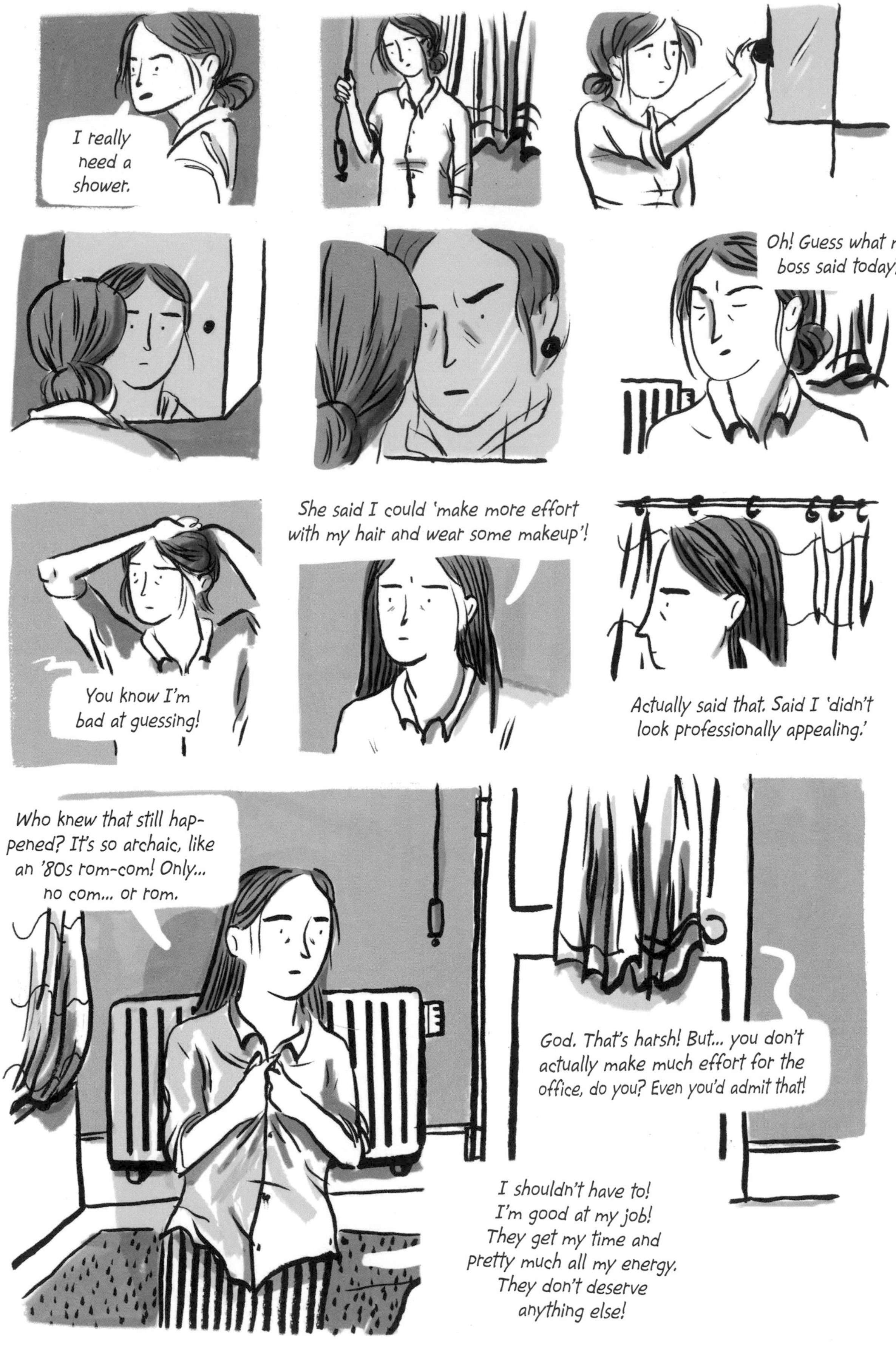

I really need a shower.
Oh! Guess what my boss said today?
You know I'm bad at guessing!
She said I could 'make more effort with my hair and wear some makeup'!
Actually said that. Said I 'didn't look professionally appealing.'
Who knew that still happened? It's so archaic, like an '80s rom-com! Only... no com... or rom.
God. That's harsh! But... you don't actually make much effort for the office, do you? Even you'd admit that!
I shouldn't have to! I'm good at my job! They get my time and pretty much all my energy. They don't deserve anything else!

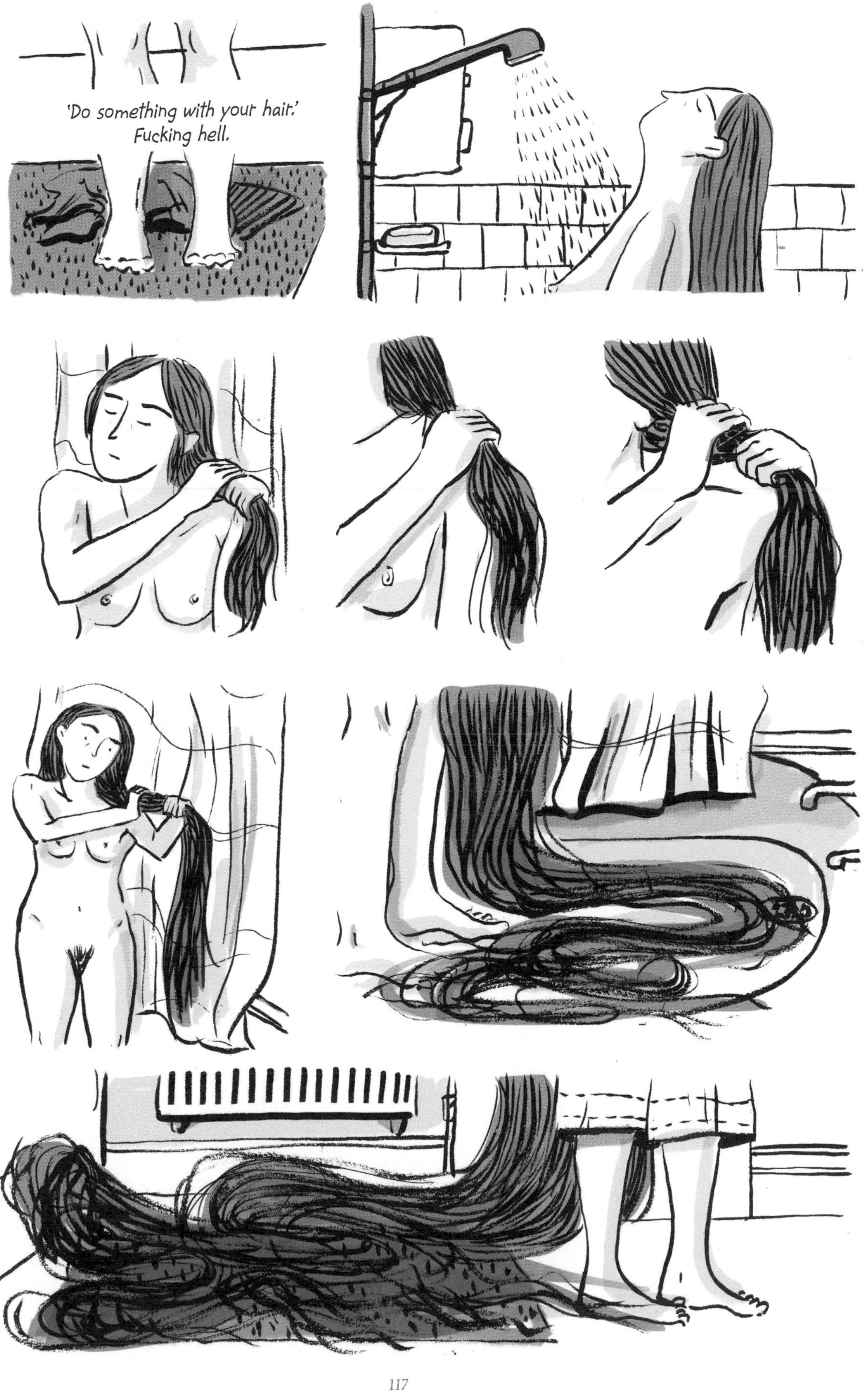
'Do something with your hair.'
Fucking hell.

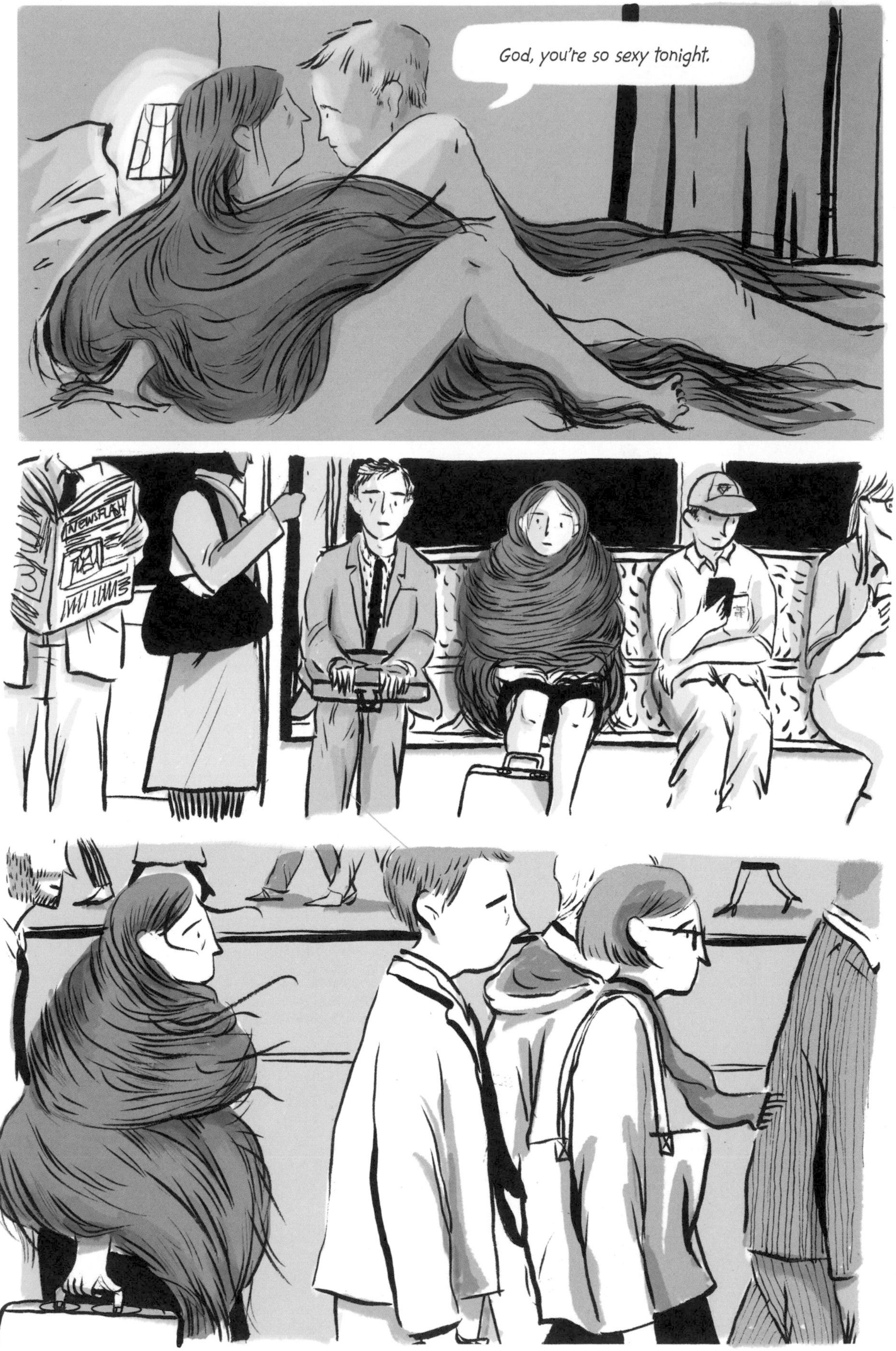
God, you're so sexy tonight.

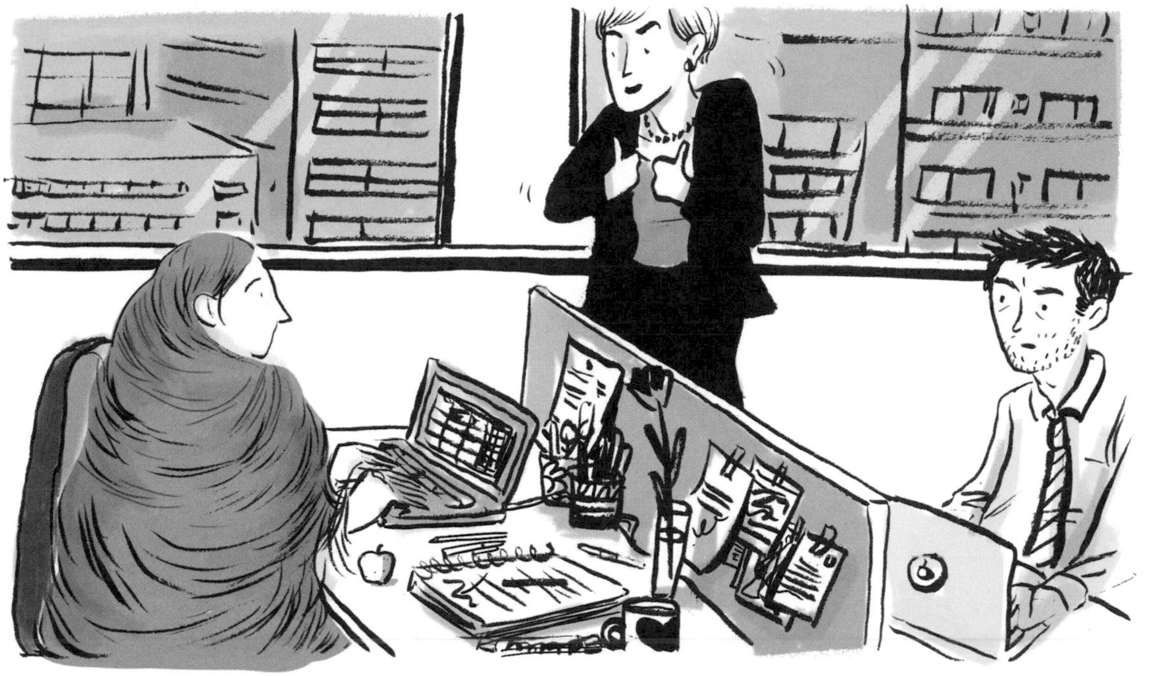

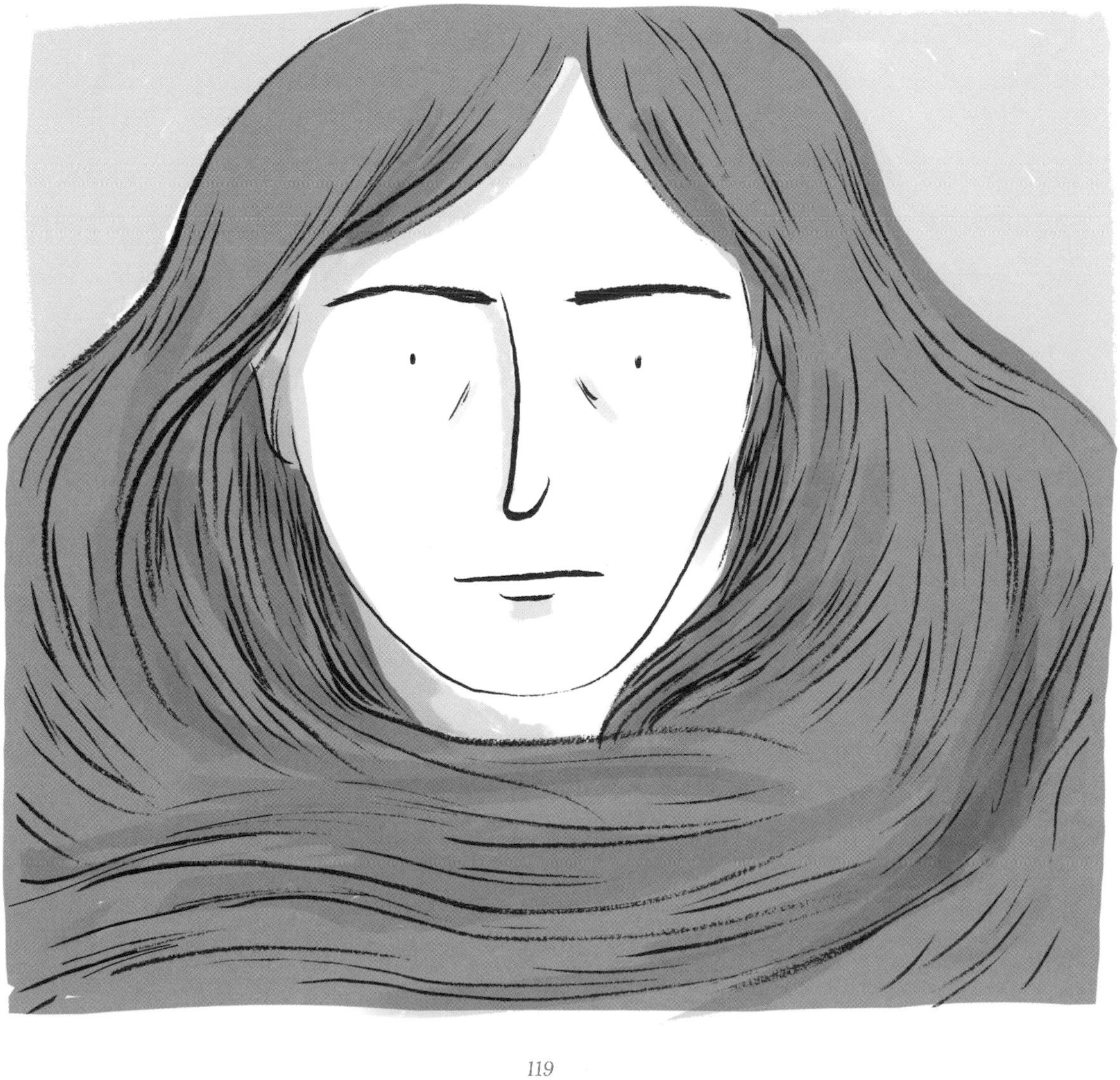

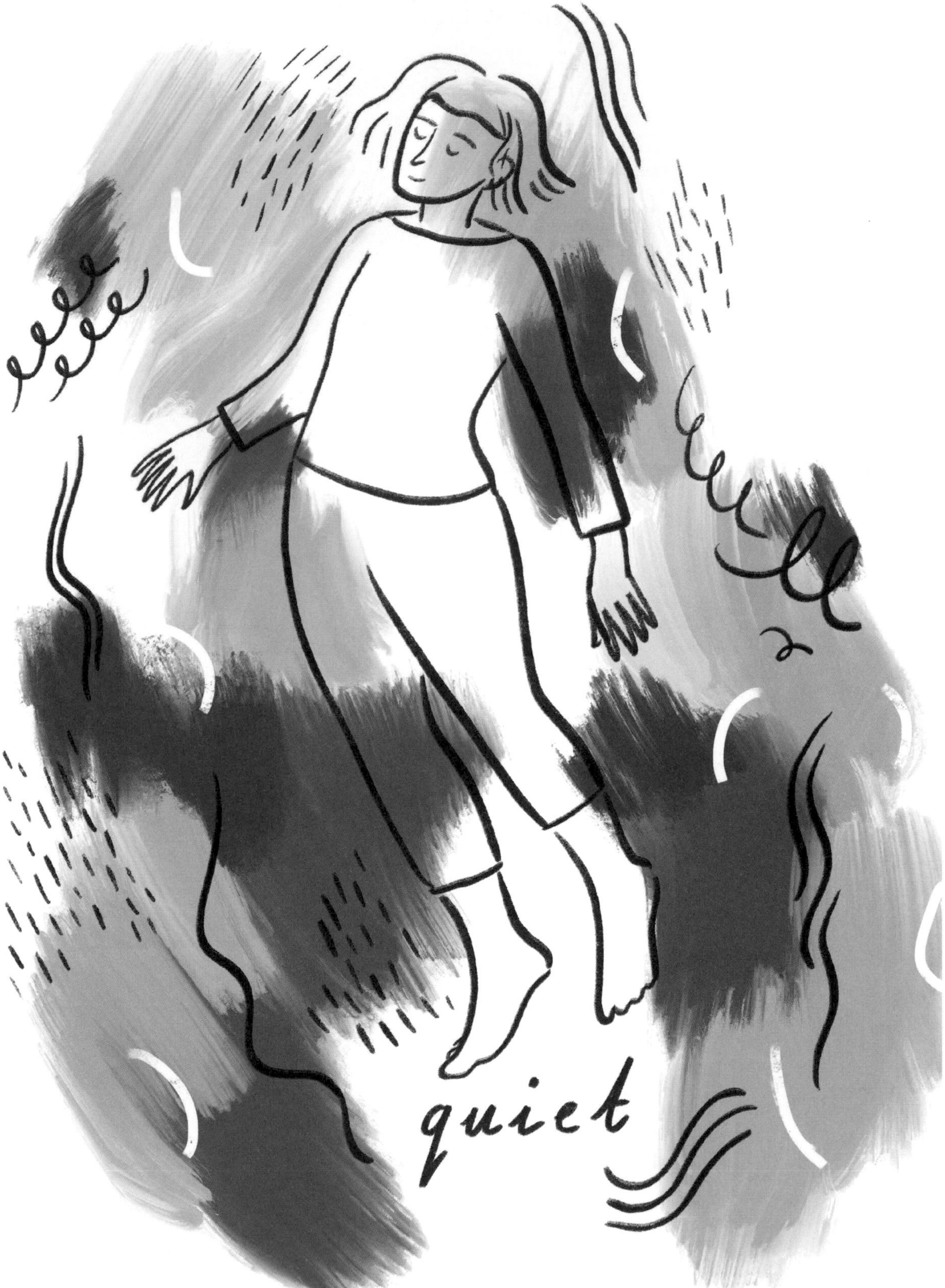
quiet

I've always been good with sounds. Years ago, I started to collect them. I think I'm probably a 'super-listener'. Is that a thing? Like a super-taster but, you know, with sound.

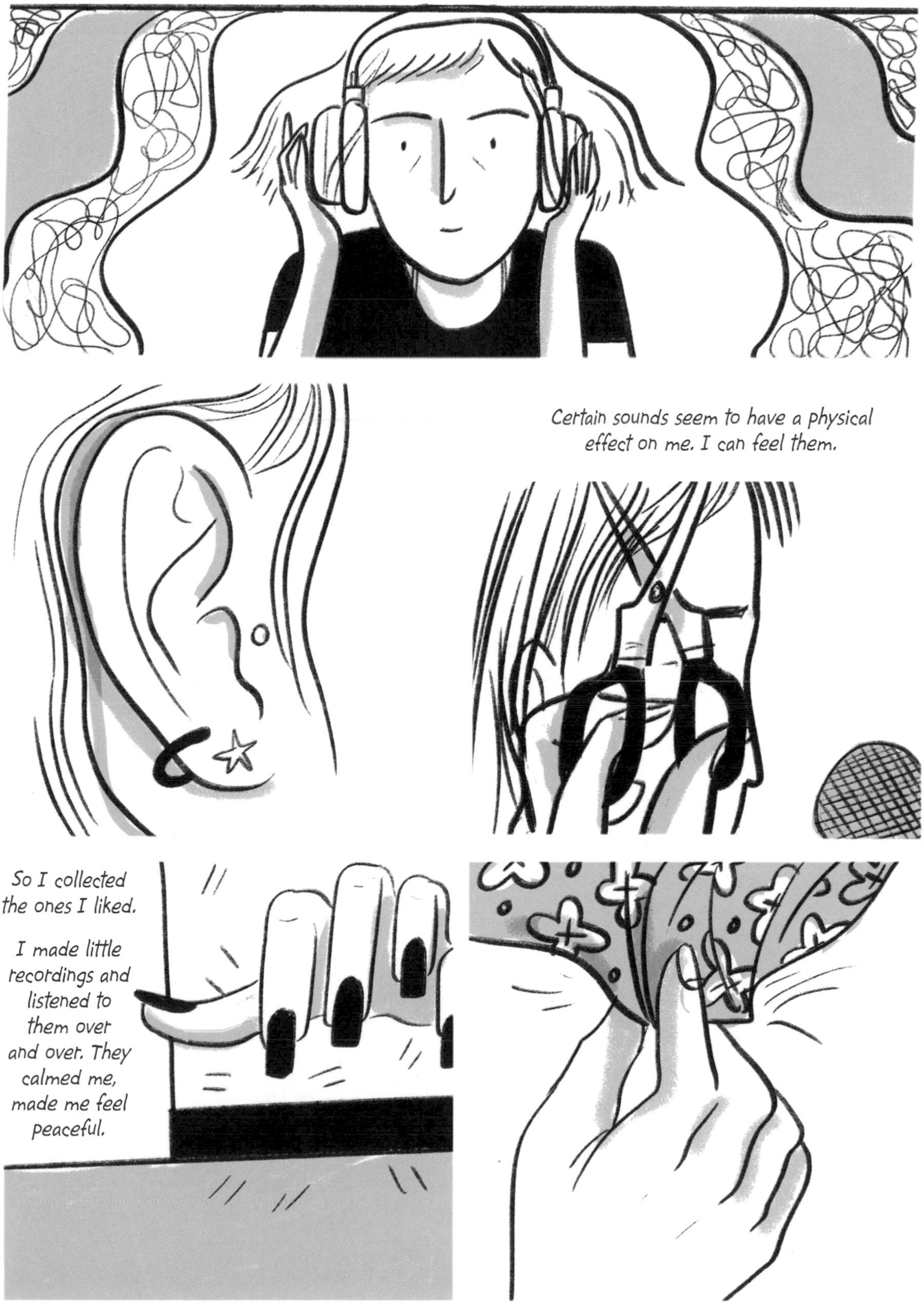
Certain sounds seem to have a physical effect on me. I can feel them.
So I collected the ones I liked.
I made little recordings and listened to them over and over. They calmed me, made me feel peaceful.

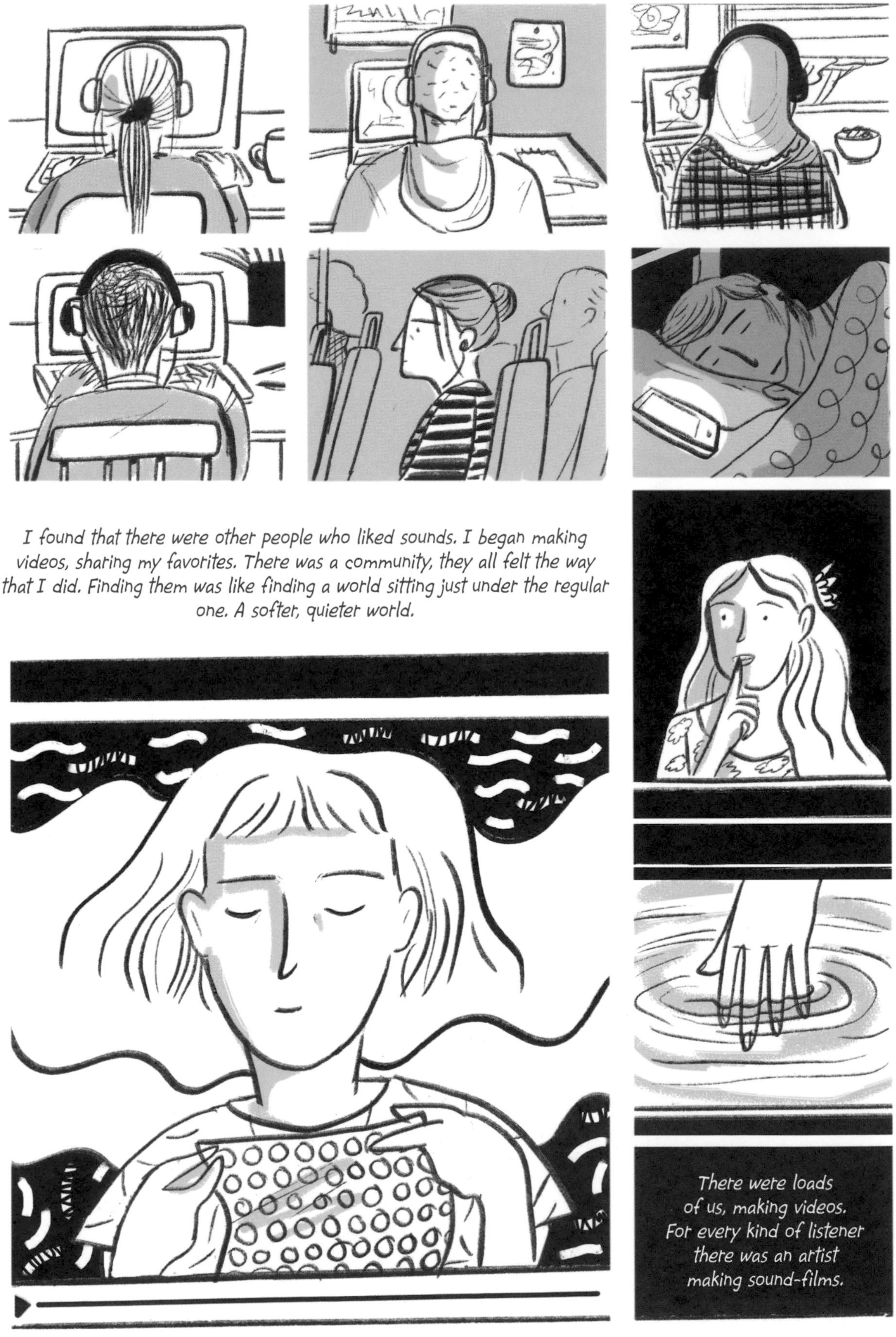
I found that there were other people who liked sounds. I began making videos, sharing my favorites. There was a community, they all felt the way that I did. Finding them was like finding a world sitting just under the regular one. A softer, quieter world.
There were loads of us, making videos. For every kind of listener there was an artist making sound-films.

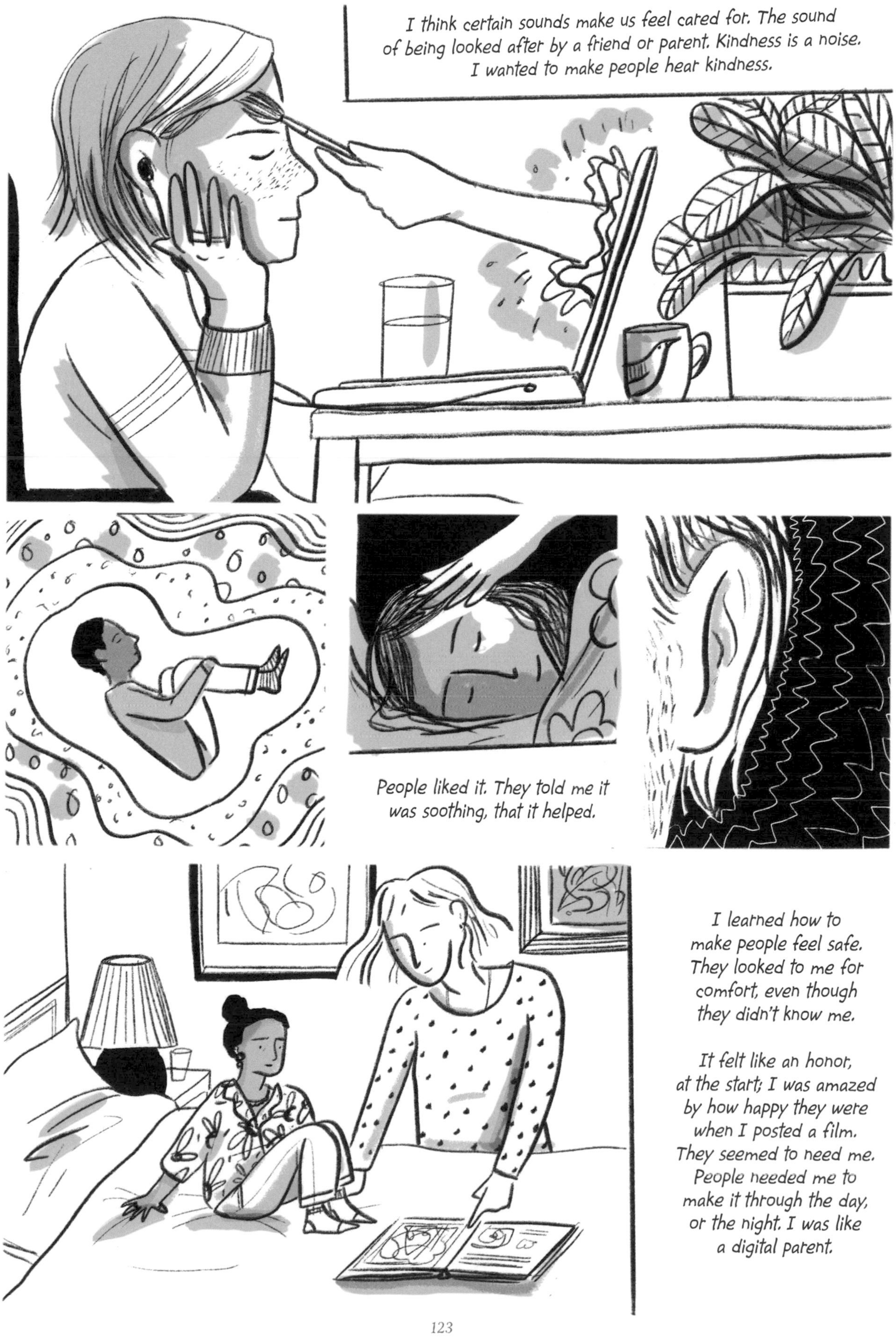
I think certain sounds make us feel cared for. The sound of being looked after by a friend or parent. Kindness is a noise. I wanted to make people hear kindness.
People liked it. They told me it was soothing, that it helped.
I learned how to make people feel safe. They looked to me for comfort, even though they didn't know me.
It felt like an honor, at the start; I was amazed by how happy they were when I posted a film. They seemed to need me. People needed me to make it through the day, or the night. I was like a digital parent.

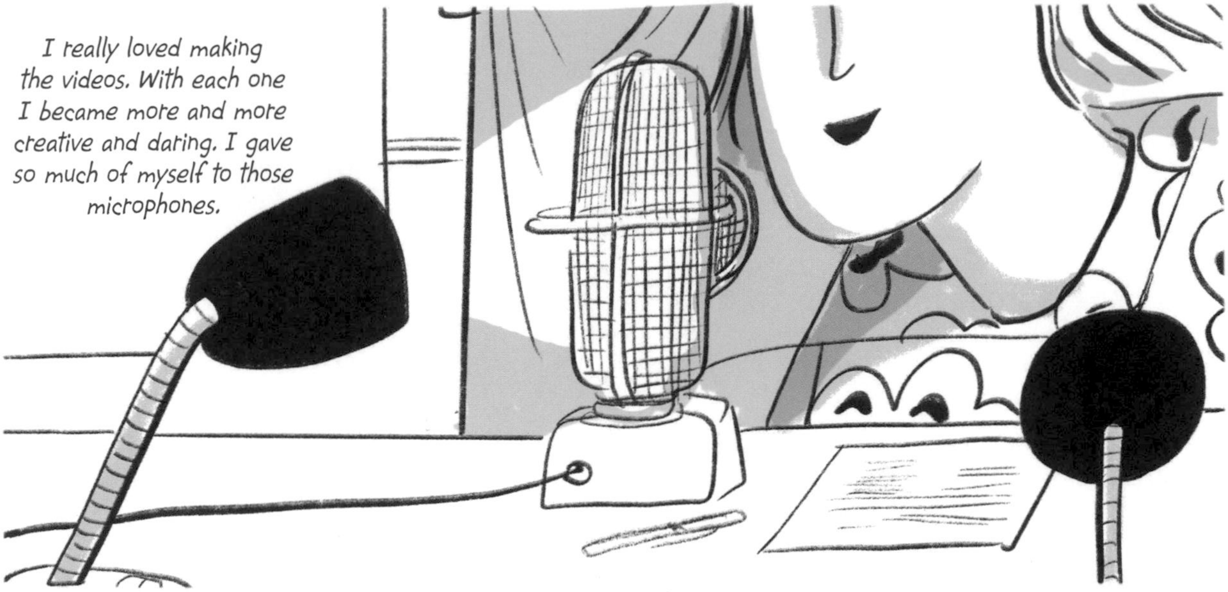
I really loved making the videos. With each one I became more and more creative and daring. I gave so much of myself to those microphones.

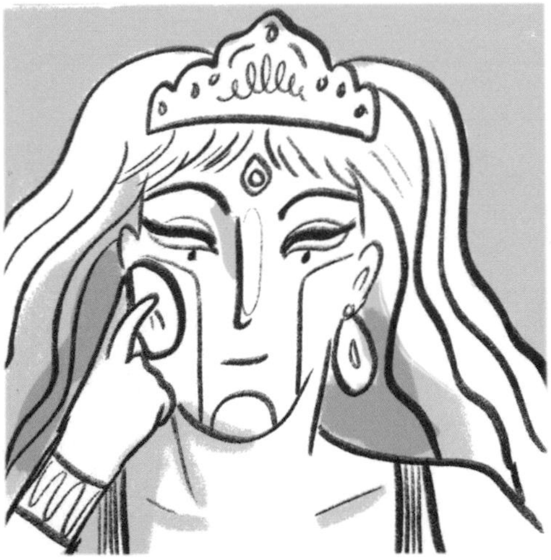

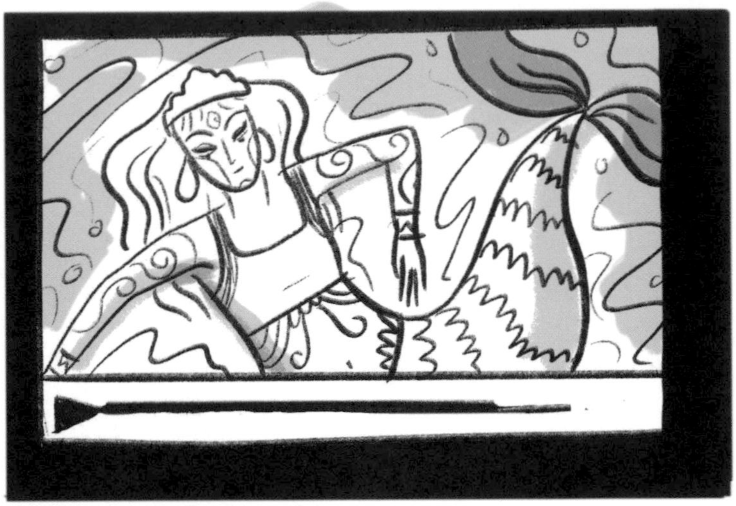

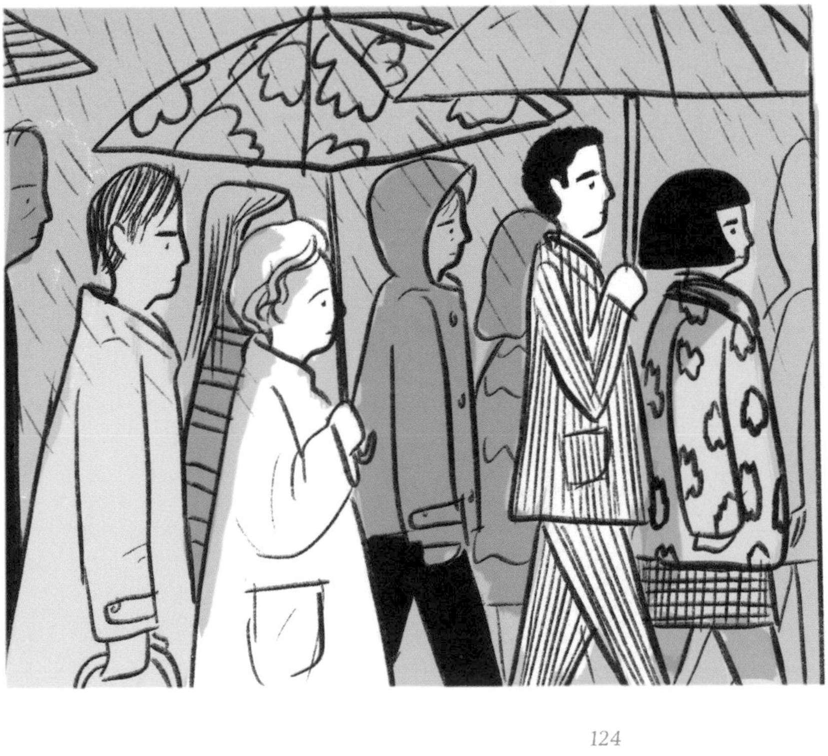

But as my own life became fuller, the world was becoming tougher. Life for most people was hard. They were tired and lonely and the news was always bad. Increasingly, they needed my work to help them wake or sleep, or simply to live. They began to ask for more. Every video had to be something new. They wanted new sounds most of all. The old sounds weren't working anymore.

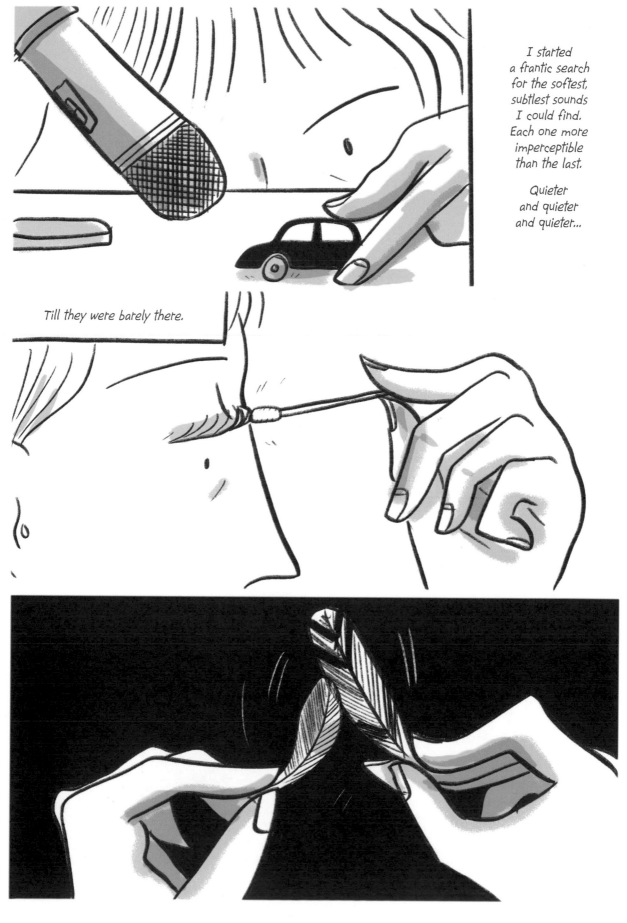

I started a frantic search for the softest, subtlest sounds I could find. Each one more imperceptible than the last.

Quieter and quieter and quieter...

Till they were barely there.

I liked this but it was SO LOUD!!!!!

You've not posted a new vid in a week! I MISS YOU!!

OMG I LOVE YOU! xxxxxxxx

Your mic is picking up too much background sound. I can hear birds.

The sound of a perfectly still glass of water.

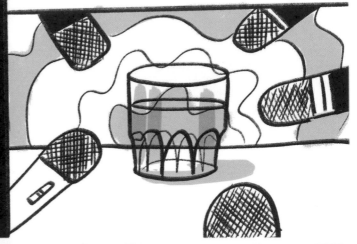

A plant growing towards the light.

A bookshelf.

Thoughts of sound.

It was never quite enough. I was so tired.

I usually sleep to your vids but this one didn't work.

You promised a cotton wool vid. WHERE???

I've said it before but your stuff is just too loud!

I liked your old stuff more. This is weird.

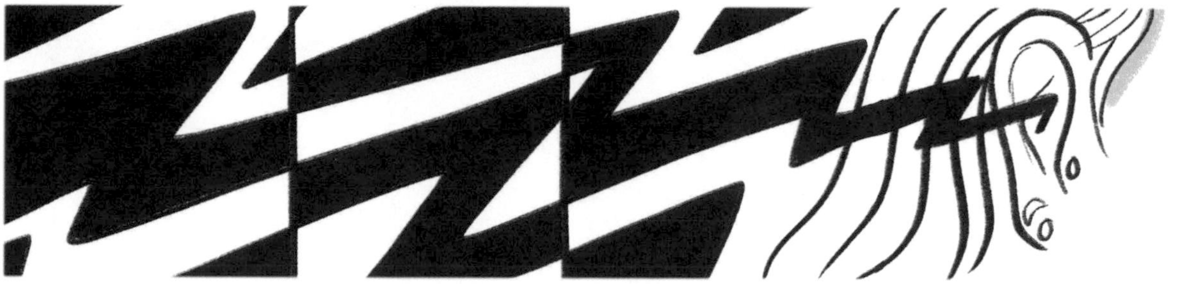

I couldn't find the joy in sounds anymore. Everything seemed too loaded and too loud.
I wondered if you could strain your ears, like you can your eyes.

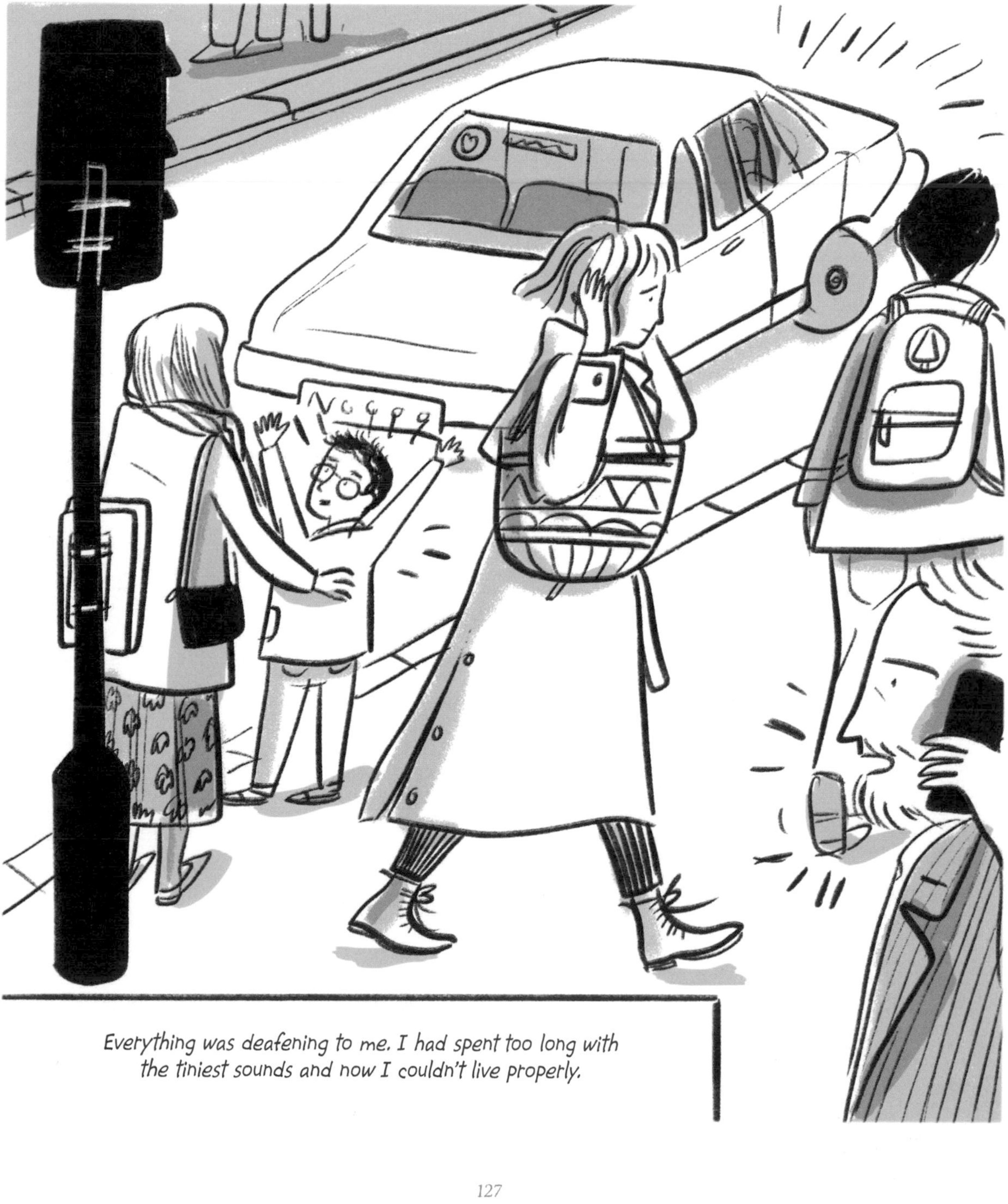
Everything was deafening to me. I had spent too long with the tiniest sounds and now I couldn't live properly.

I decided to make one last video. It was almost entirely inaudible. It was a masterwork of impossibly subtle noise. It was the sound of the smallest needle pressing against a single hair inside your ear. It was perfect.

Those who heard it couldn't stop listening to it. They sunk into deep, beautiful sleep for days at a time. They became addicted to how calm it made them. They ruined their lives with my film. I wasn't sorry.

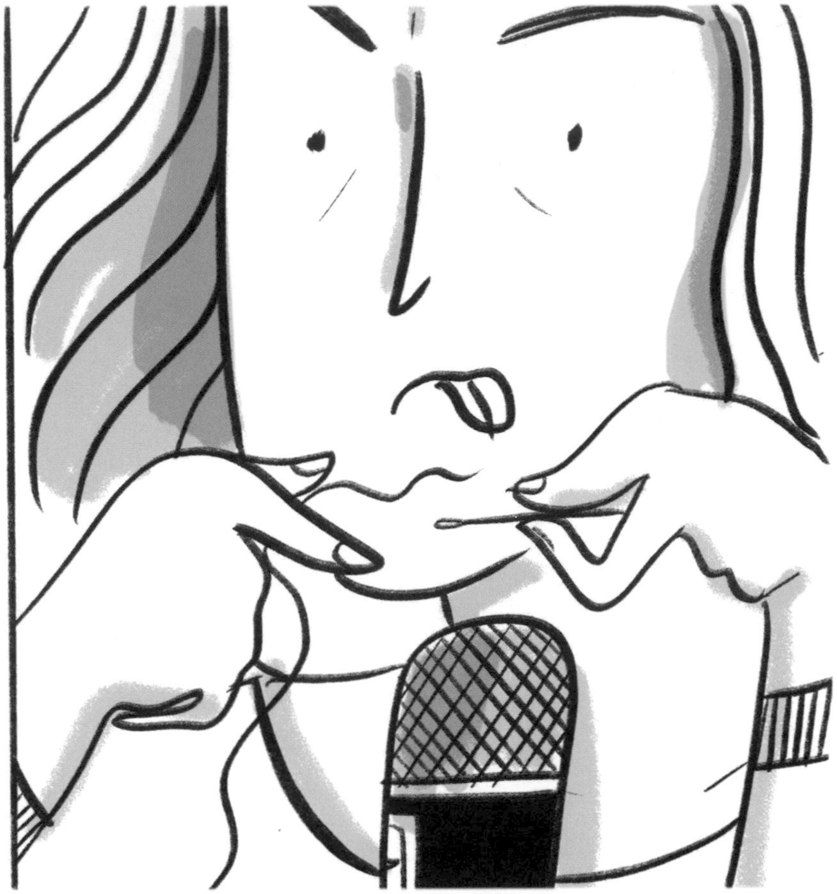

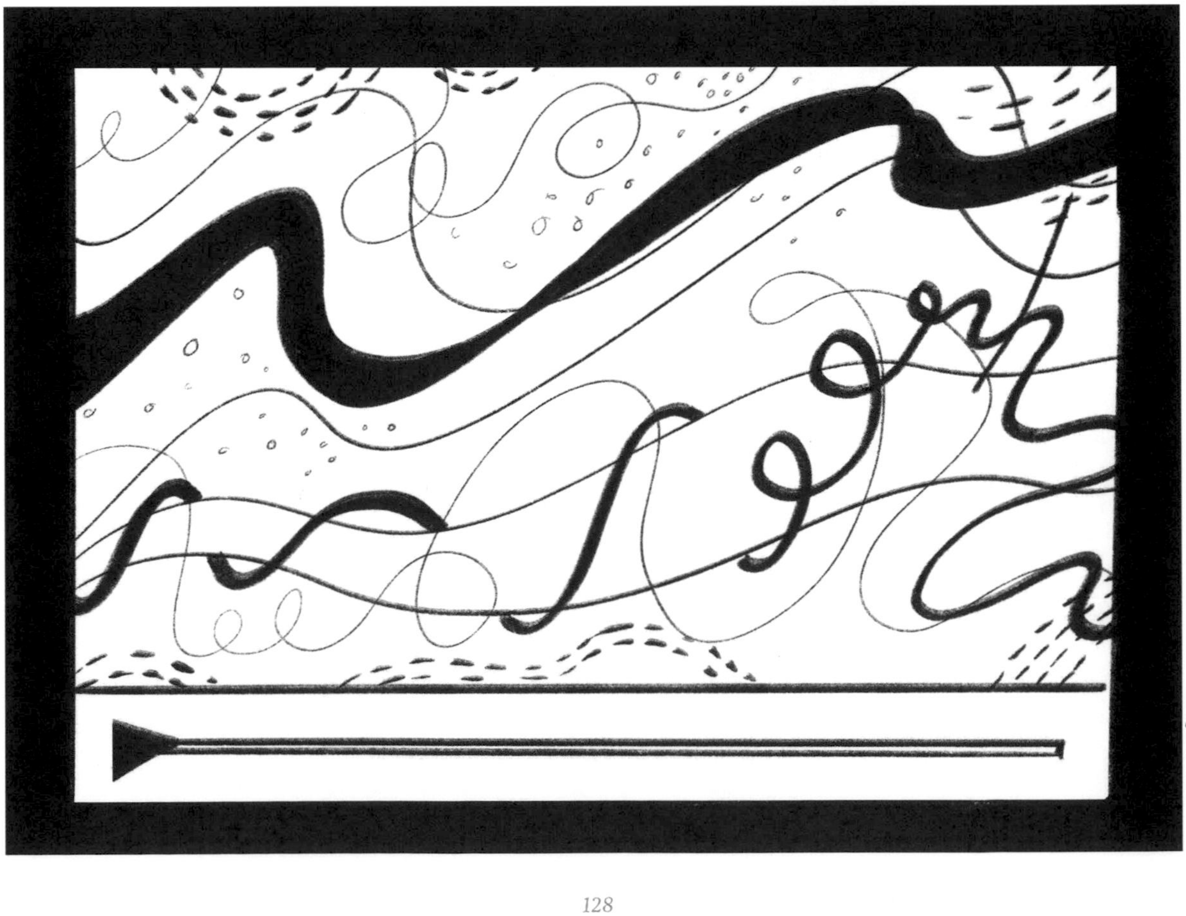

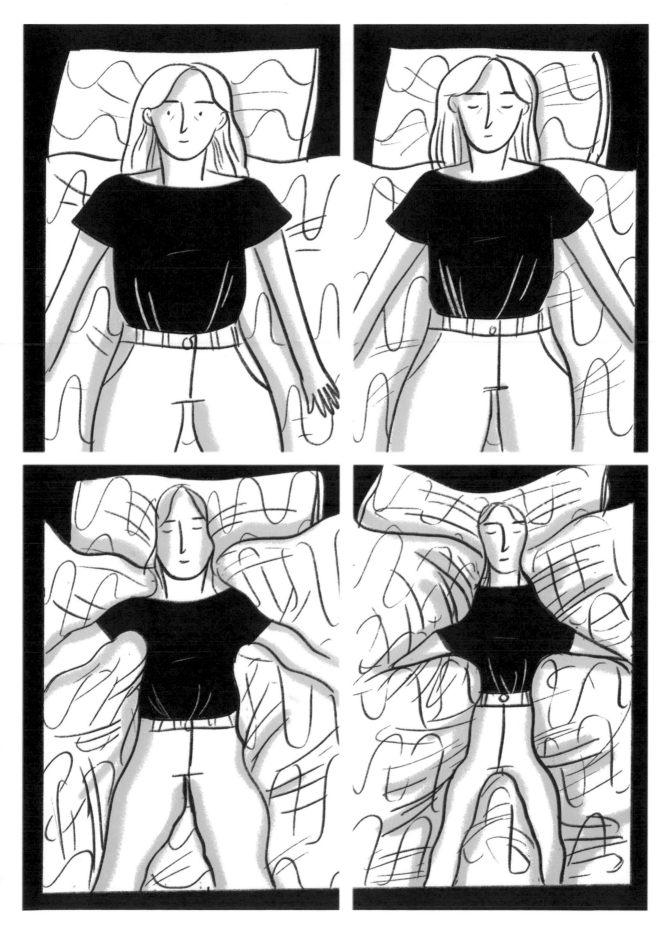

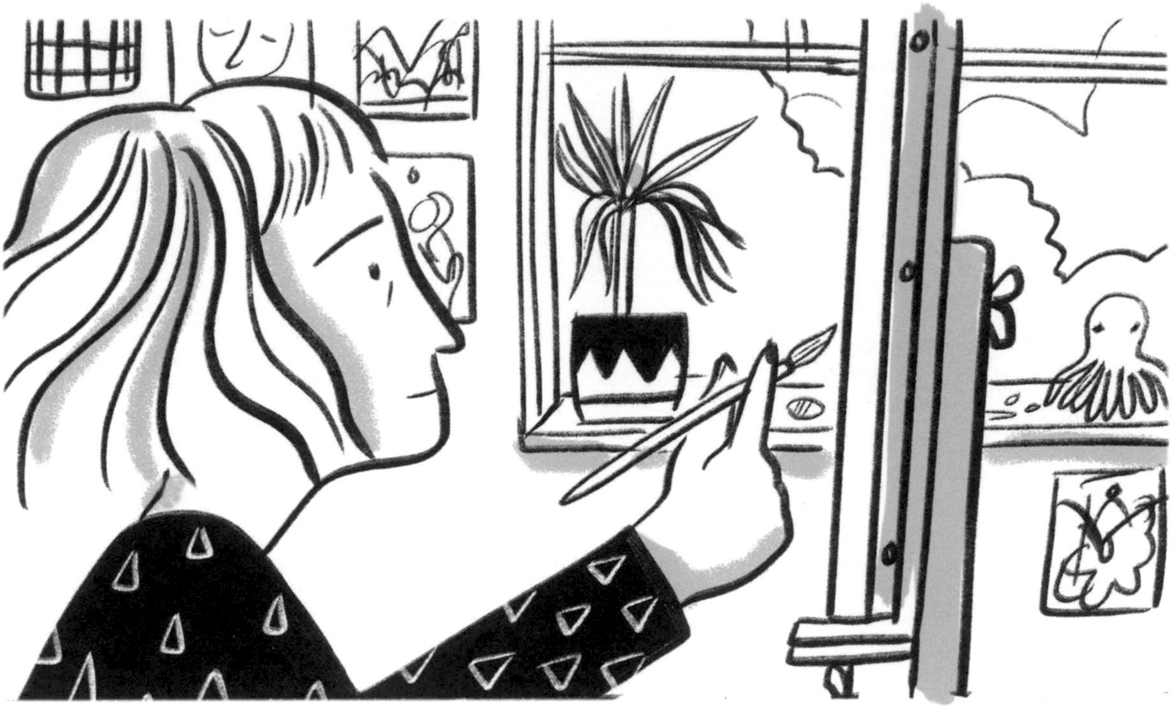

I don't collect sounds anymore. I barely notice them.
I listen to music on loudspeakers and don't even register the melody;
I paint now and I never show anyone. It's just for me, thank goodness.

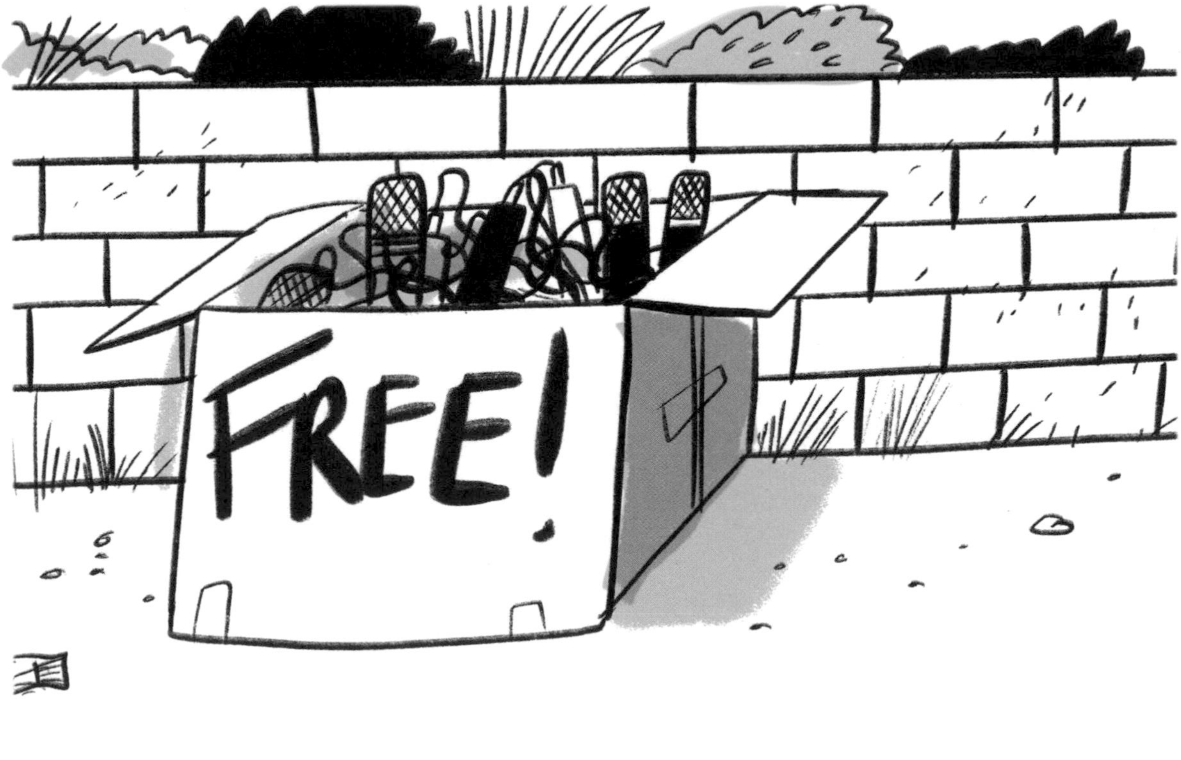
FREE!

THE WEDDING GUESTS

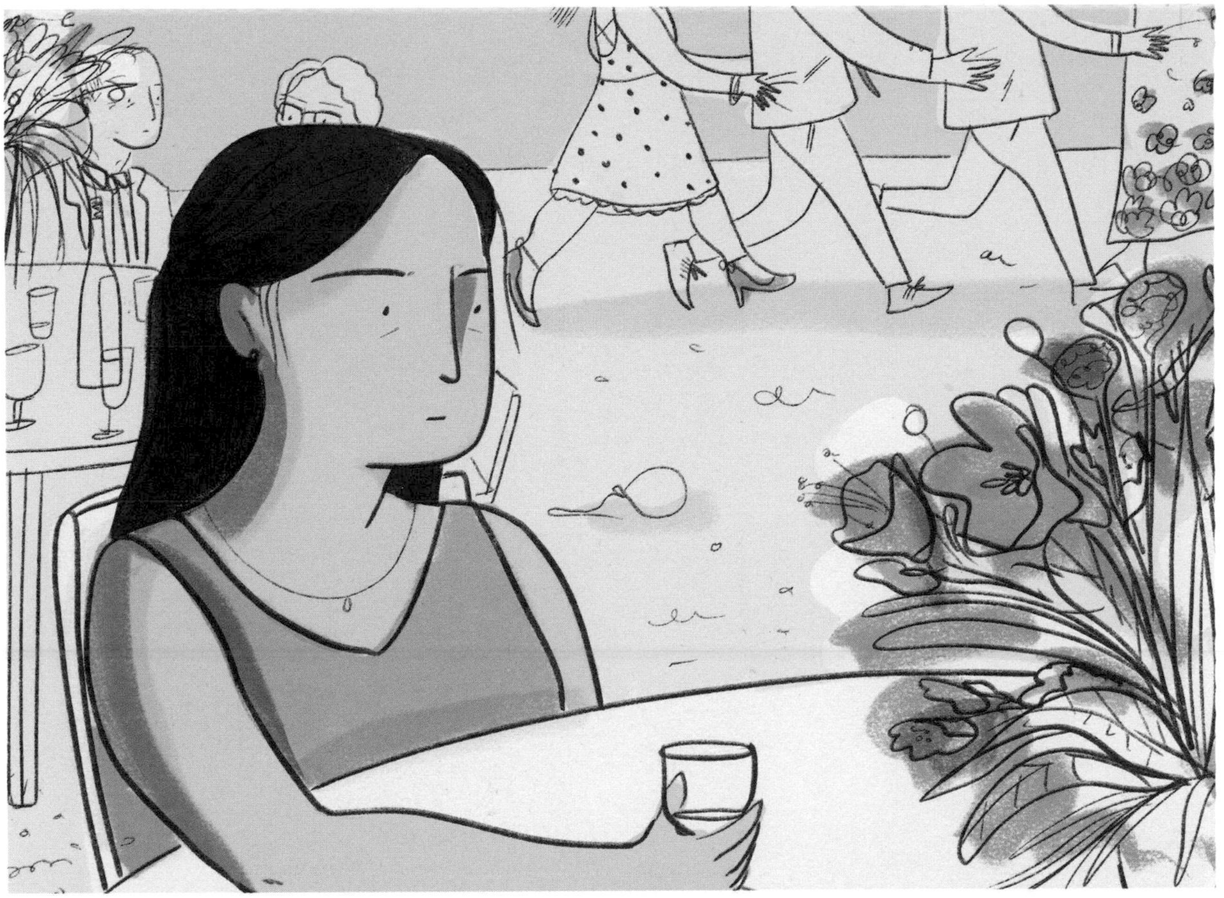

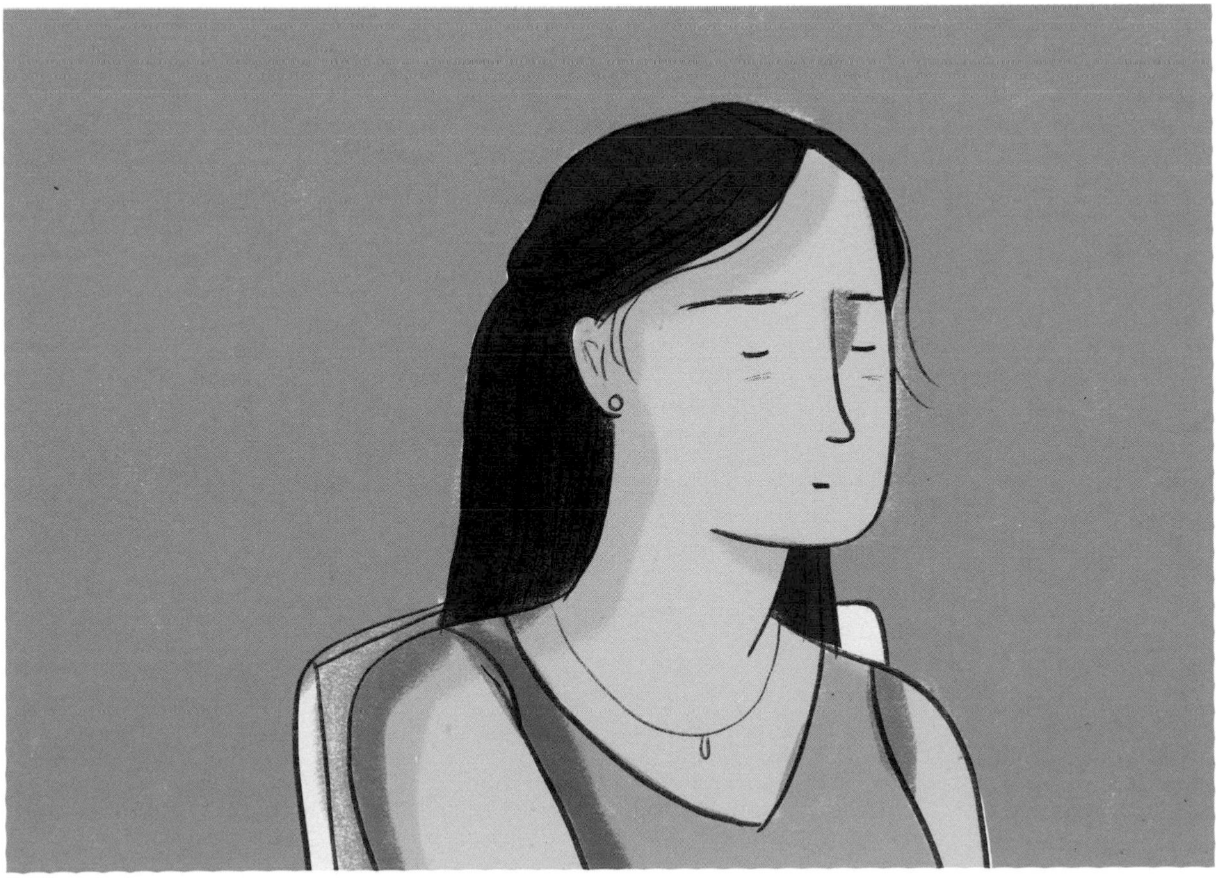

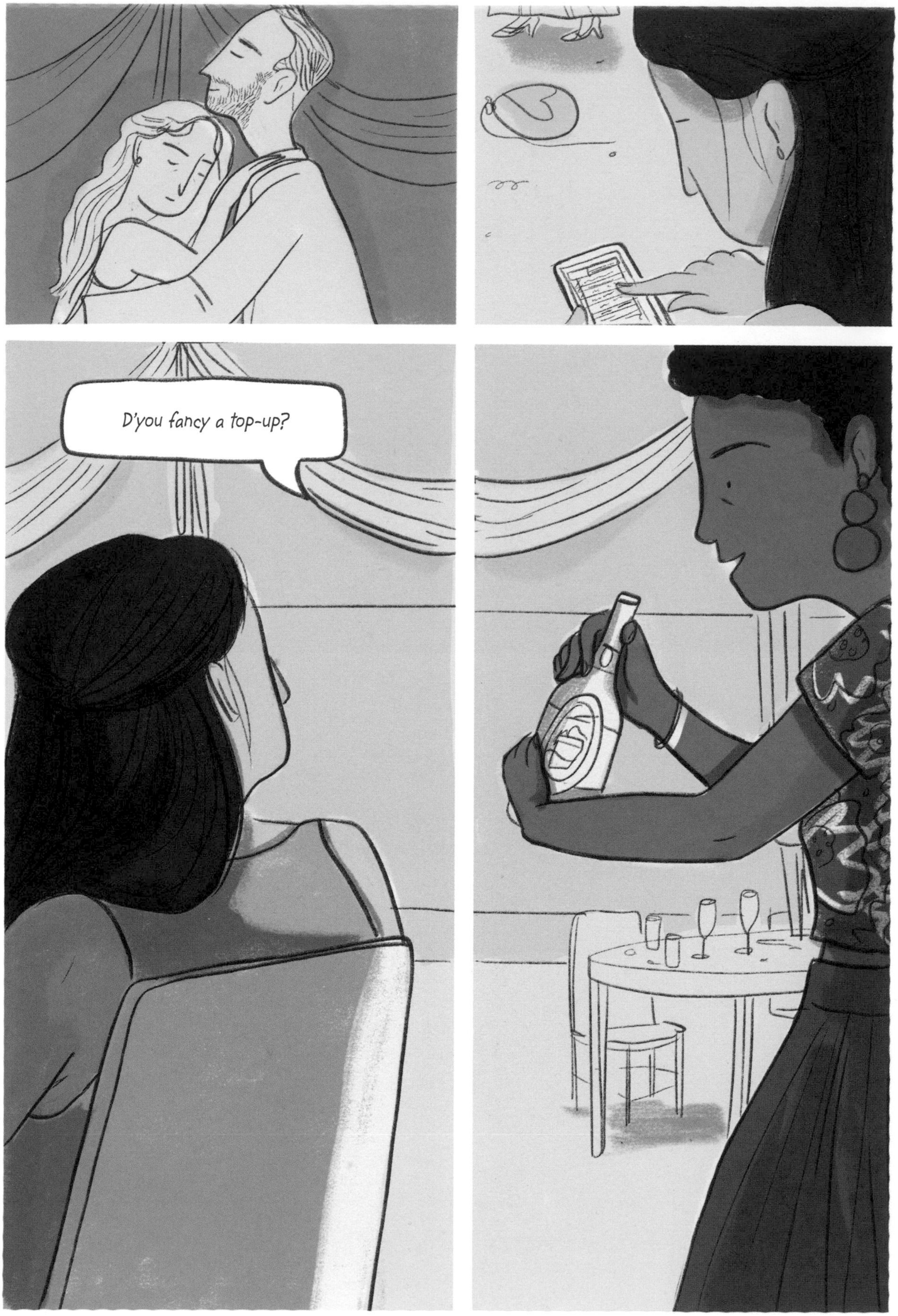
D'you fancy a top-up?

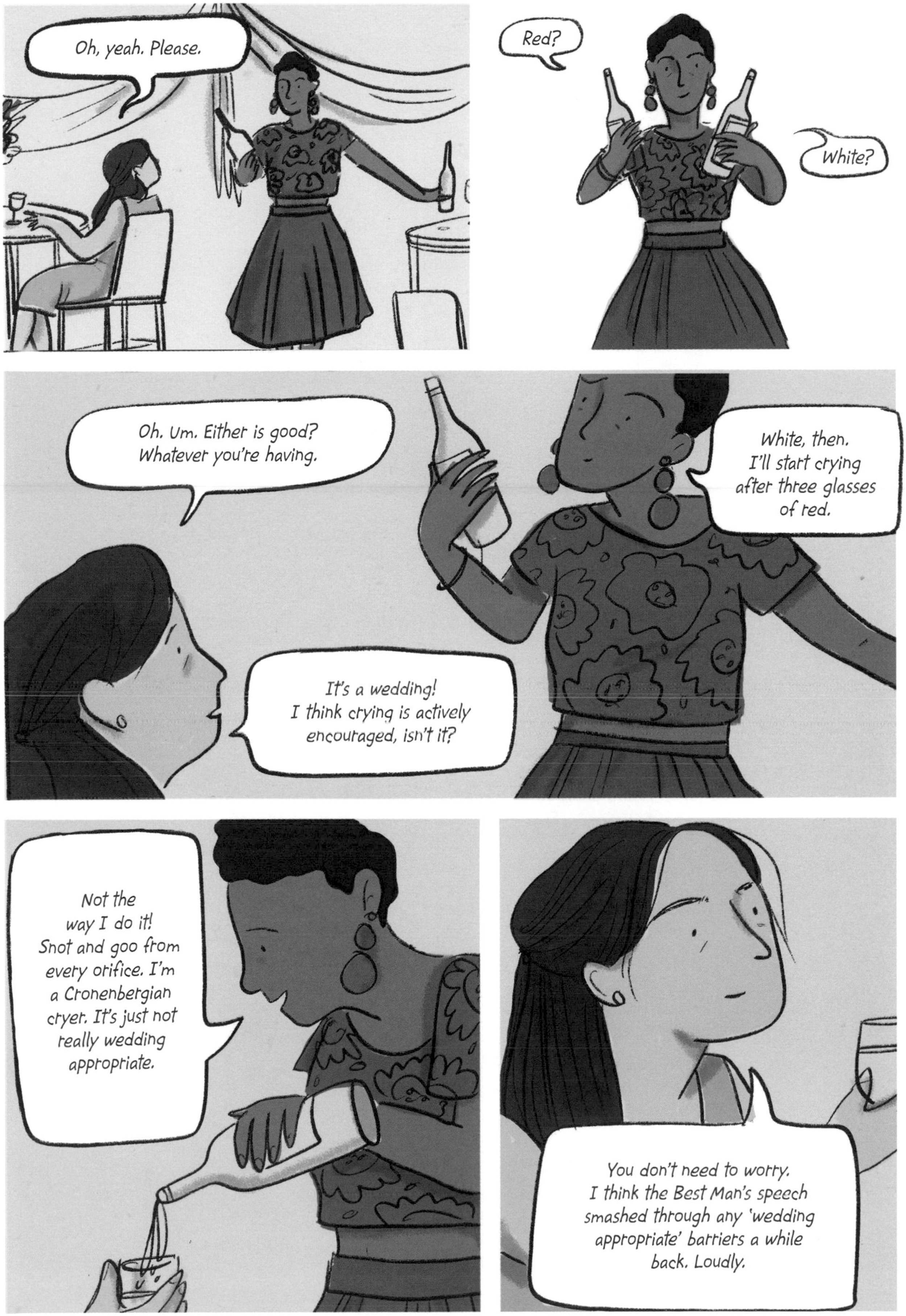

Oh, yeah. Please.
Red?
White?
Oh. Um. Either is good? Whatever you're having.
White, then. I'll start crying after three glasses of red.
It's a wedding! I think crying is actively encouraged, isn't it?
Not the way I do it! Snot and goo from every orifice. I'm a Cronenbergian cryer. It's just not really wedding appropriate.
You don't need to worry. I think the Best Man's speech smashed through any 'wedding appropriate' barriers a while back. Loudly.

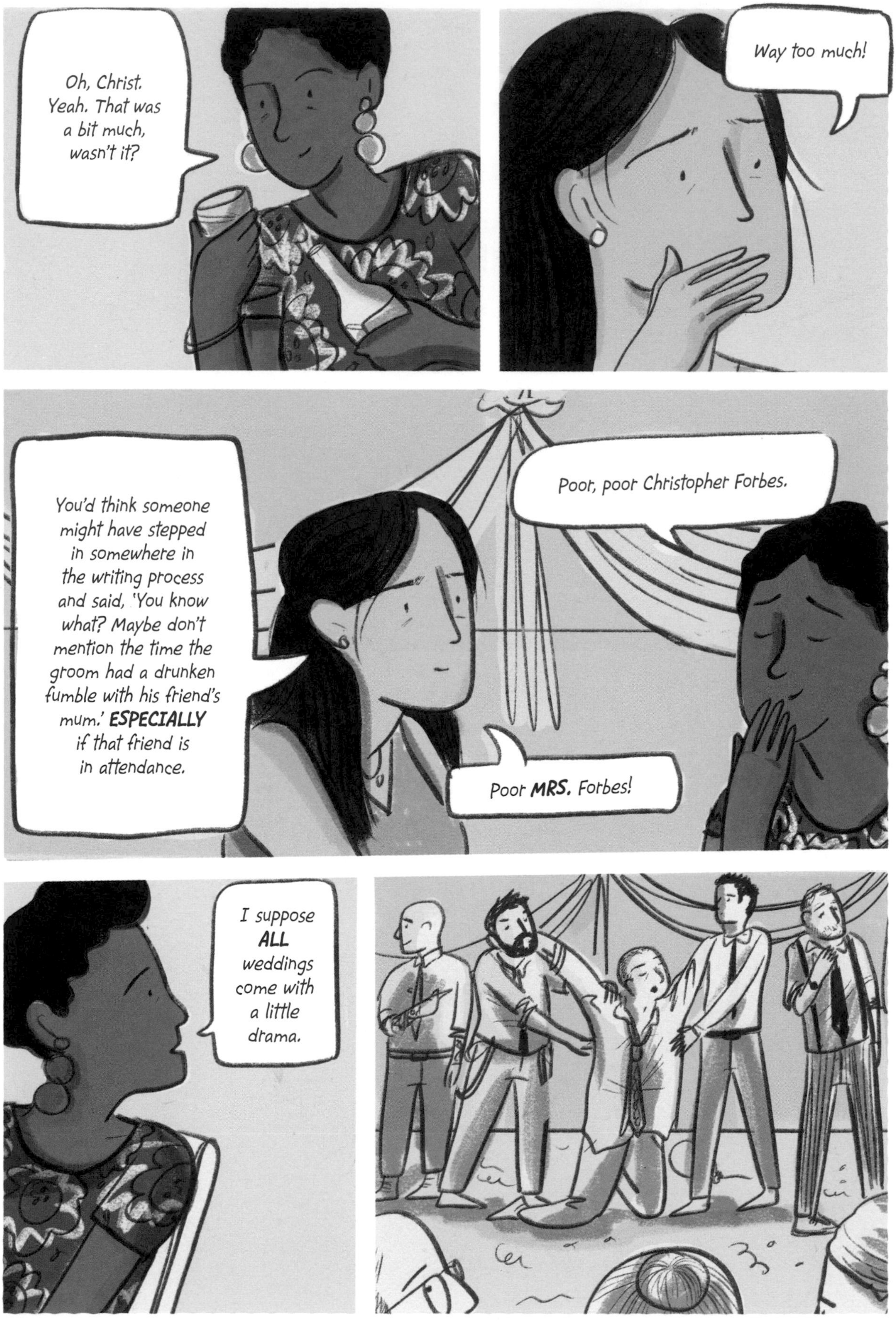
Oh, Christ. Yeah. That was a bit much, wasn't it?
Way too much!
You'd think someone might have stepped in somewhere in the writing process and said, 'You know what? Maybe don't mention the time the groom had a drunken fumble with his friend's mum.' **ESPECIALLY** if that friend is in attendance.
Poor, poor Christopher Forbes.
Poor **MRS.** Forbes!
I suppose **ALL** weddings come with a little drama.

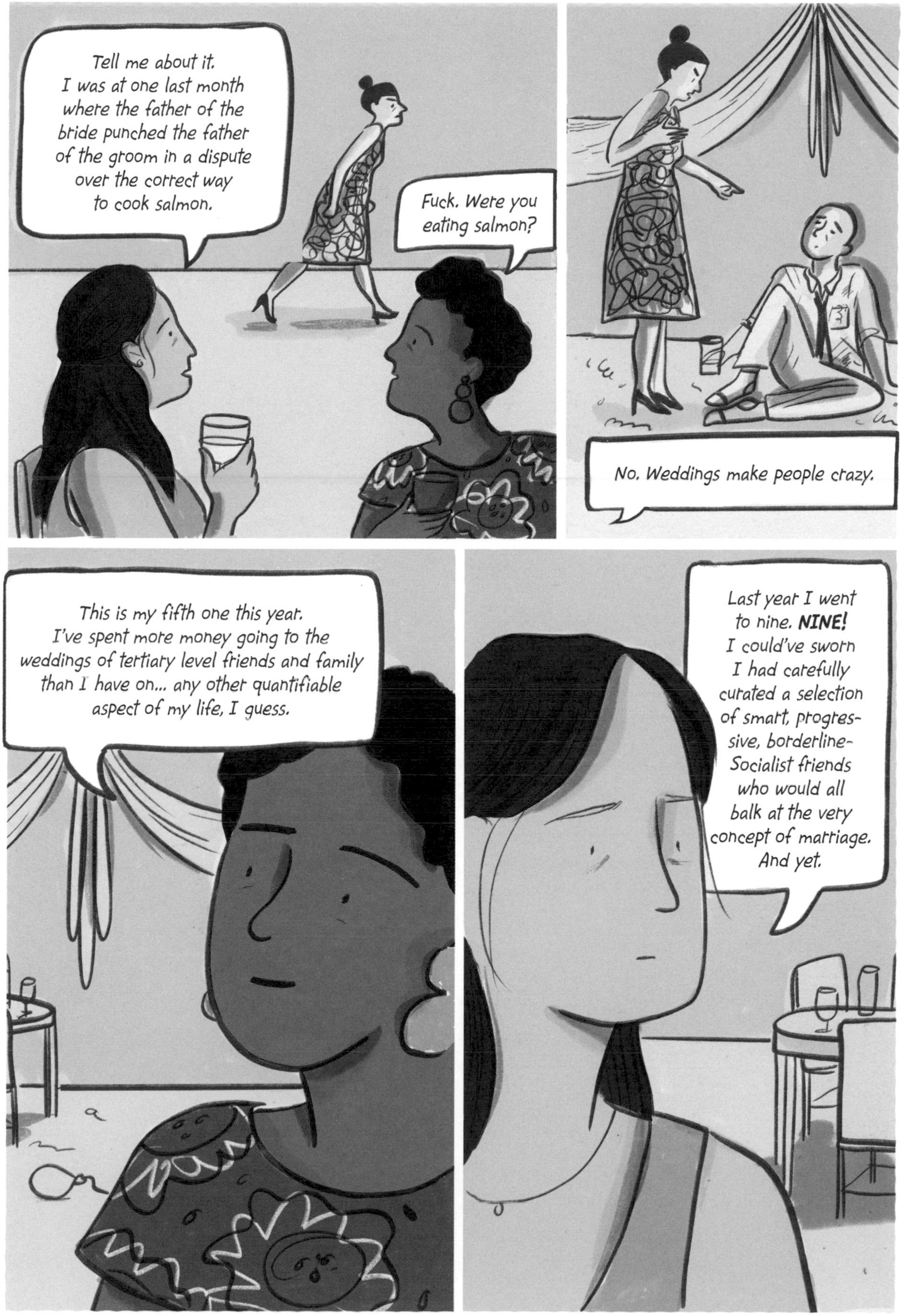
Tell me about it. I was at one last month where the father of the bride punched the father of the groom in a dispute over the correct way to cook salmon.
Fuck. Were you eating salmon?
No. Weddings make people crazy.
This is my fifth one this year. I've spent more money going to the weddings of tertiary level friends and family than I have on... any other quantifiable aspect of my life, I guess.
Last year I went to nine. **NINE!** I could've sworn I had carefully curated a selection of smart, progressive, borderline-Socialist friends who would all balk at the very concept of marriage. And yet.

HA. God, me too.
Last year I went to the wedding of a friend who I used go to fucking pro-Anarchy events with at uni. She used to bin-dive instead of food-shopping, but she still had a 25-tier cake with hand-piped flowers and someone brought in especially to fold napkins into hummingbirds.

Fuuuuuck!

Yeah. I know. We've all seen a napkin swan, but a hummingbird is impressive, right?

Haha, no, I meant...

Yeah, I know. I was being **HILARIOUS.** Remember? I'm hilarious!

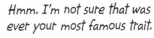

Hmm. I'm not sure that was ever your most famous trait.

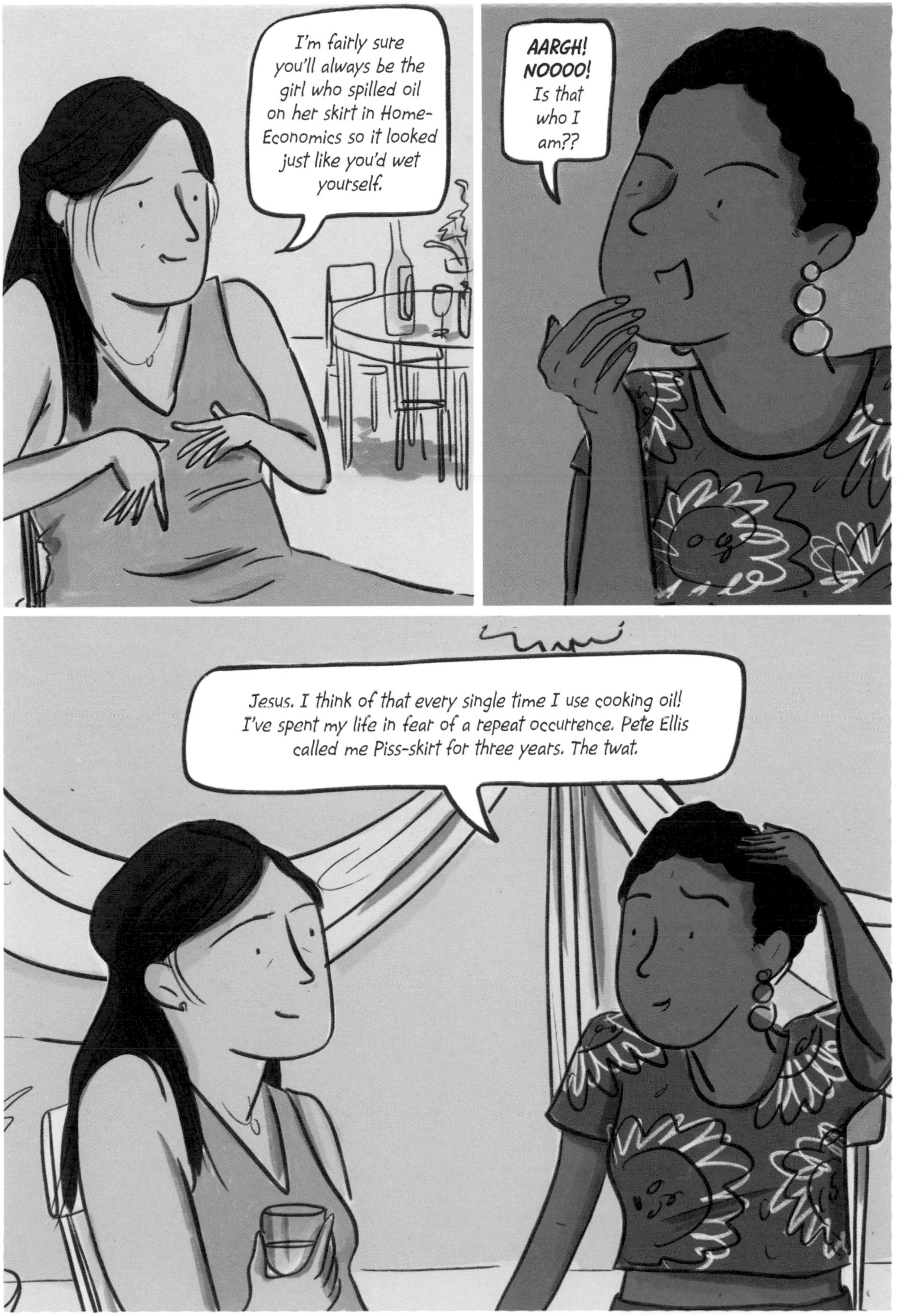
I'm fairly sure you'll always be the girl who spilled oil on her skirt in Home-Economics so it looked just like you'd wet yourself.
AARGH! NOOOO! Is that who I am??
Jesus. I think of that every single time I use cooking oil! I've spent my life in fear of a repeat occurrence. Pete Ellis called me Piss-skirt for three years. The twat.

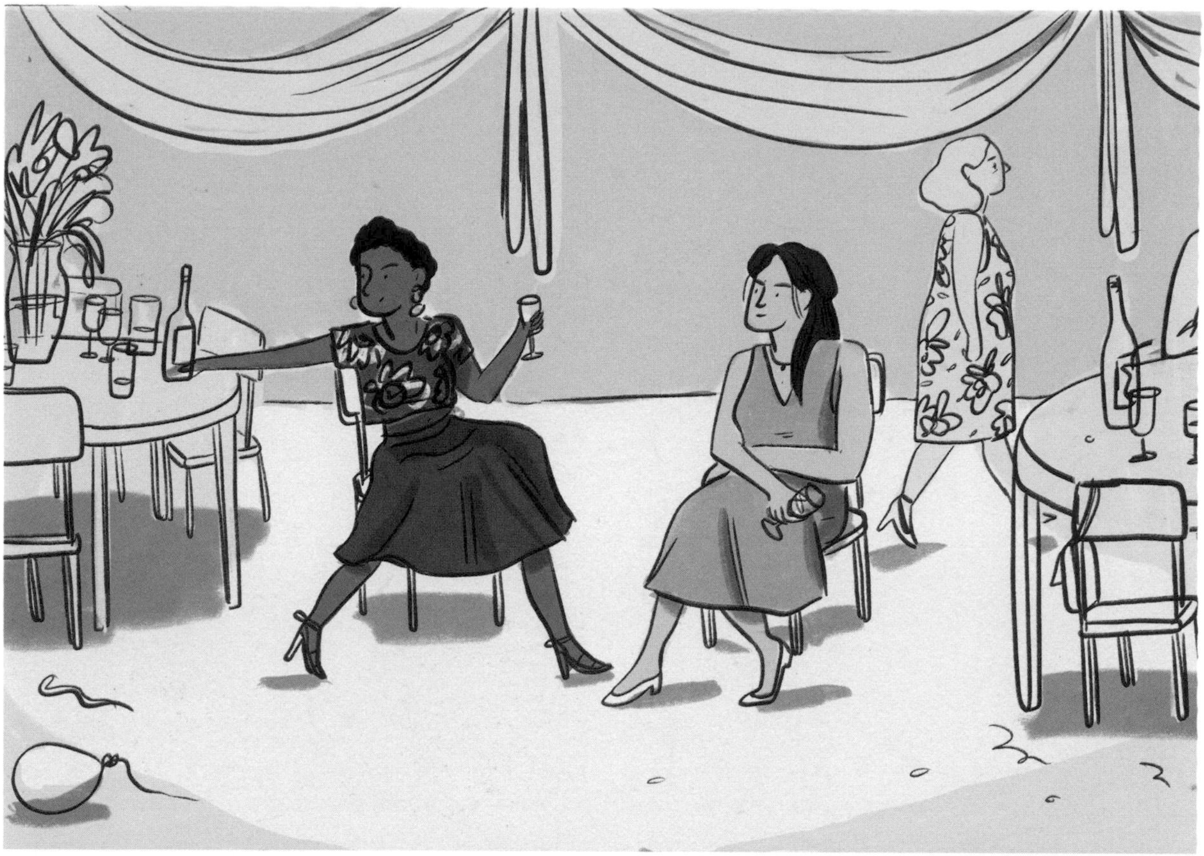

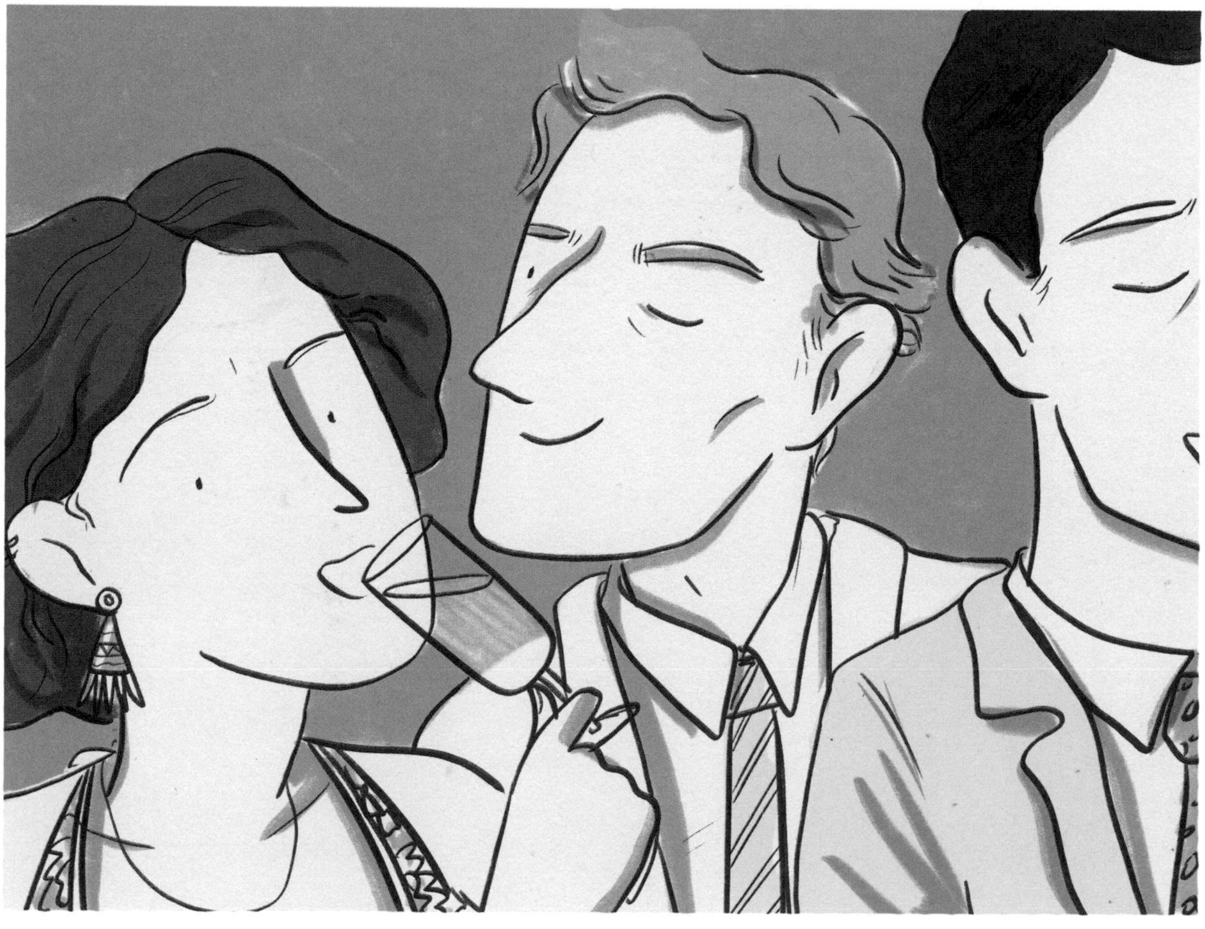

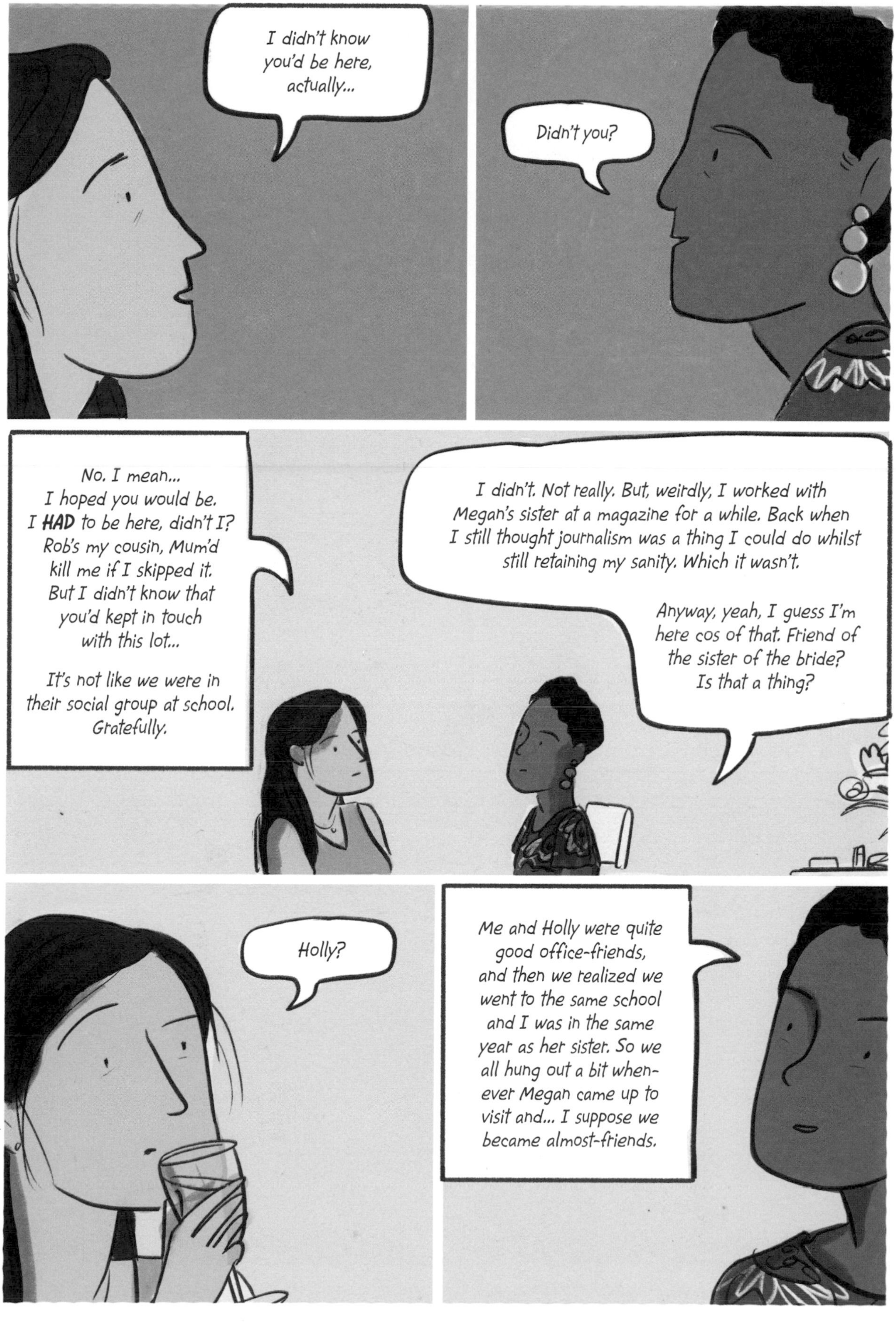
I didn't know you'd be here, actually...
Didn't you?
No. I mean... I hoped you would be. I **HAD** to be here, didn't I? Rob's my cousin, Mum'd kill me if I skipped it. But I didn't know that you'd kept in touch with this lot...
It's not like we were in their social group at school. Gratefully.
I didn't. Not really. But, weirdly, I worked with Megan's sister at a magazine for a while. Back when I still thought journalism was a thing I could do whilst still retaining my sanity. Which it wasn't.
Anyway, yeah, I guess I'm here cos of that. Friend of the sister of the bride? Is that a thing?
Holly?
Me and Holly were quite good office-friends, and then we realized we went to the same school and I was in the same year as her sister. So we all hung out a bit whenever Megan came up to visit and... I suppose we became almost-friends.

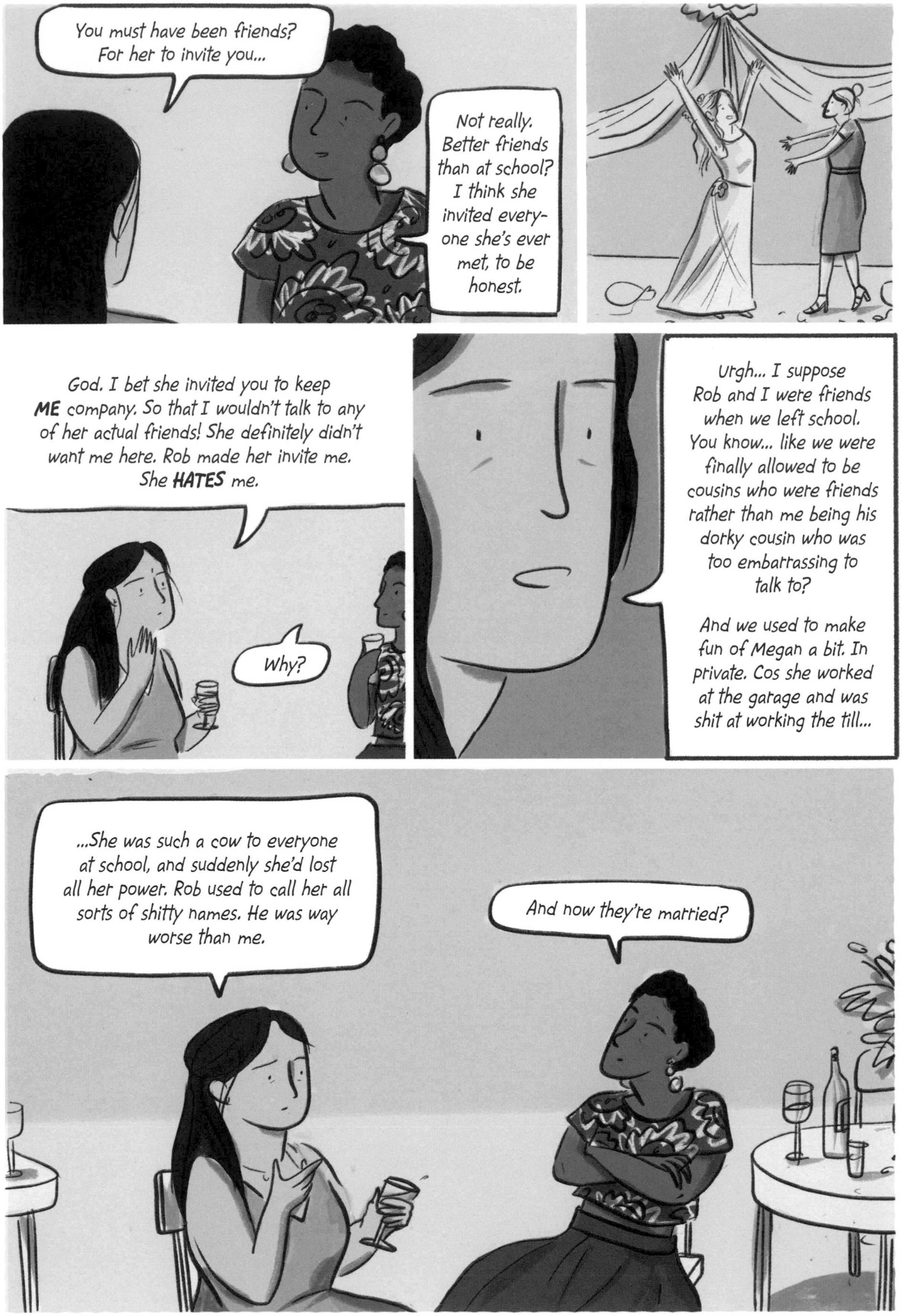
You must have been friends? For her to invite you...
Not really. Better friends than at school? I think she invited everyone she's ever met, to be honest.
God. I bet she invited you to keep **ME** company. So that I wouldn't talk to any of her actual friends! She definitely didn't want me here. Rob made her invite me. She **HATES** me.
Why?
Urgh... I suppose Rob and I were friends when we left school. You know... like we were finally allowed to be cousins who were friends rather than me being his dorky cousin who was too embarrassing to talk to?
And we used to make fun of Megan a bit. In private. Cos she worked at the garage and was shit at working the till...
...She was such a cow to everyone at school, and suddenly she'd lost all her power. Rob used to call her all sorts of shitty names. He was way worse than me.
And now they're married?

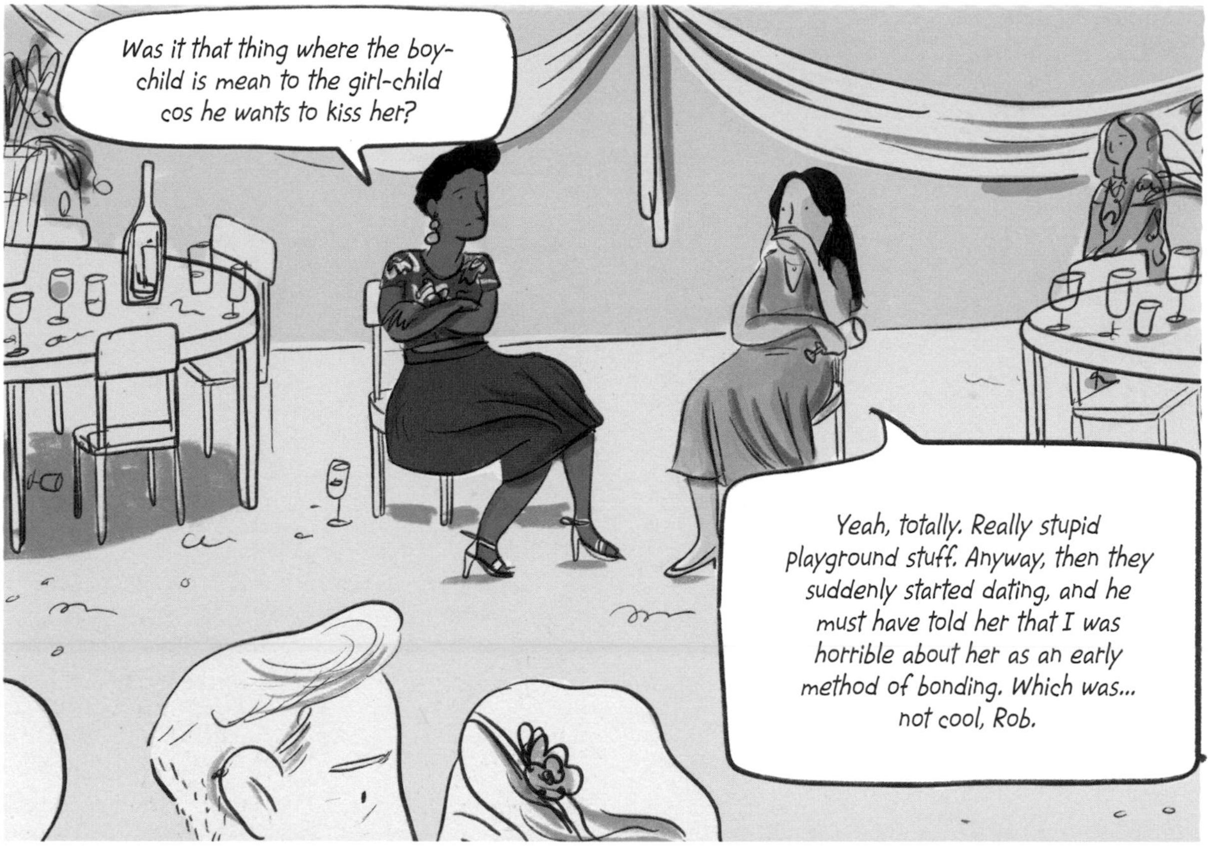
Was it that thing where the boy-child is mean to the girl-child cos he wants to kiss her?
Yeah, totally. Really stupid playground stuff. Anyway, then they suddenly started dating, and he must have told her that I was horrible about her as an early method of bonding. Which was... not cool, Rob.

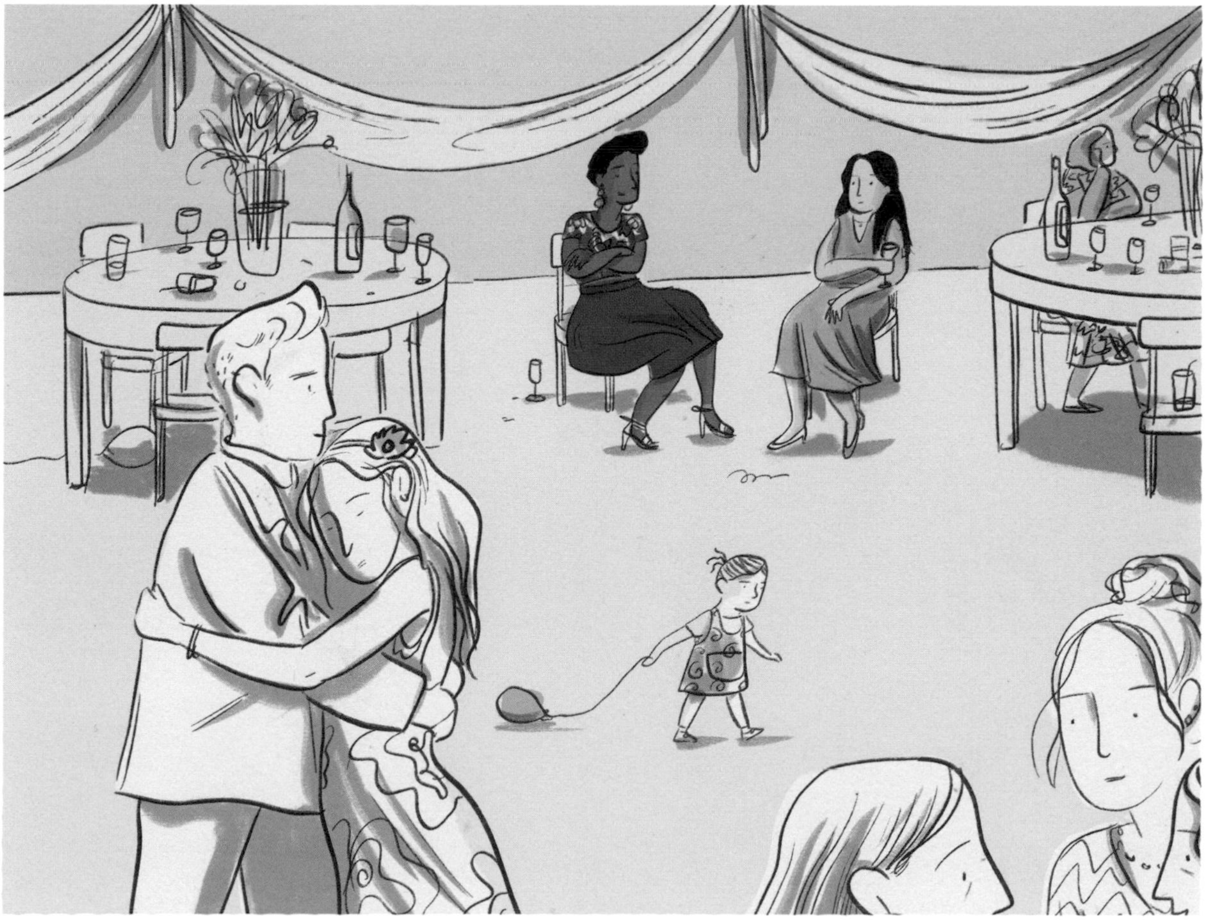

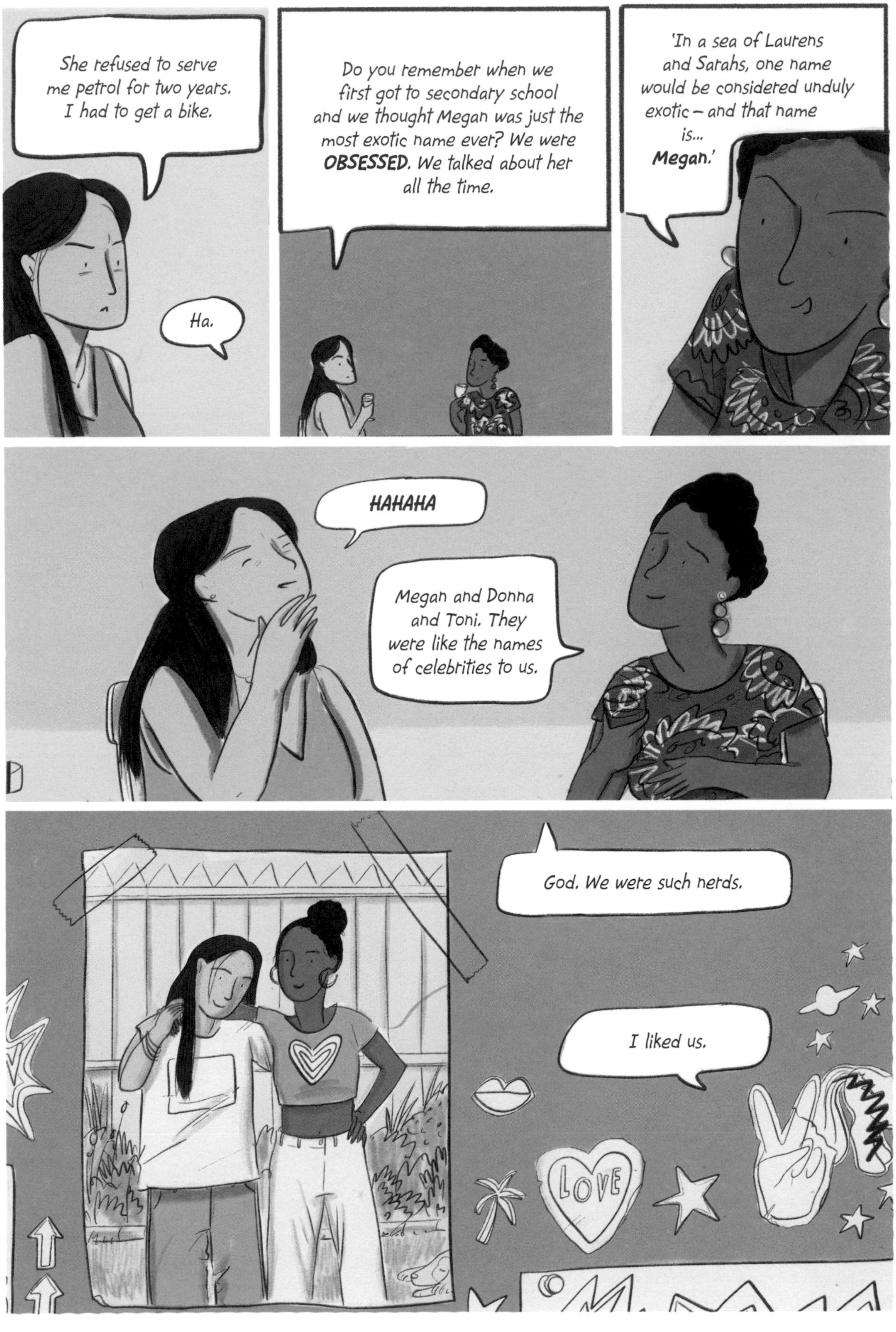

She refused to serve me petrol for two years. I had to get a bike.
Ha.
Do you remember when we first got to secondary school and we thought Megan was just the most exotic name ever? We were **OBSESSED**. We talked about her all the time.
'In a sea of Laurens and Sarahs, one name would be considered unduly exotic – and that name is... **Megan**.'
HAHAHA
Megan and Donna and Toni. They were like the names of celebrities to us.
God. We were such nerds.
I liked us.
LOVE

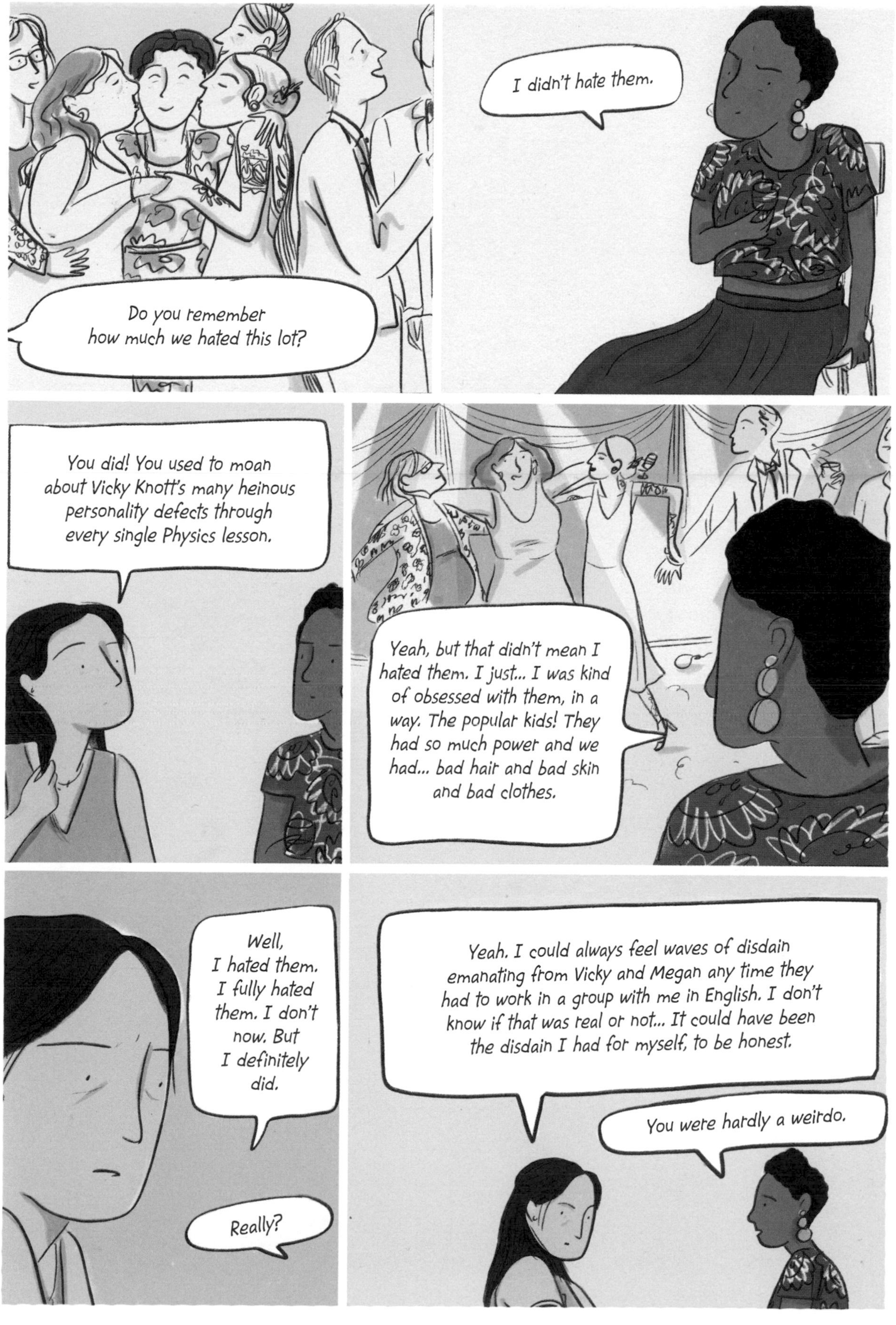
Do you remember how much we hated this lot?
I didn't hate them.
You did! You used to moan about Vicky Knott's many heinous personality defects through every single Physics lesson.
Yeah, but that didn't mean I hated them. I just... I was kind of obsessed with them, in a way. The popular kids! They had so much power and we had... bad hair and bad skin and bad clothes.
Well, I hated them. I fully hated them. I don't now. But I definitely did.
Really?
Yeah. I could always feel waves of disdain emanating from Vicky and Megan any time they had to work in a group with me in English. I don't know if that was real or not... It could have been the disdain I had for myself, to be honest.
You were hardly a weirdo.

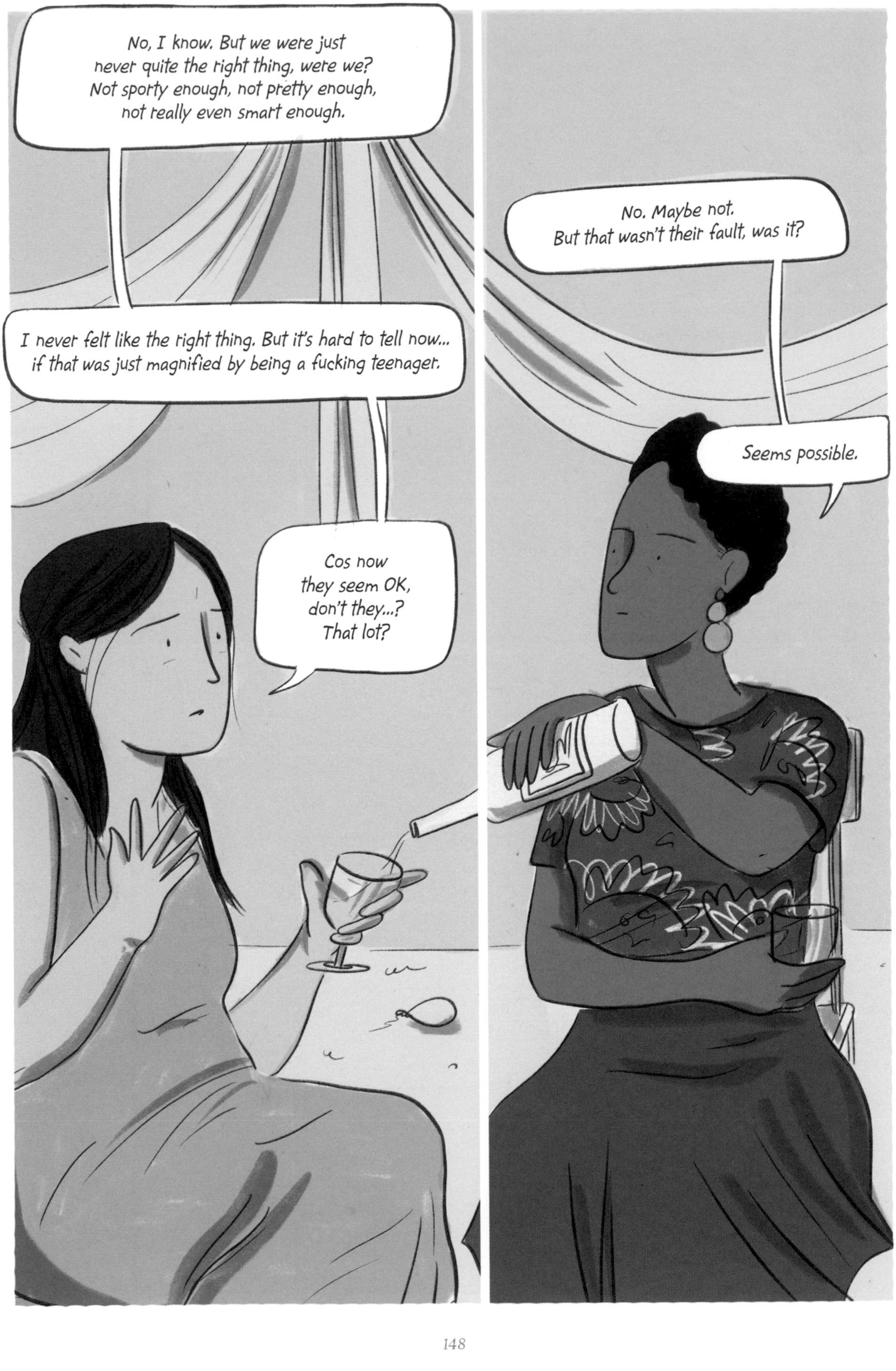
No, I know. But we were just never quite the right thing, were we? Not sporty enough, not pretty enough, not really even smart enough.
I never felt like the right thing. But it's hard to tell now... if that was just magnified by being a fucking teenager.
Cos now they seem OK, don't they...? That lot?
No. Maybe not. But that wasn't their fault, was it?
Seems possible.

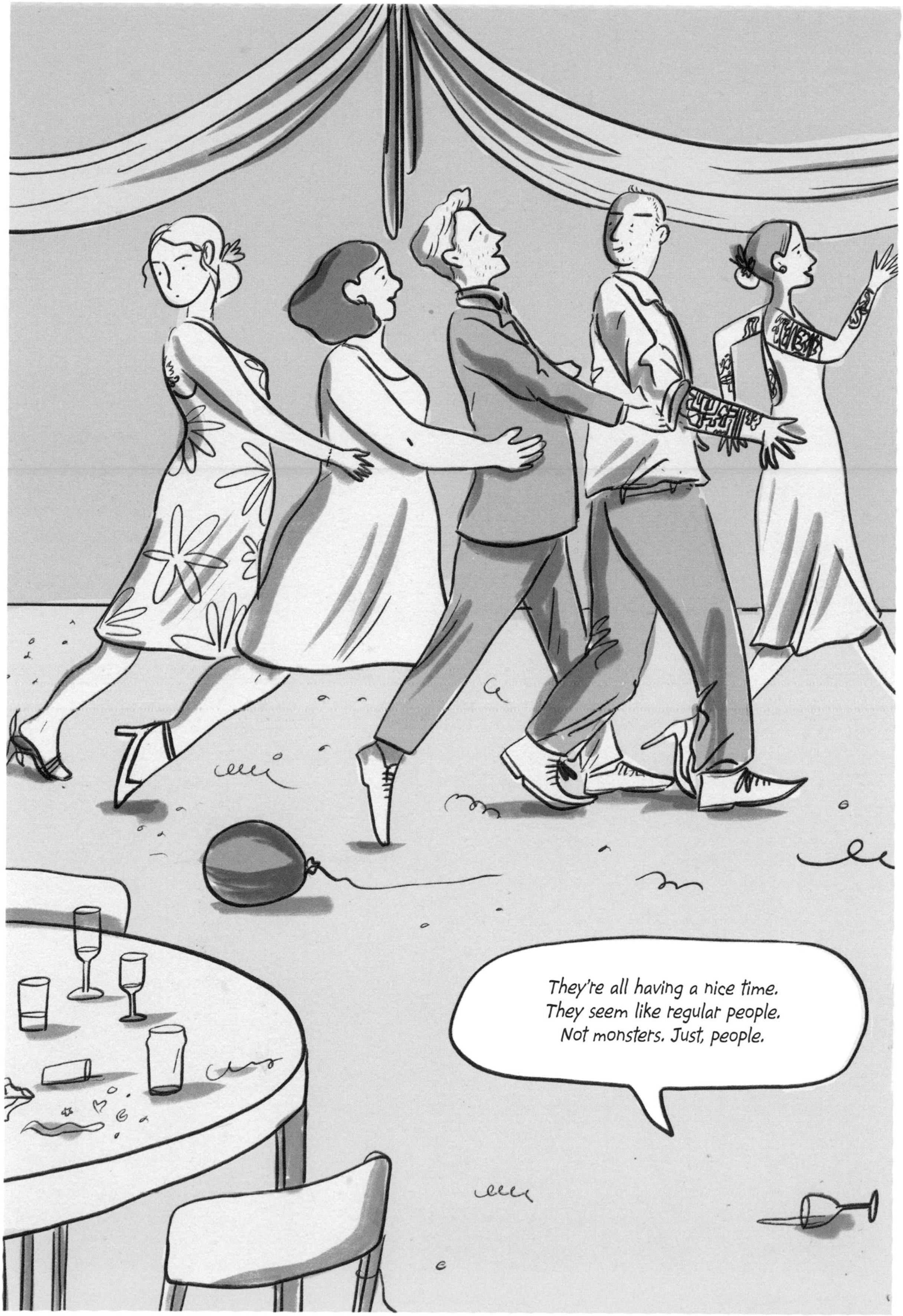
They're all having a nice time. They seem like regular people. Not monsters. Just, people.

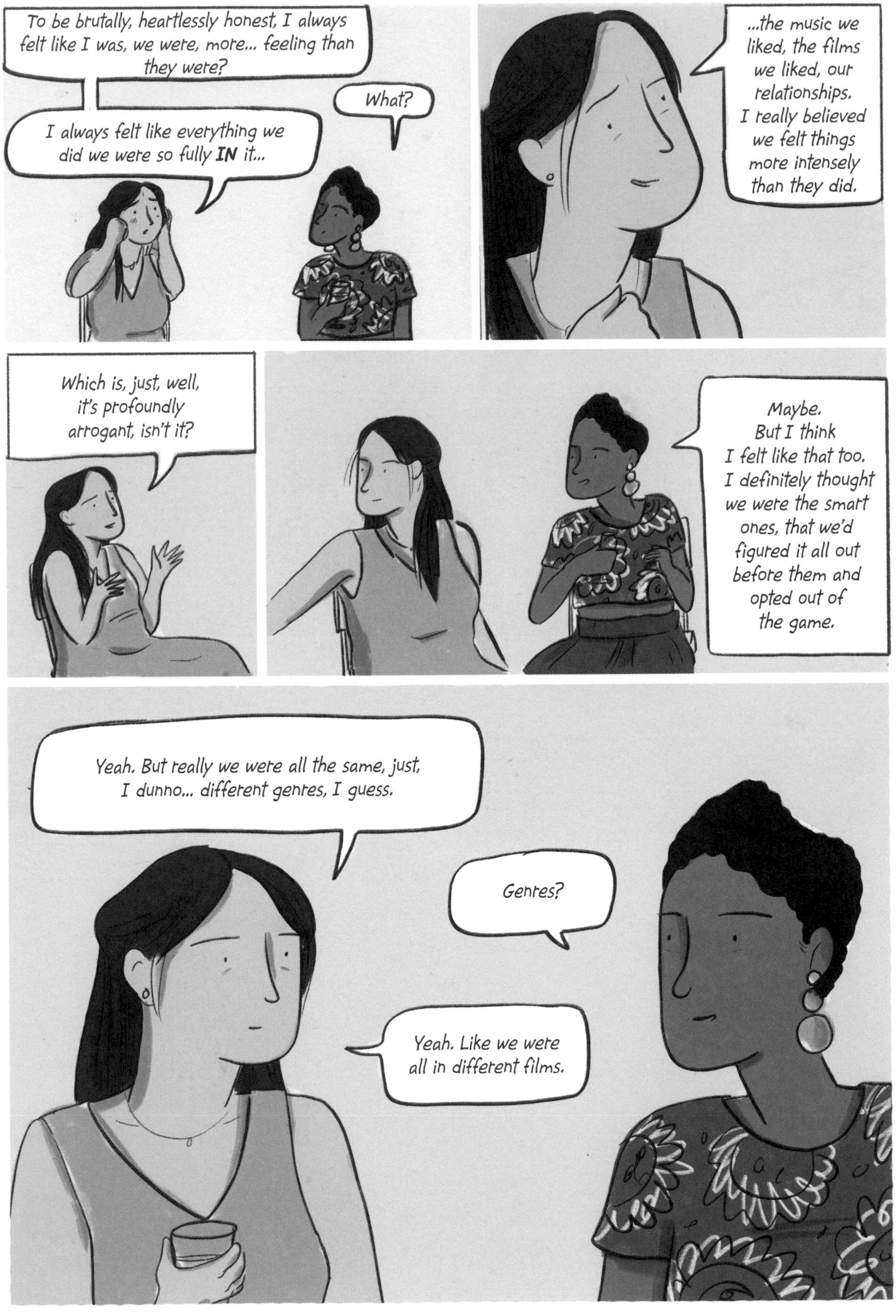
To be brutally, heartlessly honest, I always felt like I was, we were, more... feeling than they were?
I always felt like everything we did we were so fully **IN** it...
What?
...the music we liked, the films we liked, our relationships. I really believed we felt things more intensely than they did.
Which is, just, well, it's profoundly arrogant, isn't it?
Maybe. But I think I felt like that too. I definitely thought we were the smart ones, that we'd figured it all out before them and opted out of the game.
Yeah. But really we were all the same, just, I dunno... different genres, I guess.
Genres?
Yeah. Like we were all in different films.

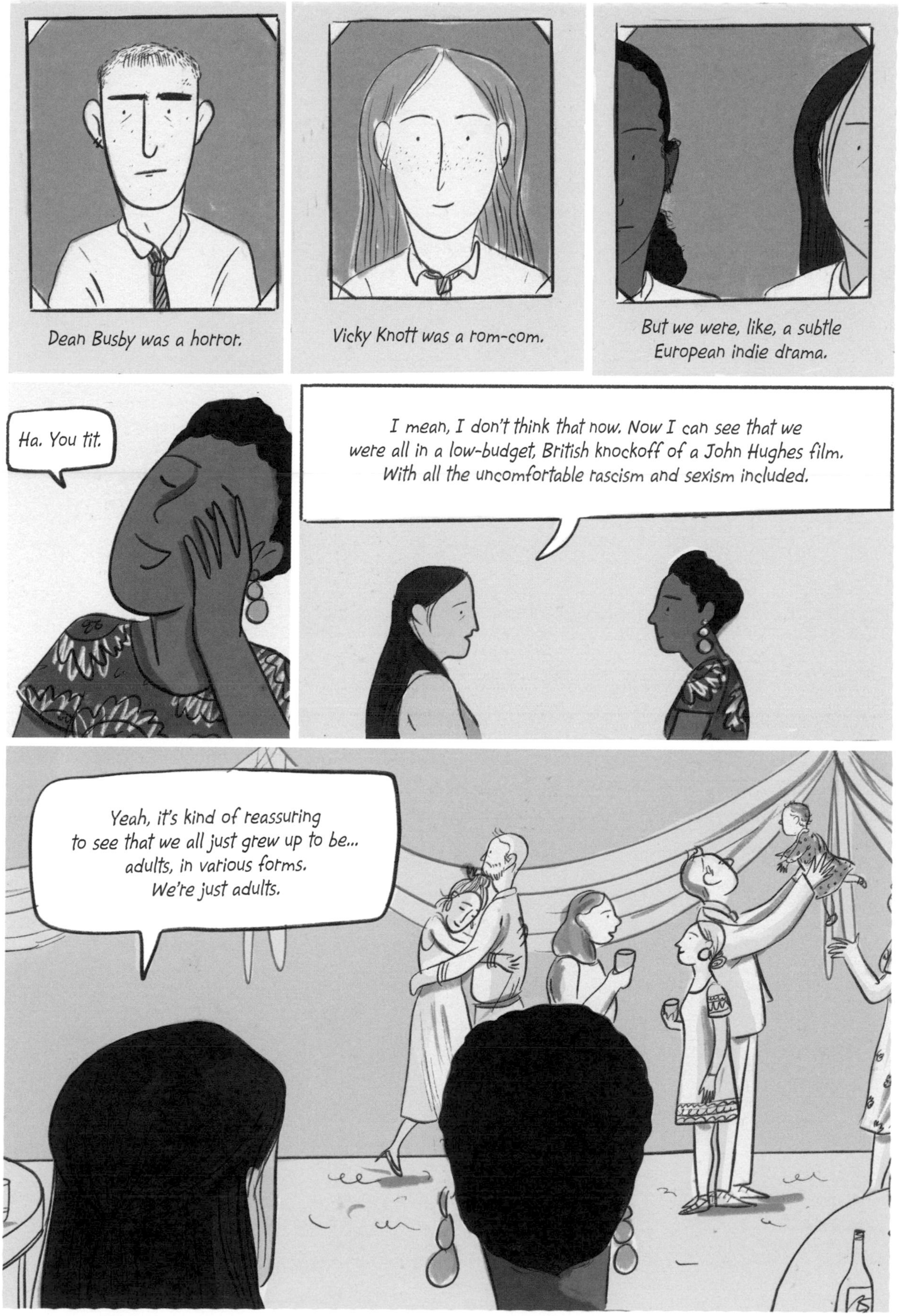

Dean Busby was a horror.
Vicky Knott was a rom-com.
But we were, like, a subtle European indie drama.
Ha. You tit.
I mean, I don't think that now. Now I can see that we were all in a low-budget, British knockoff of a John Hughes film. With all the uncomfortable rascism and sexism included.
Yeah, it's kind of reassuring to see that we all just grew up to be... adults, in various forms. We're just adults.

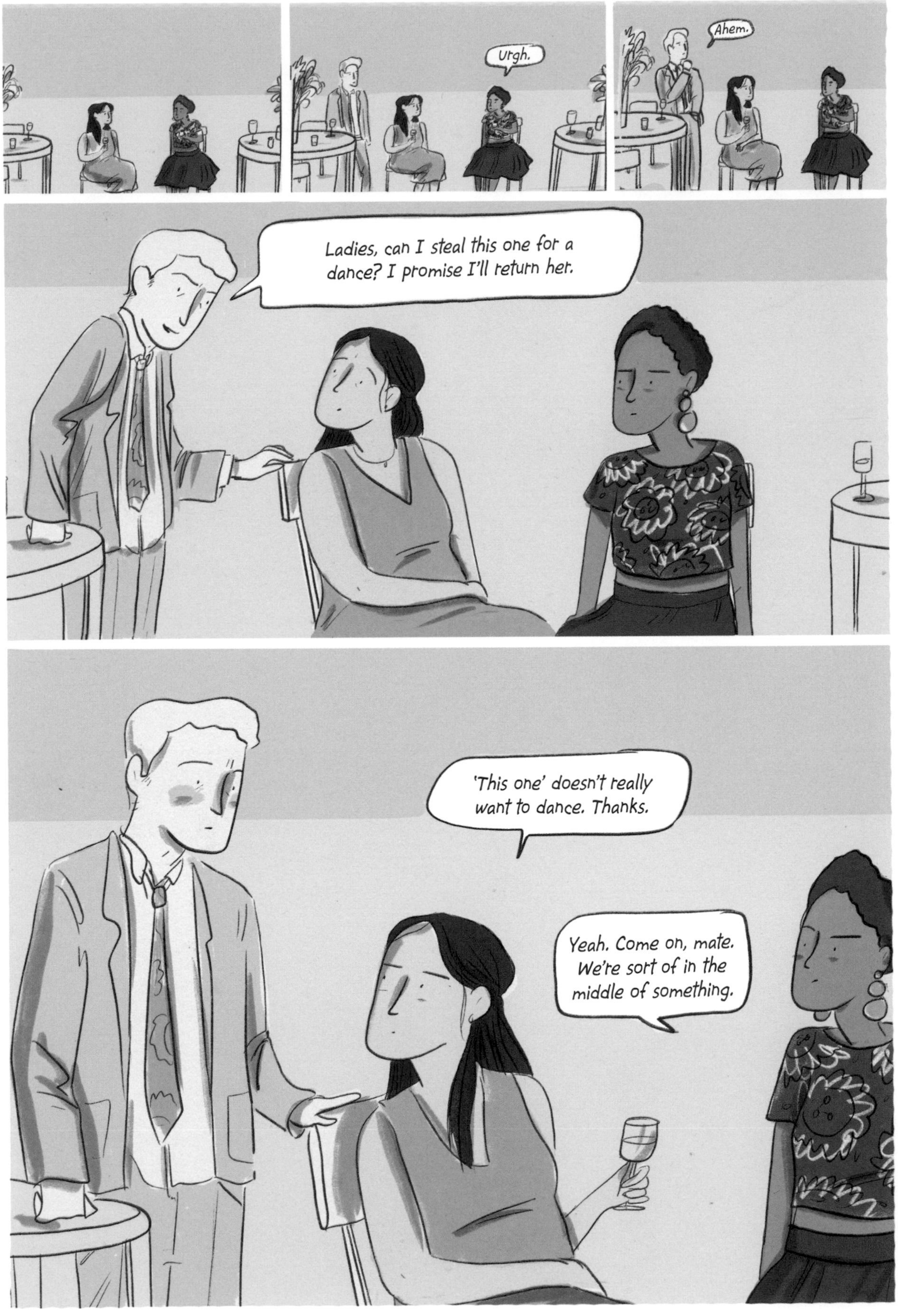
Urgh.
Ahem.
Ladies, can I steal this one for a dance? I promise I'll return her.
'This one' doesn't really want to dance. Thanks.
Yeah. Come on, mate. We're sort of in the middle of something.

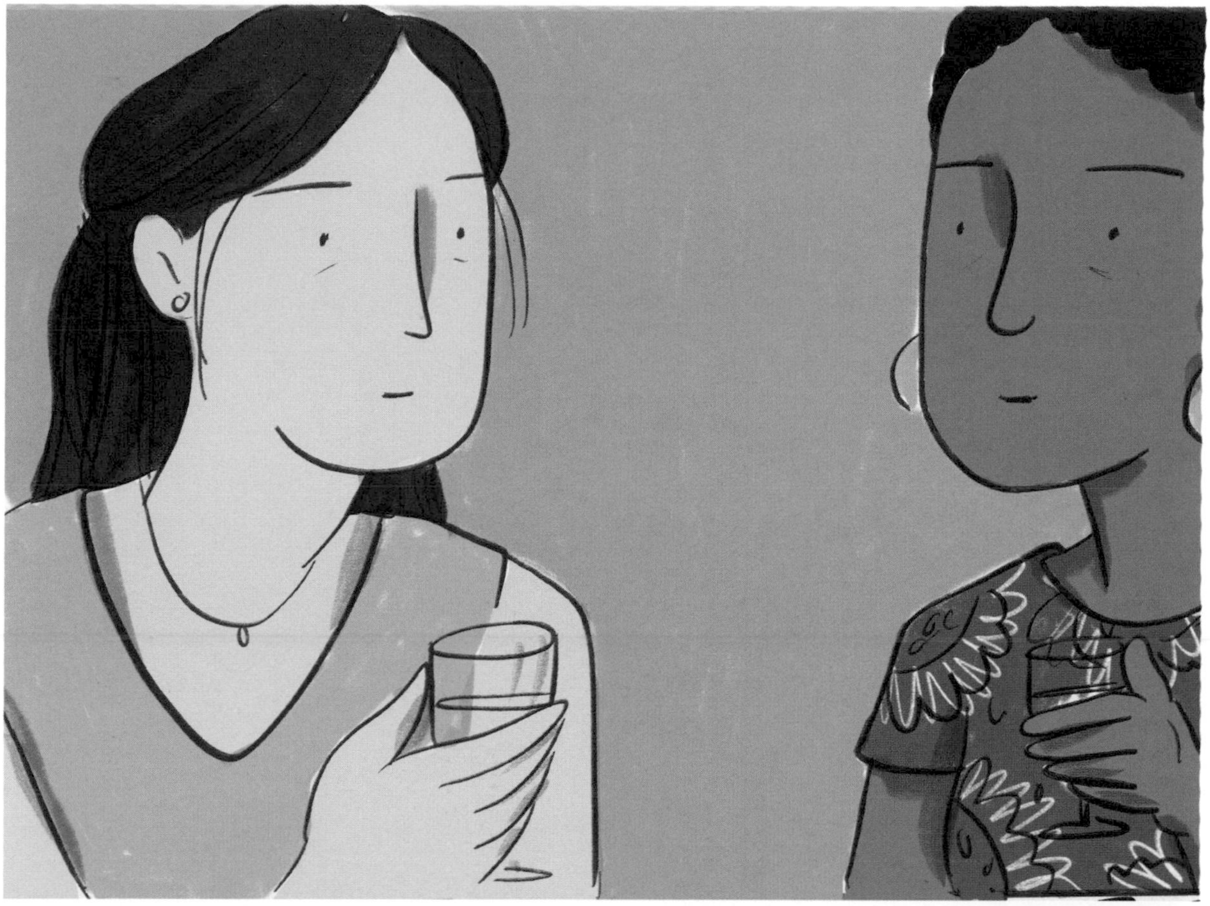

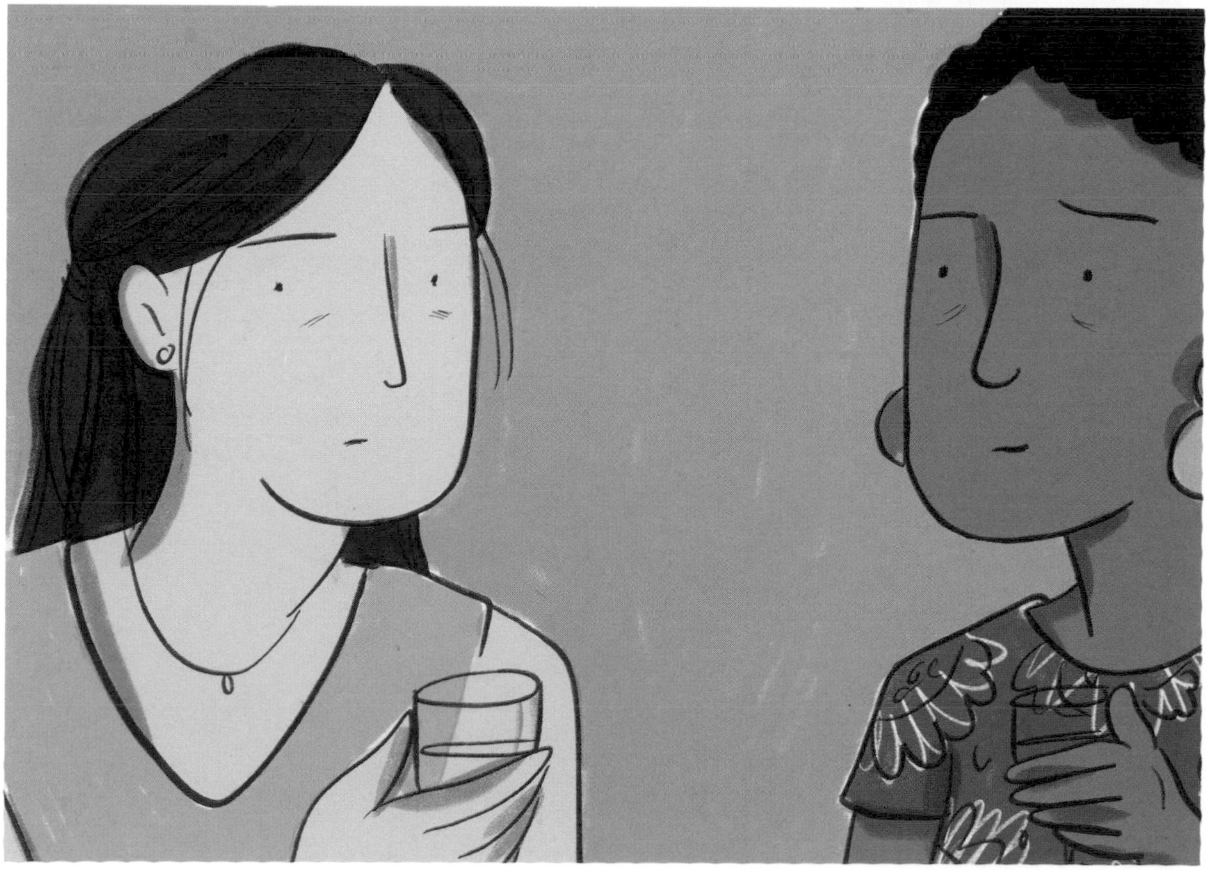

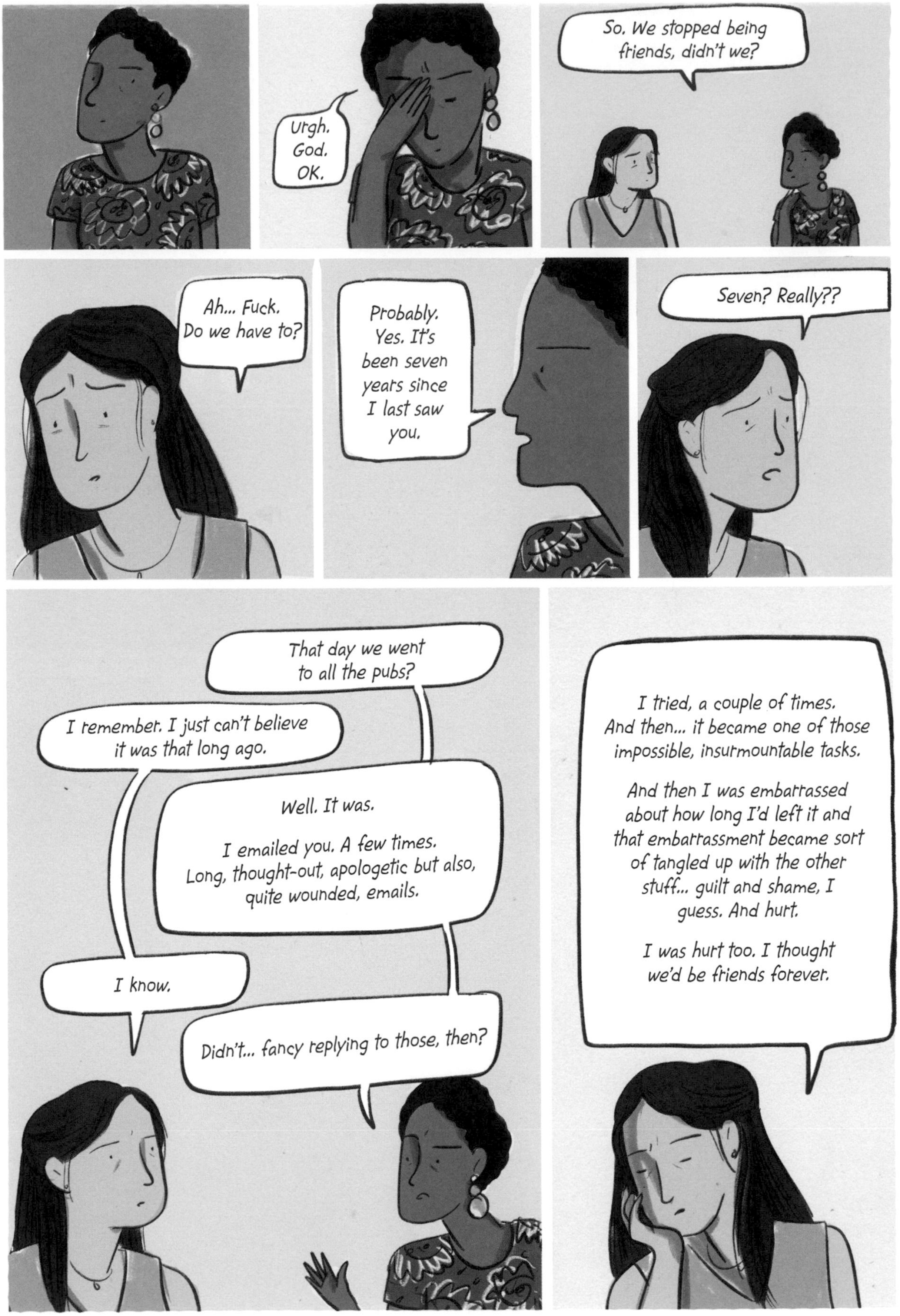
Urgh. God. OK.
So. We stopped being friends, didn't we?
Ah... Fuck. Do we have to?
Probably. Yes. It's been seven years since I last saw you.
Seven? Really??
That day we went to all the pubs?
I remember. I just can't believe it was that long ago.
Well. It was.
I emailed you. A few times. Long, thought-out, apologetic but also, quite wounded, emails.
I know.
Didn't... fancy replying to those, then?
I tried, a couple of times. And then... it became one of those impossible, insurmountable tasks.
And then I was embarrassed about how long I'd left it and that embarrassment became sort of tangled up with the other stuff... guilt and shame, I guess. And hurt.
I was hurt too. I thought we'd be friends forever.

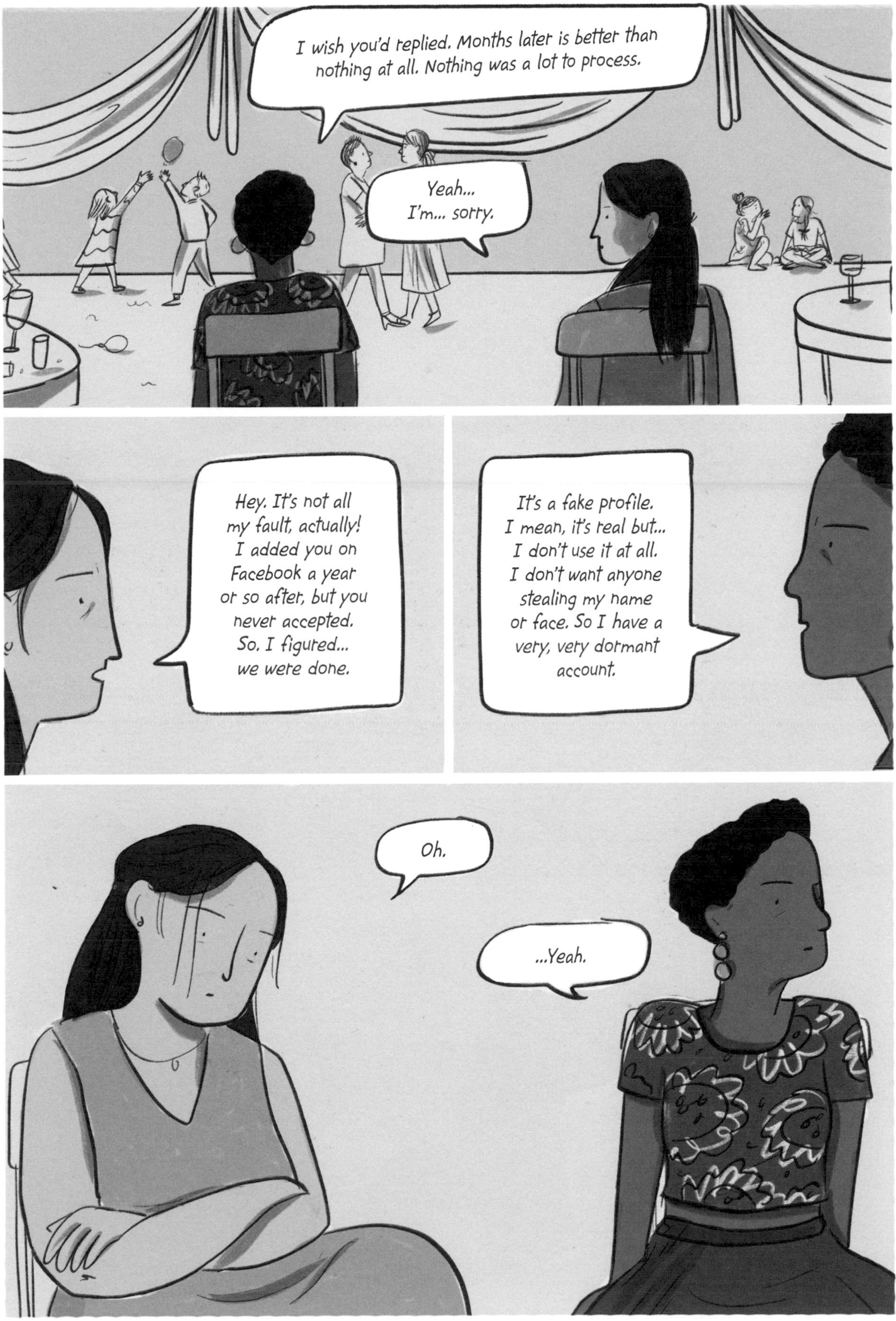
I wish you'd replied. Months later is better than nothing at all. Nothing was a lot to process.
Yeah... I'm... sorry.
Hey. It's not all my fault, actually! I added you on Facebook a year or so after, but you never accepted. So, I figured... we were done.
It's a fake profile. I mean, it's real but... I don't use it at all. I don't want anyone stealing my name or face. So I have a very, very dormant account.
Oh.
...Yeah.

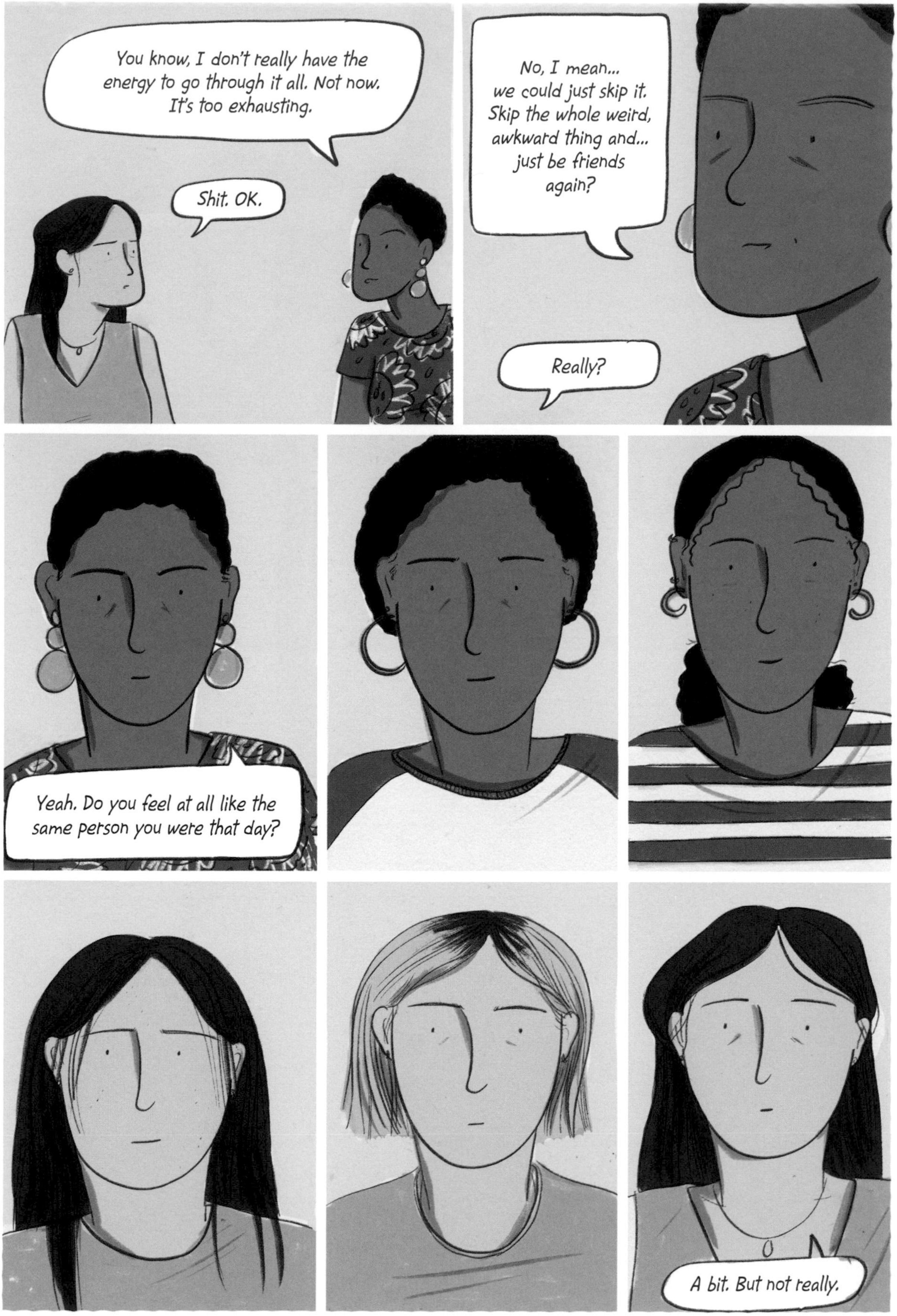
You know, I don't really have the energy to go through it all. Not now. It's too exhausting.
Shit. OK.
No, I mean... we could just skip it. Skip the whole weird, awkward thing and... just be friends again?
Really?
Yeah. Do you feel at all like the same person you were that day?
A bit. But not really.

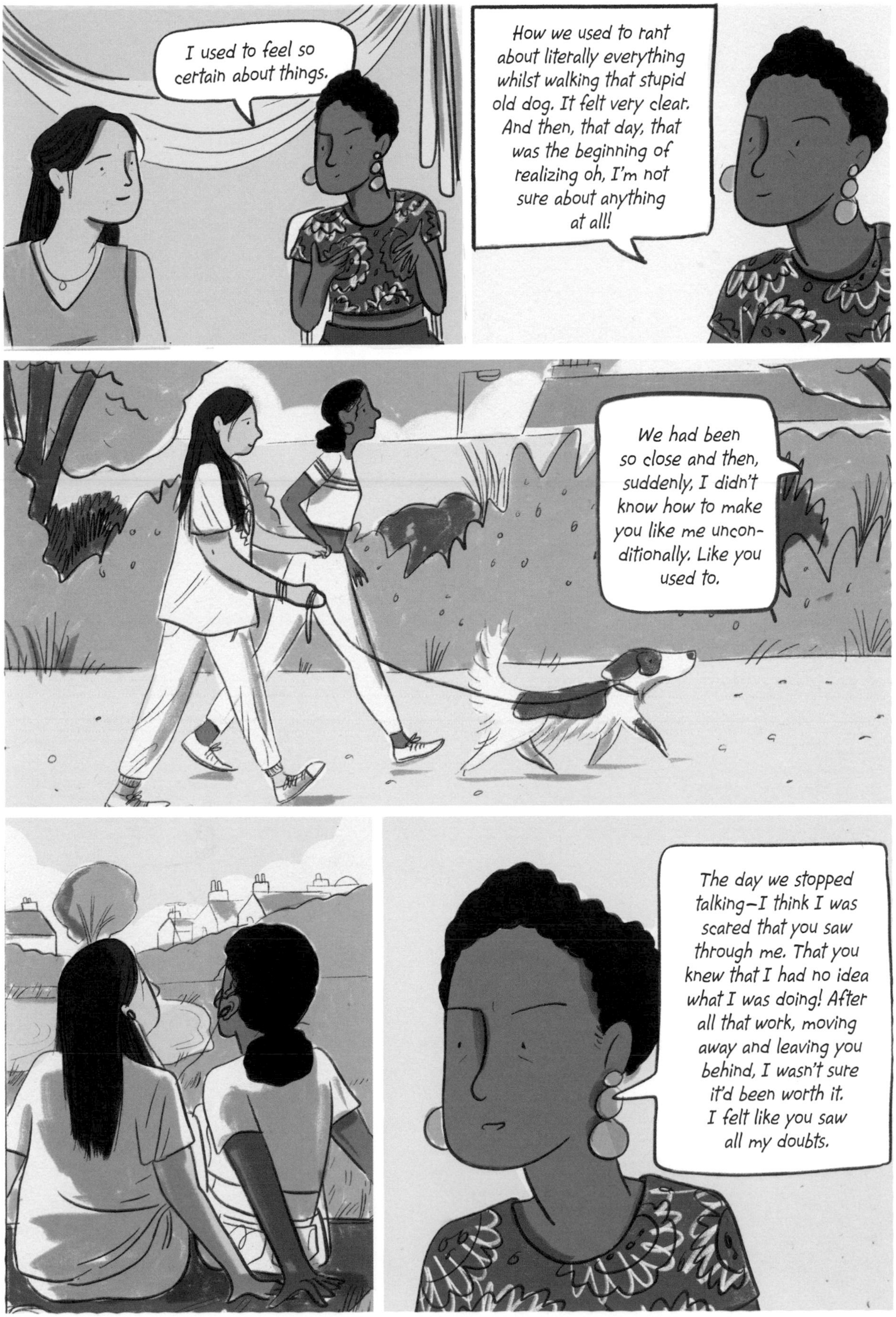
I used to feel so certain about things.
How we used to rant about literally everything whilst walking that stupid old dog. It felt very clear. And then, that day, that was the beginning of realizing oh, I'm not sure about anything at all!
We had been so close and then, suddenly, I didn't know how to make you like me unconditionally. Like you used to.
The day we stopped talking—I think I was scared that you saw through me. That you knew that I had no idea what I was doing! After all that work, moving away and leaving you behind, I wasn't sure it'd been worth it. I felt like you saw all my doubts.

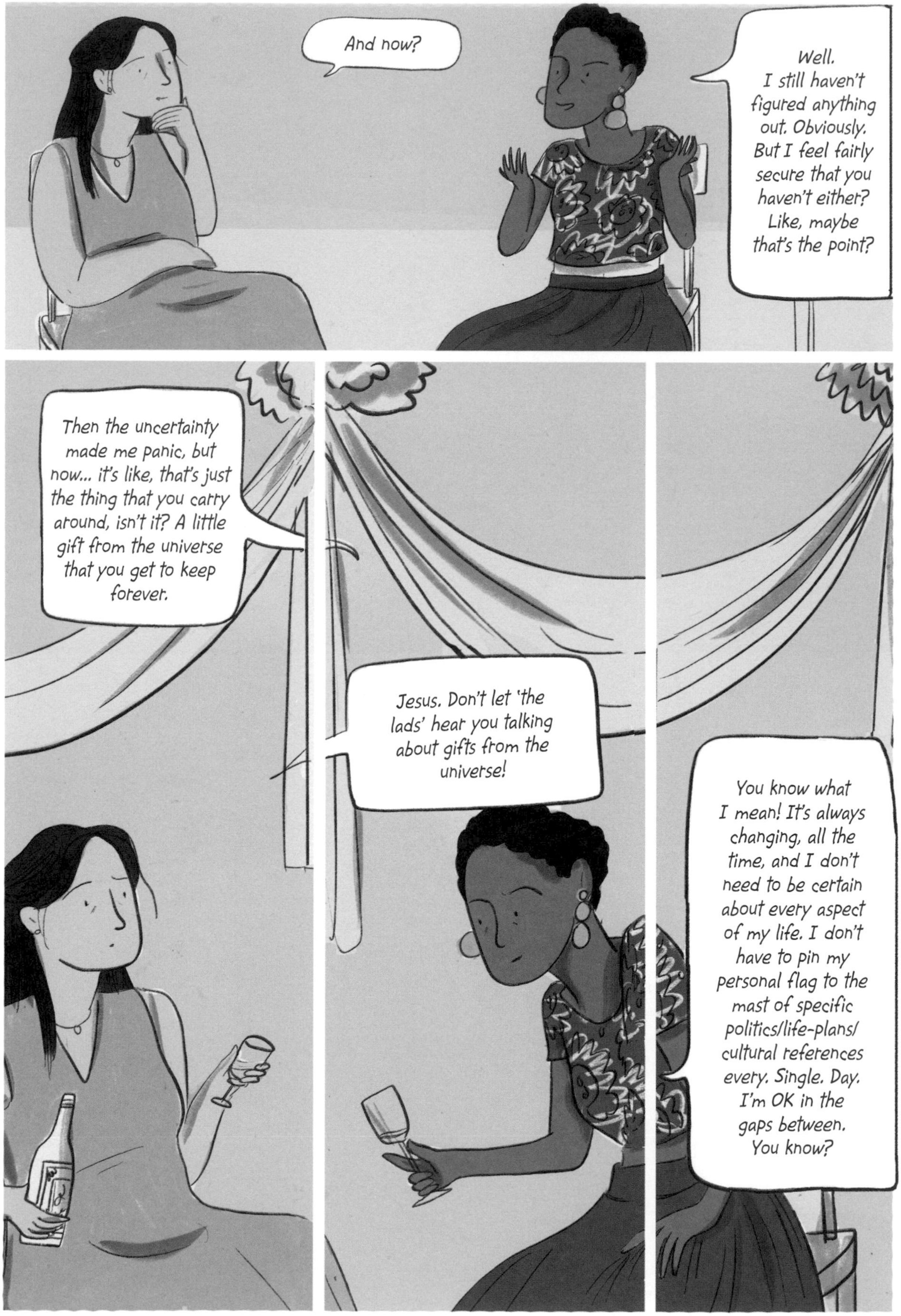
And now?
Well. I still haven't figured anything out. Obviously. But I feel fairly secure that you haven't either? Like, maybe that's the point?
Then the uncertainty made me panic, but now... it's like, that's just the thing that you carry around, isn't it? A little gift from the universe that you get to keep forever.
Jesus. Don't let 'the lads' hear you talking about gifts from the universe!
You know what I mean! It's always changing, all the time, and I don't need to be certain about every aspect of my life. I don't have to pin my personal flag to the mast of specific politics/life-plans/cultural references every. Single. Day. I'm OK in the gaps between. You know?

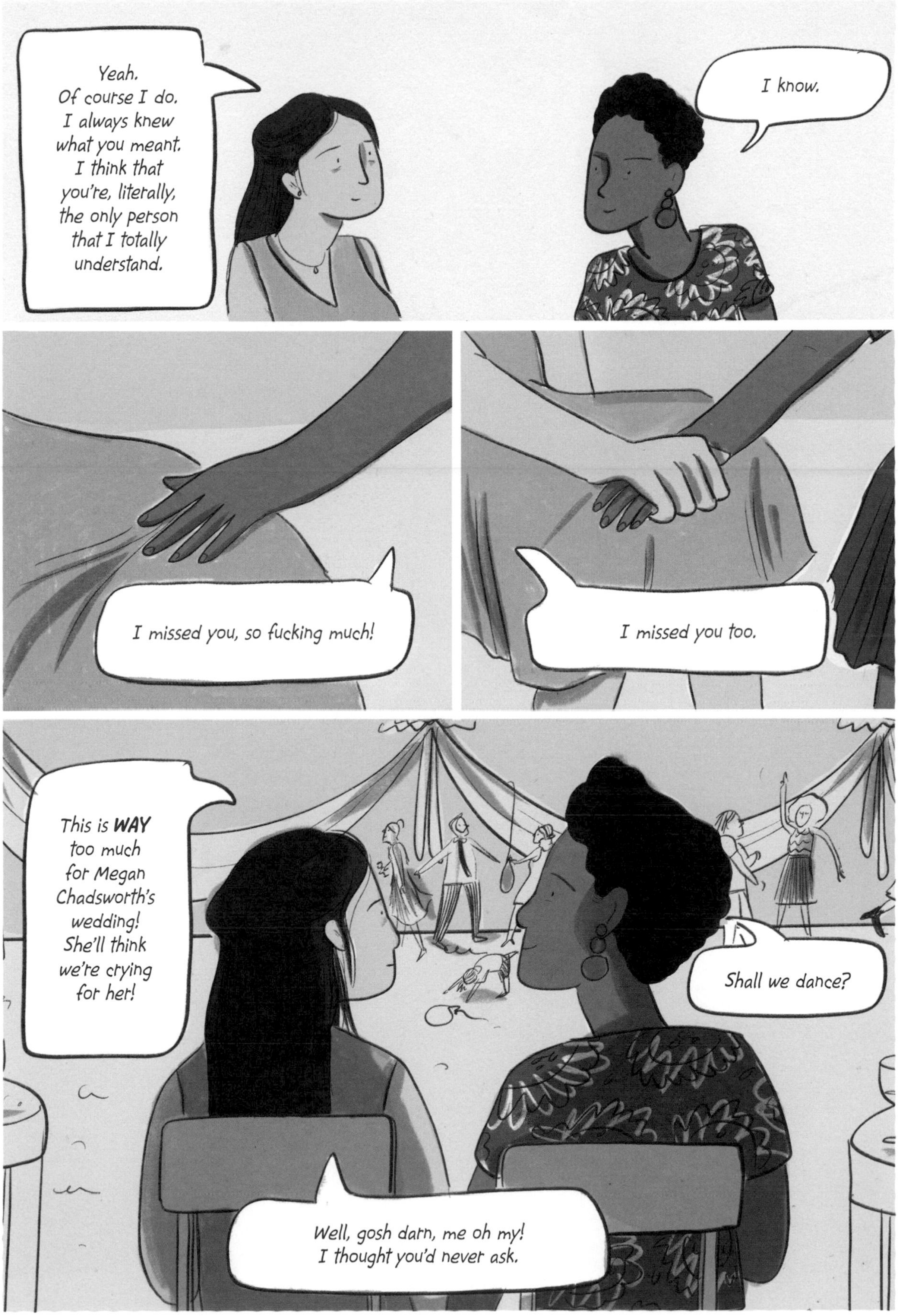
Yeah. Of course I do. I always knew what you meant. I think that you're, literally, the only person that I totally understand.
I know.
I missed you, so fucking much!
I missed you too.
This is **WAY** too much for Megan Chadsworth's wedding! She'll think we're crying for her!
Shall we dance?
Well, gosh darn, me oh my! I thought you'd never ask.

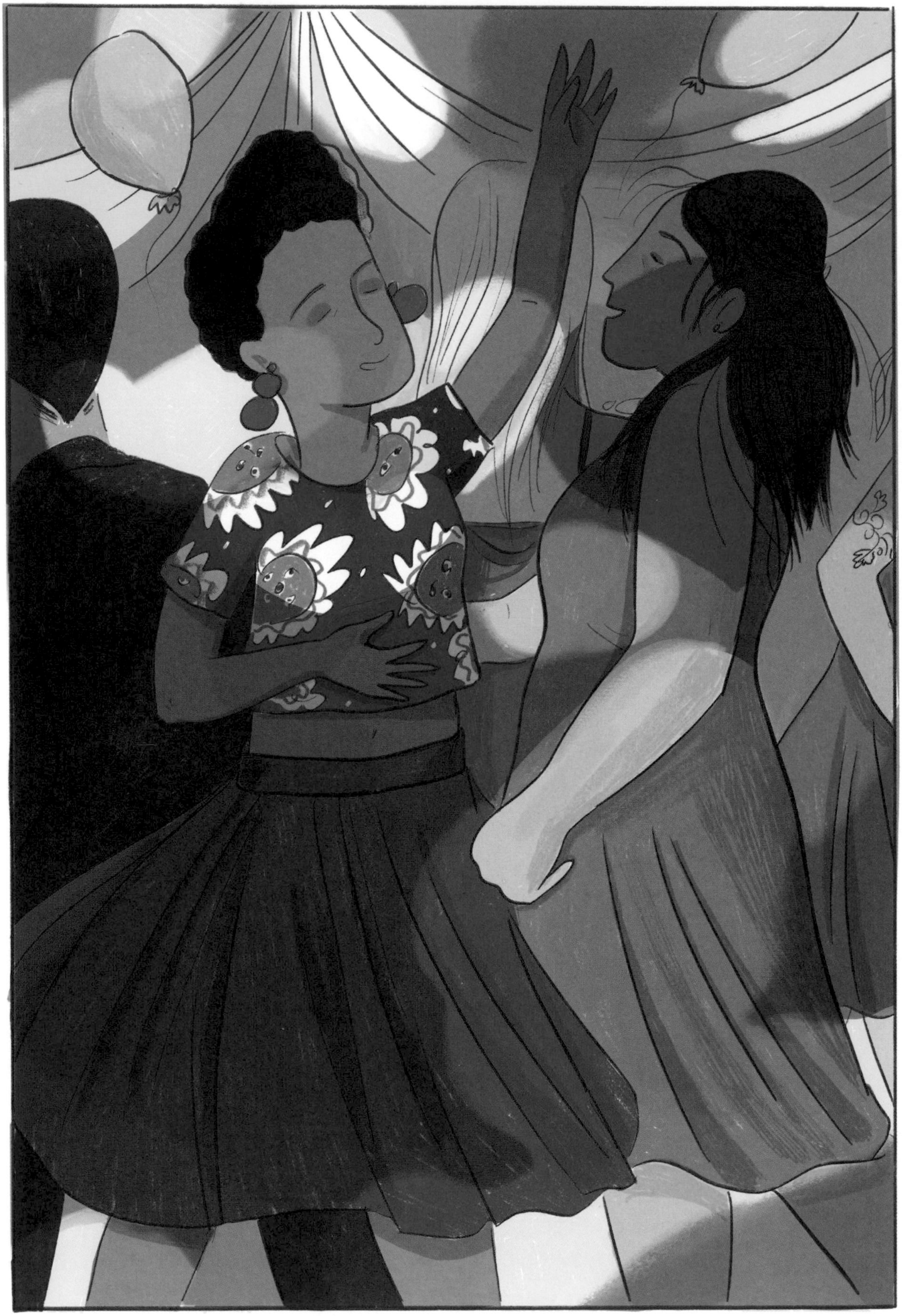